No. social housing units 2015-2023 — Strategies

Completed	completed + planned	Strategies
1,112	3,722	IMHAB council housing production
1,505		Retrofitting purchased buildings
54	378	IMHAB industrialized council housing production
156	1,074	Foundations and Zero Equity Cooperatives FZEC Agreement
	762	HMB's affordable housing production
2,306		Areas of urban regeneration *
1,747		Mobilization of empty housing **

This map is a graphic representation of the impact of each of the seven strategies to increase social and affordable housing that Barcelona City Council has been carrying out since 2015, and those planned at January 2023, the date on which the edition of this book closed. The number of homes developed by each strategy, be it building, purchasing or retrofitting, has been taken as a common element.

*

The section "Areas of urban regeneration" includes homes that have benefited from the corresponding grants (high complexity properties and urban regeneration), and the homes of vulnerable people.

**

The "Mobilization of empty housing" section accounts for homes that are dealt with by the programme to acquire social and affordable dwellings: rental exchange, transfer programme (managed by Hàbitat3) and the programme to attract tourist apartments for social rental.

gestating living

BARCELONA'S **SOCIAL HOUSING** STRATEGIES

gestating living

BARCELONA'S **SOCIAL HOUSING** STRATEGIES

Ajuntament de Barcelona | COAC
arquitectes.cat

Caterina Figuerola
Ibon Bilbao (eds.)

INDEX

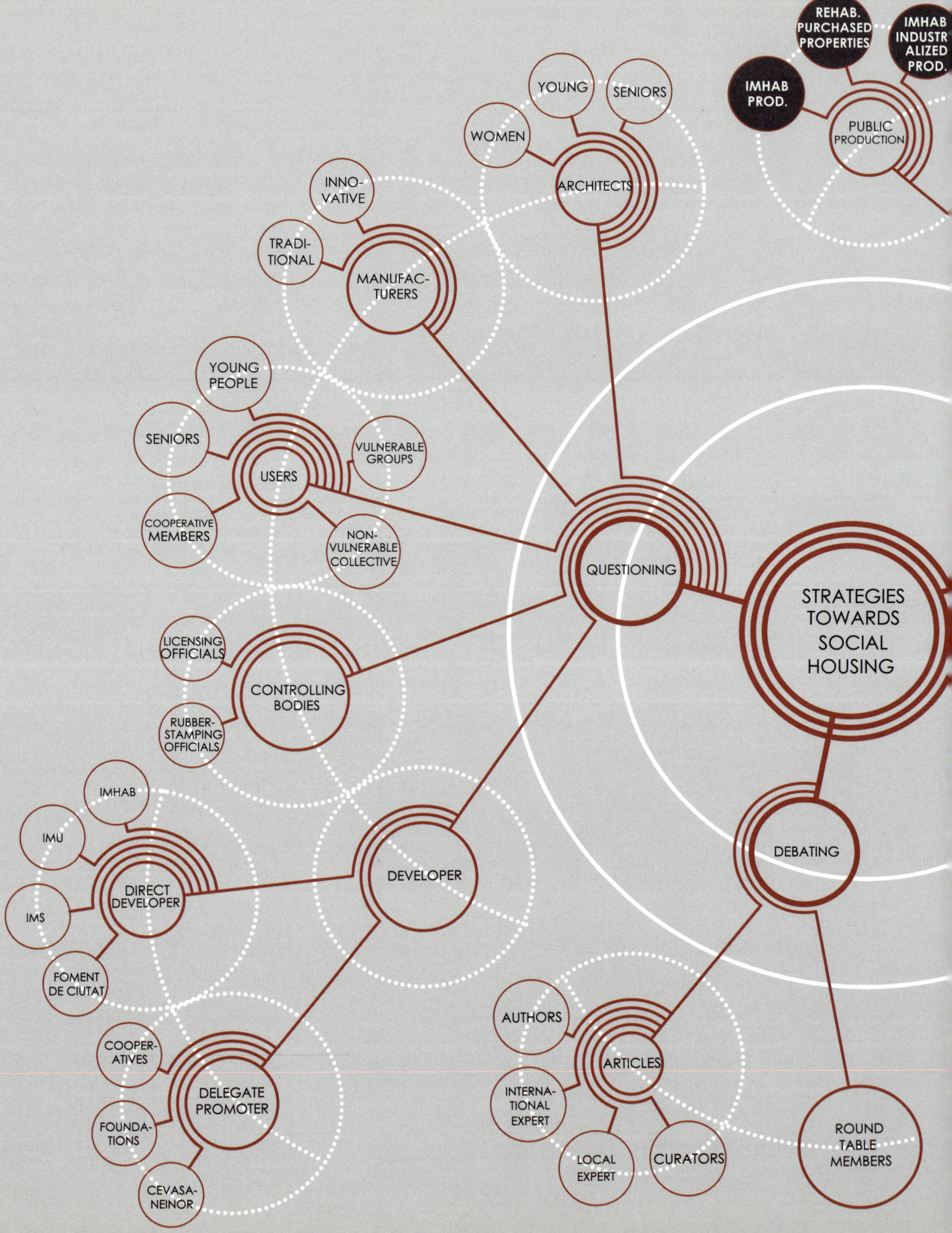

REHAB. PURCHASED PROPERTIES
IMHAB INDUSTR ALIZED PROD.
IMHAB PROD.
PUBLIC PRODUCTION
YOUNG
SENIORS
WOMEN
ARCHITECTS
INNO-VATIVE
TRADI-TIONAL
MANUFAC-TURERS
YOUNG PEOPLE
SENIORS
USERS
VULNERABLE GROUPS
COOPERATIVE MEMBERS
NON-VULNERABLE COLLECTIVE
QUESTIONING
STRATEGIES TOWARDS SOCIAL HOUSING
LICENSING OFFICIALS
CONTROLLING BODIES
RUBBER-STAMPING OFFICIALS
IMHAB
IMU
DIRECT DEVELOPER
IMS
FOMENT DE CIUTAT
DEVELOPER
DEBATING
COOPER-ATIVES
DELEGATE PROMOTER
FOUNDA-TIONS
CEVASA-NEINOR
AUTHORS
ARTICLES
INTERNA-TIONAL EXPERT
LOCAL EXPERT
CURATORS
ROUND TABLE MEMBERS

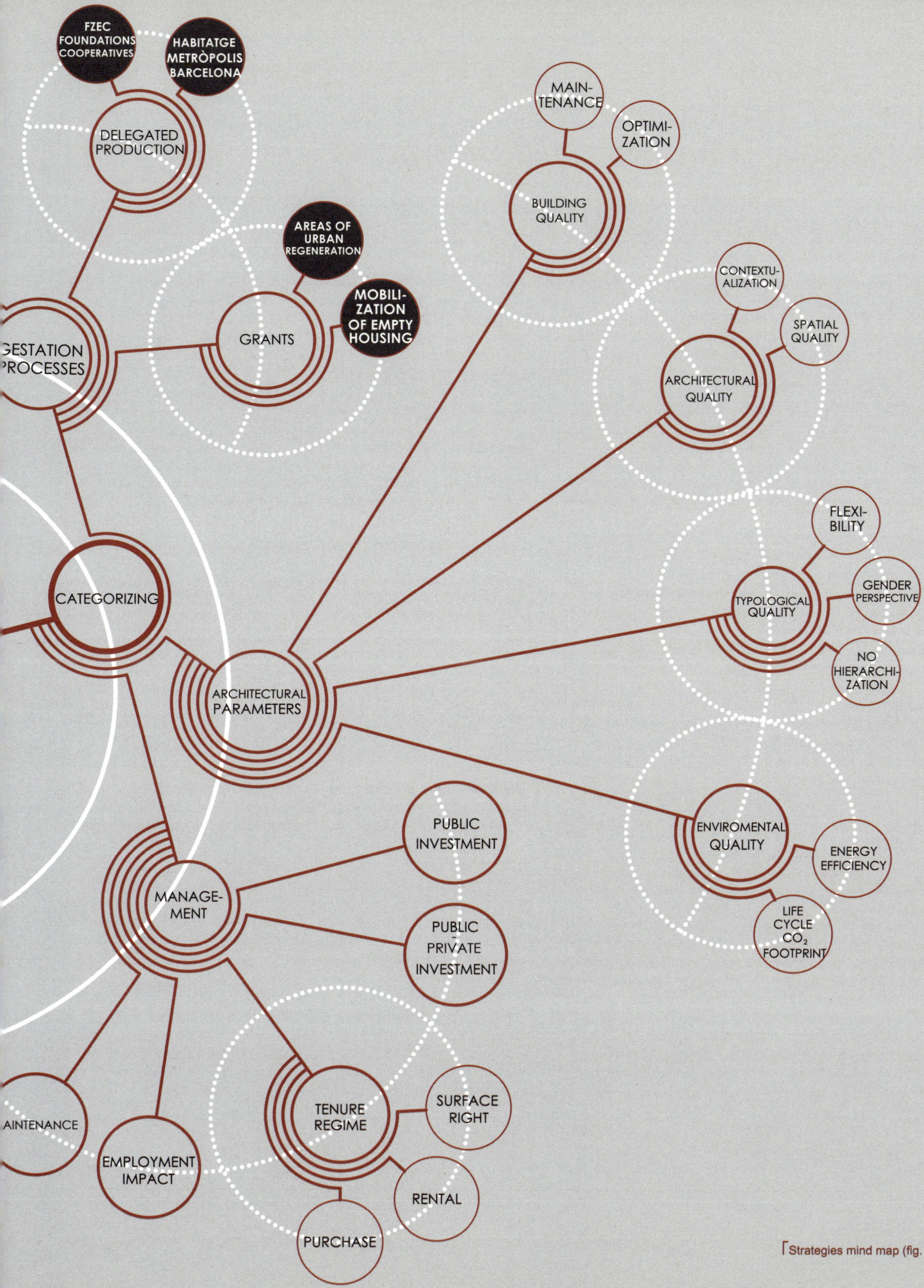

Strategies mind map (fig. 1)

Strategies for increasing social and affordable housing in Barcelona

The purpose of housing is to be lived in. This statement may at first seem obvious, but it does not always hold true. Clearly, the speculative value housing has acquired as a market commodity has on many occasions deflected it dramatically from this purpose. In the case of social housing, however, a change is occurring: we are seeing the transition from housing for sale to other forms of tenure, such as sheltered housing for rent, or transfer of use so that the land and buildings do not lose their public ownership, in this way avoiding the processes of speculation and gentrification.

This book presents and analyses the different strategies to develop and build social and affordable housing adopted in recent years by the municipal administration of the city of Barcelona. It selects a series of projects that exemplify the maximum number of work methodologies, briefs and innovative proposals, preferably already built and lived in, to be able to draw on the experience and situation of the people who live in them and get to know them at first hand.

We bring two approaches to these strategies: **GESTATING** and **LIVING**. By GESTATING we understand a whole process leading from the decision to develop these projects until the people who will live there receive the keys to their homes, via the various contracting mechanisms, project phases and construction. The protagonists of this process are all the agents involved: government, Architects' Association, architects, design and construction teams, and even users, in the case of cooperatives.

Alongside this process of GESTATING, we introduce LIVING. The inhabitants, in their everyday lives, give meaning to a home: how they appropriate the space and how they adapt it to their circumstances; how they experience all of these projects personally and how it affects them in their lives; how they live together and how they navigate the different areas of the neighbourhood, the building and the dwelling.

As curators, it seemed important to us to address the process of generating social housing due to both its urgency and its complexity. Most of the projects included in this book have been featured in other publications, but on this occasion we wanted to relate the entire journey, from planning the development to the experience of being lived in. This responds to our desire to visibilize the administrative, technical and human resources behind a complex process that we think it is vital to know in all its dimensions in order to appreciate its value.

As architects who are interested in social housing projects, we have always wanted to know precisely all the aspects surrounding the fact that people end up living in the homes we design and domesticating the spaces defined by us. It is important to say that many factors and agents intervene in a process of generating social housing, making it a complex journey in which everyone concerned has their commitment and their part to play. For a long time now, we have wanted to know about the pre-project phase, all the previous steps taken to ensure that a project is, finally, developed and built; above all, we considered it essential to know about the post-project phase, a look at life in the homes once work is complete, accompanied by the presence of the user. It is a parameter that is not often taken into account, but adding the imprint of the end user to the design process can give us guidelines for reflection about the decisions to be made when addressing the new challenges presented by contemporary housing.

As citizens, we felt the need to explore the strategic value of social and affordable housing and its capacity to generate neighbourhood and community relations, and to respond to the housing emergency in the context of a very broad range of life situations.

These are the concerns and reflections that fuel this publication, promoted by the COAC (Architects' Association of Catalonia) and Barcelona City Council. Thanks to this co-participation, it has been possible to table social housing from the point of view of architectural quality and the strategies implemented in order to produce it. We set out to produce a book that, as well as showing the built work, invites reflection on social housing in quantitative and qualitative terms.

The methodology of the book begins with the creation of three mind maps: strategies, exemplification and production, defining the conceptual framework and scope of the publication.

The **strategy mind map** (Fig. 1) organizes the explanation according to three actions developed simultaneously on the theme of social housing: categorizing, questioning and debating.

Categorizing allowed us to show and understand the parameters affecting **the quantity and the quality** of the proposed production, the various development and subsidy formulas being applied by the municipal government, and the extent to which the results meet the demands of architectural quality and the requirements of sustainability and energy efficiency.

In terms of management, the most significant fact is a commitment to tenure regimes that mean that the public administration does not relinquish ownership of the housing or land that it develops directly or by delegation. This fact introduces a new, absolutely determinant and across-the-board parameter: **maintenance** of the building, land and dwellings for the duration of their useful life.

Introduction

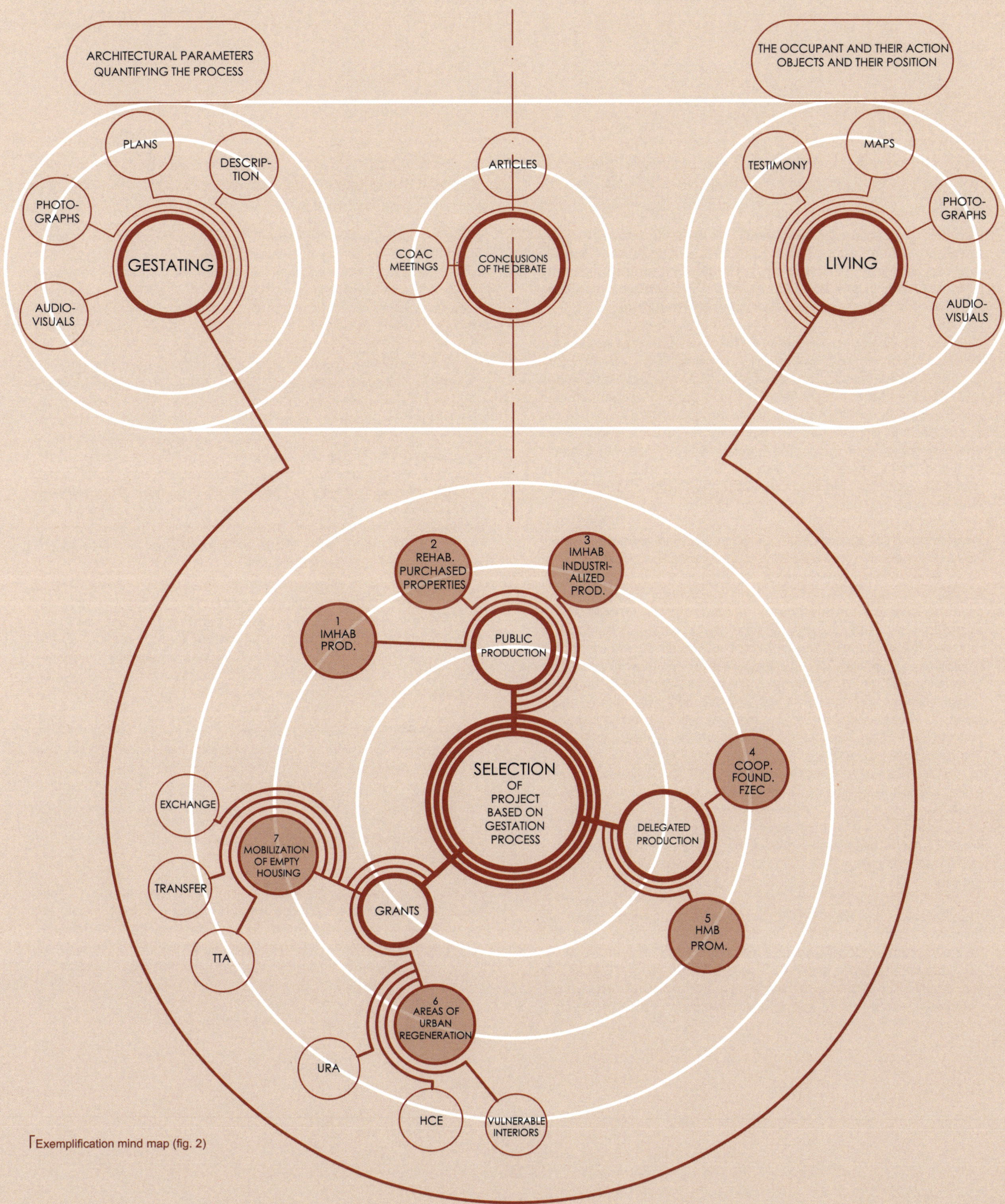

Exemplification mind map (fig. 2)

This categorization, based on the three processes of gestation (public production, delegated production and subsidies), informs the **seven strategies** for social and affordable housing outlined in this publication: **public production by the IMHAB + retrofitting of purchased buildings + industrialized housing production by the IMHAB + delegated production by foundations and zero equity cooperatives (FZEC Agreement) + delegated production by Habitatge Metròpolis Barcelona (HMB) + retrofitting of vulnerable environments + mobilization of empty housing.**

Questioning the agents involved in the development of each of the strategies has provided necessary information about forms of direct or delegated production: the administrative and design phases undergone and the time invested in each, the times of intervention and the time taken until housing is allocated. One of the aims of this approach is to expose the complexity of the process and quantify the time and human resources needed to allow people ultimately to live in social housing. We also considered it vital to record the testimony of the people who live in the projects presented that are already a reality.

Debating with all the agents involved in the management of social housing production, be they developers, government technicians, cooperative members, designers of the various projects or constructors, is an opportunity to hear the contribution of each to a process that begins with the allocation of a municipal plot for residential use. And it does not end with the handover of keys to the people or groups who will live in those homes; it will continue, in most of the strategies, for years, with the responsibility for maintenance and management. For this reason, during the process of gestation of this publication we organized two working days at the COAC headquarters, during which the teams that designed the projects exemplifying each of the strategies sat down to talk with the people from the municipal government, foundations or cooperatives responsible for developing and managing them, and the constructors who materialized them. This represented reflection on the processes of gestation.

The **exemplification mind map** (Fig. 2) developed the methodology for defining the graphic, audiovisual and written content of this book.

The transition from GESTATING to LIVING occurs when people are given the keys to their home and move in. A total of 23 case studies is presented to exemplify each of the seven strategies. Of these, 16 are lived in and are therefore addressed in terms of GESTATING and LIVING, while the remaining seven, at the design stage or not yet lived in at the time of writing, are addressed in their gestation.

To explain the GESTATION, we asked the design teams for the project documentation and most representative landmarks in the process, highlighting the documents generated in the different phases, including intermediate states, tests and waivers. The images provided by the teams represent the construction process and the finished building before it is lived in. The various administrations were asked to provide information and relevant dates in the previous and subsequent design and construction phases, ranging from the announcement of production to the adjudication or handing over of keys to users.

All the graphic and audiovisual material to document LIVING was generated specially for this publication. These are documents that illustrate the everyday lives of the occupants and their circumstances. The photographs taken by Adrià Goula show the buildings today in their urban context, and the photographs of the communal spaces and interiors of the homes taken by Maite Caramés show how they are being lived in. It was necessary to access the homes in order to map the way the spaces are occupied and to record testimonies. It was time to talk to the occupants: they explained and we took note, modelling and drawing their situation. This fieldwork meant contacting the users of 258 homes to be able finally to go into 66 of them, in 16 different buildings.

First, mapping domestic life incorporated the occupants' and users' testimony and experience of living in the chapters dedicated to each strategy. Then the specific chapter on interventions at the professional meetings organized at the COAC brought to the debate the voices of all the agents involved in the gestation of the various strategies.

The twofold GESTATING/LIVING approach further allowed us to open each chapter with two complementary articles, giving a voice to multiple agents in different disciplines who intervened personally or as experts in one of the strategies. All this forms the theoretical body deriving from the debate.

The **production mind map** (Fig. 3) presents the material produced to make the book.

As well as organizing its contents, the GESTATING/LIVING double entry also defines the book's graphic design. In every case we worked with a double page, one with a colour background for gestating and one with a white background for living, so you always know which entry the documentation you are looking at belongs to.

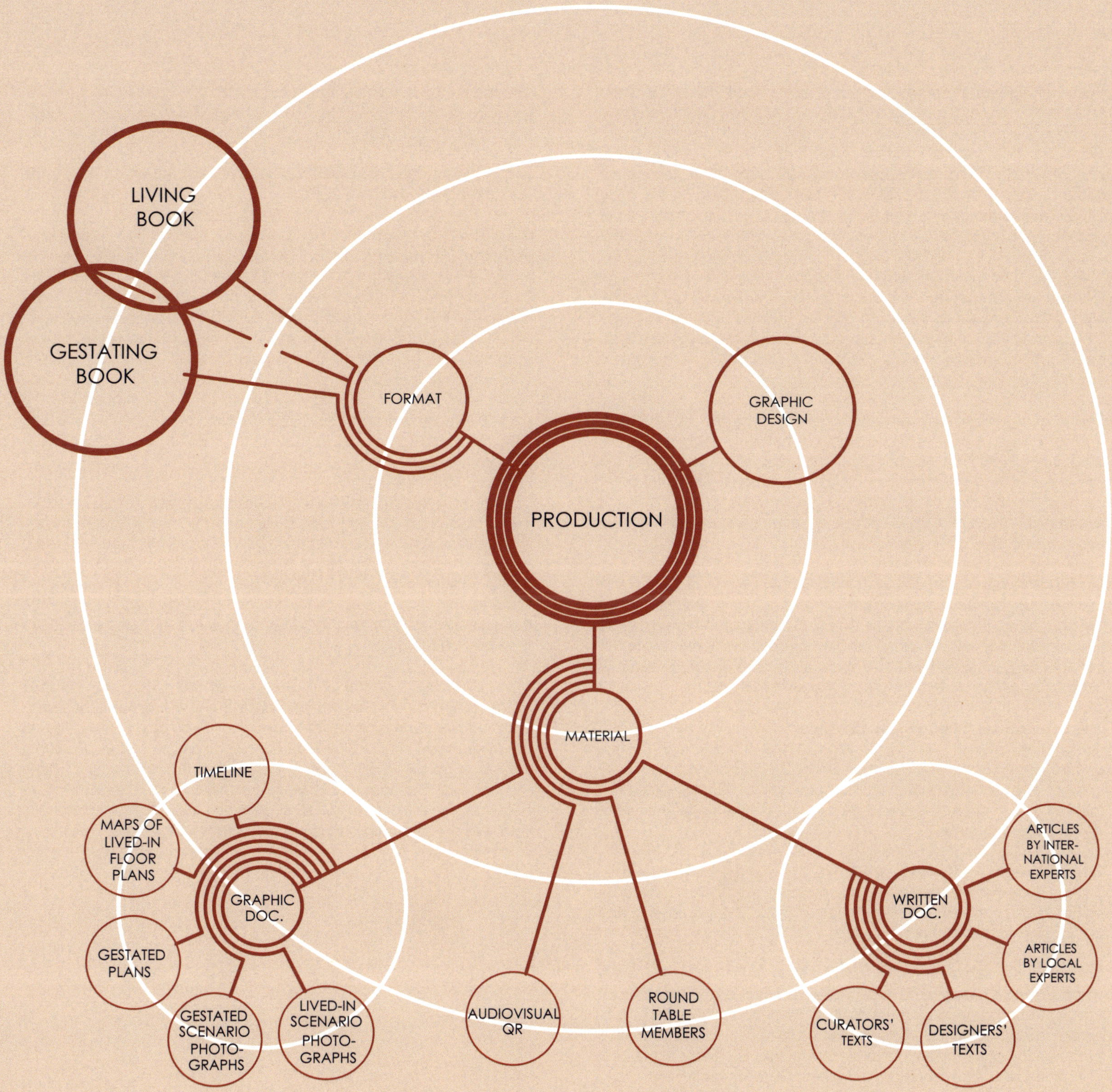

Production mind map (fig. 3)

Each of the chapters explaining a strategy is presented by the diagram of the strategy mind map as a guide to situate each example in each category, and opens with two articles about gestating and living. The first graphic information we find in each example is the project timeline. This is followed, page by page, with documents about gestating by the design teams and about living by the team of curators. In the central part of the chapter, the photographs of occupation occupy a double page to compare different ways of living.

The graphic documentation of the gestation provided by the design teams was redrafted to unify the graphics, and specific documents were generated about the living process for this publication in the form of articles, timelines, floor plans, audiovisuals with user testimonies, photographs of the buildings in their current urban context and comparative images.

The book opens by unfolding the cover to show the **quantitative map of social and affordable housing developments in Barcelona**, where each of the strategies to develop social housing in the city is quantified and shown graphically by district. The total number of social housing units developed between 2015 and 2023 and scheduled at January 2023, the date on which the edition of this book closed, was quantified.

Various **articles** are proposed to introduce the words GESTATING/LIVING into the discourse on housing and reflect on its direction in the near future. The book opens with two institutional forewords and two introductory articles about the two approaches, written by international experts. Each strategy opens with two articles by national experts as a lead-in to the projects that exemplify it.

The **production timeline** is a document showing the sequence of the different phases and significant dates in the process of each production. It begins with the decision by the Council to start development of a plot and ends with the handover of keys to users. The fold-out document that closes the book is a comparative timeline of all the developments.

Based on the editable files provided by the teams that designed the 23 developments selected, **all the graphic material of the gestation was redrawn** to unify the graphics of the publication and present comparable material.

Thanks to the fieldwork carried out on each of the visits, the **lived-in floor plan** of each home was drawn, producing 16 experiences. The floor plan is seen as a support for information collected to represent reality, like a map of an instant at which objects are seen as a prolongation of the subject, and the interaction with them of the user is what gives them meaning and makes them complete.

The map shows a whole series of objects that have to be seen not as isolated but in the context of a home, where someone invades a space with their way of living. It is this space that we have to understand, based on each particular case. These graphic documents aim rigorously and accurately to transmit and represent the condition of the everyday —of living.

We wanted to record, on an audiovisual support, our **interviews with the inhabitants** of the various developments studied. We made 21 recordings in 16 different buildings. We asked just three questions that were deliberately very open so as not to direct the occupants towards a specific topic: what is the neighbourhood like? what's the building like? what's your home like? Addressing three scales, from the urban to the domestic, including the community, but with the idea that each person should talk about the issues they considered relevant on each. Listening to the occupants in their context provided a great deal of information to compare. You can view the videos by using the QR code printed next to a still from the interview.

Adrià Goula **photographed the buildings in their urban context.** Years later, he returned to the buildings in question to photograph them with an eye to the relationships being created between them and public space, to the ability of housing to create city. Each chapter establishes a dialogue between the infographics of the imagined building, the photographs of the finished building contributed by the design teams involved in the gestation process, and photographs of the now lived-in building.

Maite Caramés took the **photographs of the communal spaces** of the 16 buildings and the **comparative photographs of living** in 66 homes. She entered them with her eyes set on the different neighbourhood relationships and the very diverse ways of seeing the same space in terms of everyday life. In the middle of each chapter is a photograph of the same space in four representative homes of the building in question. We think that her text expresses very well the meaning and value of these photographs:

"The photographs that form part of this book were taken with the aim of creating a comparison that showed the diversity of ways of living in similar spaces in various homes in Barcelona.

This posed a number of technical challenges for a photographer. One of them was repetition: in order to present the contrast between almost identical spaces, it was important always to find the same viewpoint. But this was not easy due to the variety of layouts: where one family had an open-plan space, another had placed a piece of furniture that got in the way; where someone had their television, someone else had piled boxes that obstructed the view. And this was the case with so many things.

Another challenge was working with natural light and doing it at times of day that we could not choose, because we were dependent on the availability of the occupants of the spaces to take the photographs. This meant that on some occasions you would come up against backlighting and on others you would find a dull, milky lighting, and, on yet others, a series of contrasts made it impossible to produce a halfway decent image.

A final challenge was the harmonious combination of people and spaces. People are the heart of the project, but so are the spaces they occupy, and the lens that is used to cover as much surface as possible, often used in architecture photography, is rarely the best for portraits of people. This challenge was also consistent with the realist principle inherent in this type of project: the idea was to present scenes in keeping with people's real habits –to compile a small assortment of typical portraits that show how these people live in certain homes in Barcelona, and to do so in a credible, varied way.

But all of these challenges had great rewards: the first was coming into contact with lives that speak of realities I was unaware of, that inhabit the same city in which I was born and where I also live. All the people who opened their door to us did so disinterestedly and kindly. In some cases there was prior contact and consent, but others were cold calls: a knock at the door, unknown faces, cameras, a few words about the project, suspicion. And yet, in the end, they let us in.

The other great reward was being able to discover, in the company of a generous, committed team, the more tender face of architecture, the face that gets excited when it discovers the life that beats inside the homes that have been gestated."

Maite Caramés

Guim Costa
President of the Architects' Association of Catalonia-COAC

gestating

According to the dictionary of the Catalan language, the meaning of the verb gestate is "to form and develop, in the females of viviparous animals, the embryo in their entrails until the moment of birth".

It is no coincidence that this word is included in the title of this book, since the process by means of which we first imagine, then design and, finally, physically build a home is, ultimately, a figurative process of gestation that culminates with the delivery of a unique and specific project in response to the original functional brief and prior specifications.

Each home has to allow each person and each cohabitation unit to shape their particular microcosm in keeping with their way of living, incorporating dynamics and elements to make it a comfortable and, at the same time, energy-efficient private space.

Accordingly, when this book talks about gestation, it aims to emphasize this process of embryonic development up until the moment of birth—in this case of a home that allows the development of its users, with their particularities and circumstances, and with the appropriate expenditure of energy.

The Universal Declaration of Human Rights (1948) states that everyone has the right to a standard of living that ensures their health and well-being, especially as regards food, clothing, housing, medical care and necessary social services.

The regulation of the right to housing in the Universal Declaration was the first time that housing was recognized as fundamental to living a decent life, to a personal identity, especially as regards privacy, but also to everyday life and the creation of life expectations.

The Spanish Constitution, furthermore, recognizes the right to housing as a guiding principle of socio-economic policy, so the public authorities must try to protect it, as they do universal medical services and the public education network. From the viewpoint of equal opportunities, they must also guarantee that citizens have access to it, by means of public intervention avoiding social exclusion.

Today's urban concentration and the economic and environmental crisis raise the need to review the process of creating housing — whether by means of major retrofitting or new construction— and to manage it in cities to provide coverage for all needs.

This task corresponds to the government, which must regulate land use and the major processes of remodelling the existing urban fabric, seeking the general interest, avoiding speculation and, further, implementing new innovations and proposals to generate healthy, energetically-sustainable spaces, in order to avoid overexploitation of the environment and citizens.

The right to housing is, then, a right that tends to eradicate social differences, and it is in this aspect that the book you have before you aims to present a new line of work: public intervention in the field of housing in order to give this social right effective content, but with an innovative approach that, for the past eight years, Barcelona City Council has been carrying out in collaboration with the other integral parties in the process: architects, developers and contractors.

This book therefore presents the learning process represented by the development of these social projects and conclusions that can be drawn to show not just successful projects, but also possibilities for improvement in the future.

Each of the parties involved, with their expertise, contributed in a coordinated, crosscutting process to designing a global system that culminated in the production of a series of homes to meet various social needs in which, with the leadership of the Administration, the process is actively coordinated with all interested parties.

Without doubt, it is a task that invites reflection on the strategy to be followed in an urban context in which space is scarce, and vulnerabilities and needs are numerous, all the more so at a time like the present, when the economic, social, energy and environmental situation is particularly delicate.

living

Anna Vergés
Architect. Co-Director of BIAU Living on the Fringe

Housing and habitability

Access to adequate housing is a right because it is a guarantee of safety and health. From a strategic or political point of view, to make an analogy with the field of health, we understand the importance of solid information and ongoing research to providing appropriate responses to the diversity of specific diseases. Housing policy follows the same premise and complexity. And in order to address the issue of housing in the city of Barcelona, the first thing that the Housing and Rehabilitation Department of Barcelona City Council did was to promote a housing observatory at metropolitan level to collect all the necessary information about the state of housing, especially with regard to difficulties accessing it. "If it can't be measured, it doesn't exist", as Antón Costas reminded us at the first meeting of the scientific committee.

This publication reflects the results obtained by this task of measurement and deploys a range of varied proposals that seeks to democratize flexible options for access to affordable housing, with a housing stock that is still limited but which is calling for a change of perspective and attitude to new ways of living.

Internationally, problems of access to and maintenance of housing are accentuated, especially among the most disadvantaged population. A housing famine has been growing, turning housing into a scarce and inaccessible commodity for many, with situations in which citizens see their expectations for the future limited. Now, more than ever, it is necessary to focus the debate on how to "feed" cities and neighbourhoods with adequate housing to face present-day emergencies and propose humanized environments in which people can grow, relate and progress towards inclusive, productive and creative societies –and do so by rethinking a strategy to address the social, environmental and economic challenges of our living environments.

Problems and solutions

In the economic field, the context generated by persistent crises merely aggravates inequalities in the socio-economic reality of the population. This situation increases the need to access care support and affordable or social housing. In Spain, the difficulties are endemic, given the existing low percentage of social housing (2.5% compared to an average of 9.1% in Europe). This problem is due, in part, to the lack of diversity in housing policies in recent decades, focused on developing sheltered housing for disqualified sale, causing the loss of the opportunity to accumulate a volume of adequate social housing.

This fact is reflected in the property market, where the prices offered do not meet the needs of a significant part of the demand, especially in the rental field. This form of tenure is increasing compared to ownership, especially in the city (38.4% rentals in 2019), given the difficulties of repaying a mortgage loan, so that young people, single-parent families, the migrant population, etc., are excluded even from this option.

In the city, sustainable development goals promoted by the United Nations show that urban environments are increasingly populated spaces, with 54% in 2015 worldwide (74% in Europe) and a forecast for 2035 of 62% (79% in Europe). Cities therefore have even more responsibility for guaranteeing good habitability and developing strong housing policies.

But inequalities also affect the type of population according to gender, age and origin, leaving certain population groups with specific needs more unprotected. Progressive changes in the makeup of families reduce the number of people per household and modify the usual forms of cohabitation. This fact increases the number of housing units needed in more populated areas and calls for forms that are more flexible in time, with more complex management. Alternative forms of tenure such as cooperatives, housing exchange, cohousing, urban occupation agreements or temporary accommodation are new formulas required by different ways of living, and are promoted by the municipality in Barcelona through the Foundations and Zero Equity Cooperatives Agreement.

These changes are also reflected in urban planning and design. The car is beginning to cease to be at the centre of the urban structure, with policies turning towards sustainable mobility, which places citizens at the centre and allows for improved coexistence. We are seeing a collective determination to make the city more domestic and liveable, promoted by an inclusive urban planning that takes gender, race and age into account in the characteristic features of its design and promotes relationships between its actors.

Added to these factors is another very important challenge, the environmental one, determined by the effects of climate change and the need to mitigate the impact of construction and the CO_2 emissions of existing construction, particularly housing, which represent over 40% of the total volume of emissions in Europe.

The strategic change involves recycling existing buildings: retrofitting and adapting this stock must serve to reduce the excessive consumption of fossil fuels and the use of unsustainable construction materials. This challenge must guarantee continued maintenance of housing and reverse the negative effects on health caused by the expenses that arise from it.

The recent European New Generation funds are an opportunity to reverse the situation, especially necessary in the city of Barcelona, where the residential stock is quite old, and to make the necessary grants or loans available to owners to improve the conditions of their homes.

Transversality

All of these challenges that arise from living in and building social housing stock cannot be considered solely as the task of government agencies, and must be shared with the private sector, social bodies, cooperatives, etc. They represent a solid basis that is growing bigger and stronger every day in Barcelona, encouraging entrepreneurship in the form of innovative shared projects, such as the Habitatge Metròpolis Barcelona project and the Foundations and Zero Equity Cooperatives Agreement.

If we look at developing countries, with a virtually non-existent public system, we see how informality grows, often becoming a majority option: a system that guarantees access to precarious housing, with the emergence of participatory initiatives, that are collectively managed to improve the living conditions of the immediate environment. They are an example of an attitude that, with the necessary support, could become a strategy, a seed of a policy to undertake projects to improve housing, based on the diversity of existing needs.

In Europe we have an enviable welfare system, inclined to see the emergence of shared public initiatives. In Barcelona, these policies have been built on the basis of solid information, making it possible to address various strategies to promote and provide responses in keeping with the specific needs of certain collectives, as shown in the projects included in this publication.

There is still a long way to go, committing to the promotion of affordable rent, exchange and cooperation, in the desire to bring about a change of perspective that places citizens at the centre of the collective imaginary, makes housing and habitability central challenges in the coming years.

Tackling the housing crisis and shortage: a perspective from Vancouver

Alex Hemingway

Senior Economist. Canadian Centre for Policy Alternatives

Like many other jurisdictions, my home city of Vancouver and the province of British Columbia (BC) is facing a housing crisis and shortage. From a policy perspective, there are many facets to the housing crisis and multiple policy solutions needed from all levels of government. These include demand-side measures like property tax reform[1] and the regulation and taxation of empty homes[2], as well as the strengthening of rent controls, tenant protections and an organized renters' rights movement.

In this article, however, I focus on two key factors underlying the housing crisis on the supply side: a chronic shortfall of public investment in dedicated affordable housing, and the overall housing supply shortage relating to land use policies. In the Canadian context, national and provincial governments have important roles to play in financing affordable housing, but local governments have the capability to make significant progress even in the absence of senior government support.[3]

The policies needed here may shed light on other jurisdictions with their own dynamics and complexities. I trust that readers with deeper knowledge of local conditions in Barcelona and other jurisdictions will draw on what is useful and applicable in this analysis and disregard what is not.

One key reason for the housing shortage in BC is that austerity-minded governments —at both the federal and provincial levels— for two decades largely abandoned their traditional roles in financing dedicated affordable housing. Over the past few years, a modest reinvestment in housing by both senior levels of government has been helpful, but has fallen far short of the scale required.

A massive increase in public investment in non-market housing is one of the most effective approaches governments can take to tackle the housing crisis. An important but little understood fact is that public investment in middle-income housing can be designed to largely pay for itself. The reason is straightforward: like private rental development, the financing costs of upfront capital investment in public rental housing can be paid for through the stream of income that residents pay in rent.

But in the case of public investment in housing, rents can be set at moderately below market rates and still break even. This is because the public sector can finance the upfront capital investment at lower interest rates than the private sector; it can amortize costs over a longer period; and it can forgo the roughly 15 % that private developers typically allocate for their own profit in a rental project.

Rents in these types of break-even public and non-profit housing projects can also remain more stable over time since they are tied to covering costs rather than maximizing profits. Using this self-financing model, which I outlined in a report in 2022, a huge amount of non-market housing aimed at middle income earners can be built without competing with other priorities for tax dollars.[4]

To achieve rents substantially below market rates, affordable to those on lower incomes, further measures are needed. These include funding separate subsidy streams and grants, using cross-subsidization between market-rate and affordable units in a building, acquiring and contributing public land, upzoning low-density areas and scrapping expensive parking requirements.

Alongside a major expansion of public and non-market housing, the overall housing supply shortage must be taken into account.[5] There is no way out of the housing crisis in BC without a huge effort to end the chronic shortage of homes, which helps drive up rents and creates a steady churn of displacement and exclusion. Any housing plan worth its salt —including plans focused on public and non-profit housing— must ensure that rents fall across the board, rental vacancy rates rise, and there are homes for all.

From an affordability perspective, the empirical pattern is clear: when vacancy rates are lower, rents rise more quickly. When vacancy rates are higher —that is, when more homes are available to those looking — rents rise more slowly or fall. This is why corporate landlords like real-estate investment trusts fear increased housing supply and the prospect of having to compete for tenants who have a range of housing options available. They disclose these as "risks" in reports to shareholders and regulatory filings.

A growing body of academic research also highlights the benefits of increasing housing supply, including market rate housing. As higher-income renters move into new buildings, this "loosens the housing market in middle- and low-income areas even in the short run ... [and] is likely to improve affordability outside the submarkets where the new construction occurs and to benefit low-income people".[6]

As the same study finds, adding new social housing eases the pressures of housing shortages through the same "moving chain" mechanism, but even more effectively. New social housing units are also themselves immediately more affordable. If a plan to add new public and social housing isn't big enough to drive down overall rents —including for those who are stuck in pricier market rate units— it is either too small and needs to be expanded, or it needs to welcome new market housing as a complement.

Another key matter is where housing is built. Single-family zoning policies in places like Vancouver (and other municipalities) effectively ban apartments on most of the city's residential land. This drives up the price of the scarce parcels where multifamily housing is allowed and makes construction of new homes more difficult and expensive for public, non-profit and private rental developers alike. It also causes the displacement of renters by steering new housing development toward existing apartment sites.

Local land use policy should ensure should ensure housing is available in all neighbourhoods, prioritizing development in exclusionary, high-priced, low-density areas. Democratic processes relating to land use planning must also begin to fulsomely include the voices of renters who are currently excluded or priced out of a city or neighbourhood, not just those of incumbent homeowners and residents.

Tackling a deep-seated, and long-standing housing crisis and shortage in places like BC requires an all-of-the-above approach: a massive increase in the supply of housing across the board with as much public, non-profit, co-op, and rental housing as possible; strengthening tenants' rights and rent controls; building renter power through organizing, and taxing land wealth to pay for deeply subsidized housing.

Alejandro Echeverri
Distinguished Visiting Professor in Urbanism at TEC Monterrey

I love the words neighbourhood and neighbour, because they always include people, the relationship between them and the spaces they inhabit. They contain sociocultural and sociospatial dimensions. They speak of the inhabitant, the resident, the citizen. They include the value of caring, the value of trust. Of the meeting points, of places close by. Neighbourhood and neighbour always give us a human dimension of the place where we live. However, today we tend to forget these values when speaking of social housing as a response to an immediate need. I suggest that, when we seek to create a new place to live, we replace the impoverished word housing with the more complete neighbourhood and neighbour.

The city of Medellín has been mobilized by crises; we suffered, but we also learned from them. The drama of the 1980s and 1990s —"the difficult years" that Jorge Orlando Melo wrote about in his book— left us a complex, living city, with its contradictions and its progress. We went from living in a place with dark streets, enclaves and fears to a city of contrasts and intense encounters. And in the recent crisis, with the virus, the shadows made their presence felt again, but so too did the lights of our city. Many of these lights were extraordinary responses that occurred mainly where people dwell, sleep and live, especially popular neighbourhoods. The value of care, solidarity and trust became visible; the value of the Minga; of the collective co-production of living spaces.

We were privileged to live close by many stories of our friends from these neighbourhoods and to learn from them. El Aka and Las Doñas, the mothers, live in Comuna 13, located on the western outskirts of the city. This neighbourhood is a synthesis of the history of Medellín, revealing the drama of marginalization and violence, but also the loveliest mobilizations of solidarity. This community represents the value of the collective construction of a territory immersed in a tragedy of violence that has occurred due to a process of memory recovery. Where El Aka, Agroarte and Las Doñas, many of whom have lost their children, weave a new identity by sowing gardens of colours in dark corners of the neighbourhood. It has been a process in which the intimate places of the homes and collective meeting spaces are illuminated by the sowing of flowers to build a new story out of the memory of each family.

In the district of Santa Cruz, in northeast Medellín, there is a theatre created by popular initiative, Casa Amarilla, from which some of the loveliest and valuable stories of solidarity emerged during the most critical days of the two crises in Medellín. Jorge Blandón, Erica Muriel and a unique group of artists built the only space in the district that was free of fear during the difficult and most violent years of the nineties. There, at Casa Amarilla, all the neighbours of that time, good and bad, knew for a fact that their children were free from bullets for at least a few hours, and also that they were learning through art, conversation and theatre. In these 30 years, Casa Amarilla has become the district's space of solidarity and trust, and community initiative. In the pandemic, during the critical days of isolation, for the districts of Santa Cruz and El Sinai it was the only agent that brought food and words. Markets for families, and the "words that found their way in through the windows", filling boys and girls, and, through them, their homes, with culture and affection by means of telephone conversations.

In the 1980s, the district of Moravia, in Medellín, was known as "rubbish heights"; today, more than 40,000 people live there, an intense, complex place. Rubbish heights was true enough; it was the city's landfill until 1985. When you are talking about community leadership in our city and want to explain it, this place is a prime example. Cielo, Yeizon, Luz Mila, their families and lots of neighbours embarked on a journey of exemplary territorial protest, local improvement and solidarity economy. The process of what was originally a neighbourhood of recyclers consolidated a vital economic centrality in a unique environment of community solidarity. It has been a progressive, organic process of years, of human fabrics and housing improvements, where the value of time has been vital. But their future is still uncertain, as they have been constantly threatened with expulsion. However, I am certain that they will win this fight for their collective territory; I know of no better solidary construction of the economy of life than the one of this neighbourhood.

I have had the privilege of forging a friendship with these extraordinary people, learning and building together at Urbam, our urban planning and environment laboratory at Eafit University. I am convinced that it is impossible to carry out sustainable social and urban transformation processes with inclusive housing without local leadership and capacity in each district. We can also apply this learning to the challenge of social housing now facing our public policies, where we lack good examples of building and consolidating supportive environments of neighbours and vital ecosystems.

Where the value of districts with identity creates memorable places. Shaped by local environments and spaces of solidarity and trust. That promote and facilitate the vitality of local economies. Where the stories of El Aka and Las Doñas, of Jorge and Erica, of Cielo, Yeizon and Luz Mila can unfold. I ask myself: how could we achieve some of these attributes in our new social housing projects? What do we need to include in our design principles, management models and timelines, financing schemes and social support programmes to build real neighbourhoods?

1 Hemingway, A., "BC's speculation tax is a key piece of the housing affordability puzzle", *Policy Note*, 25 October 2018
2 Hemingway, A., "Property taxes in Vancouver are still too low, fueling inequality and speculation", *Policy Note*, 2 December 2019.
3 Note that some of the analysis and text in this article is drawn from previous published work of mine including those referenced in the preceding and subsequent footnotes.
4 Hemingway, A., "Financing public housing: how a massive expansion of rental homes can literally pay for itself", *Policy Note*, 21 April 2022.
5 Hemingway, A., "Five reasons supply matters to the housing crisis", *Policy Note*, 14 September 2022.
6 Bratu, C., Harjunen, O. and Saarimaa, T., "City-wide effects of new housing supply: evidence from moving chains", VATT Working Papers, 2021.

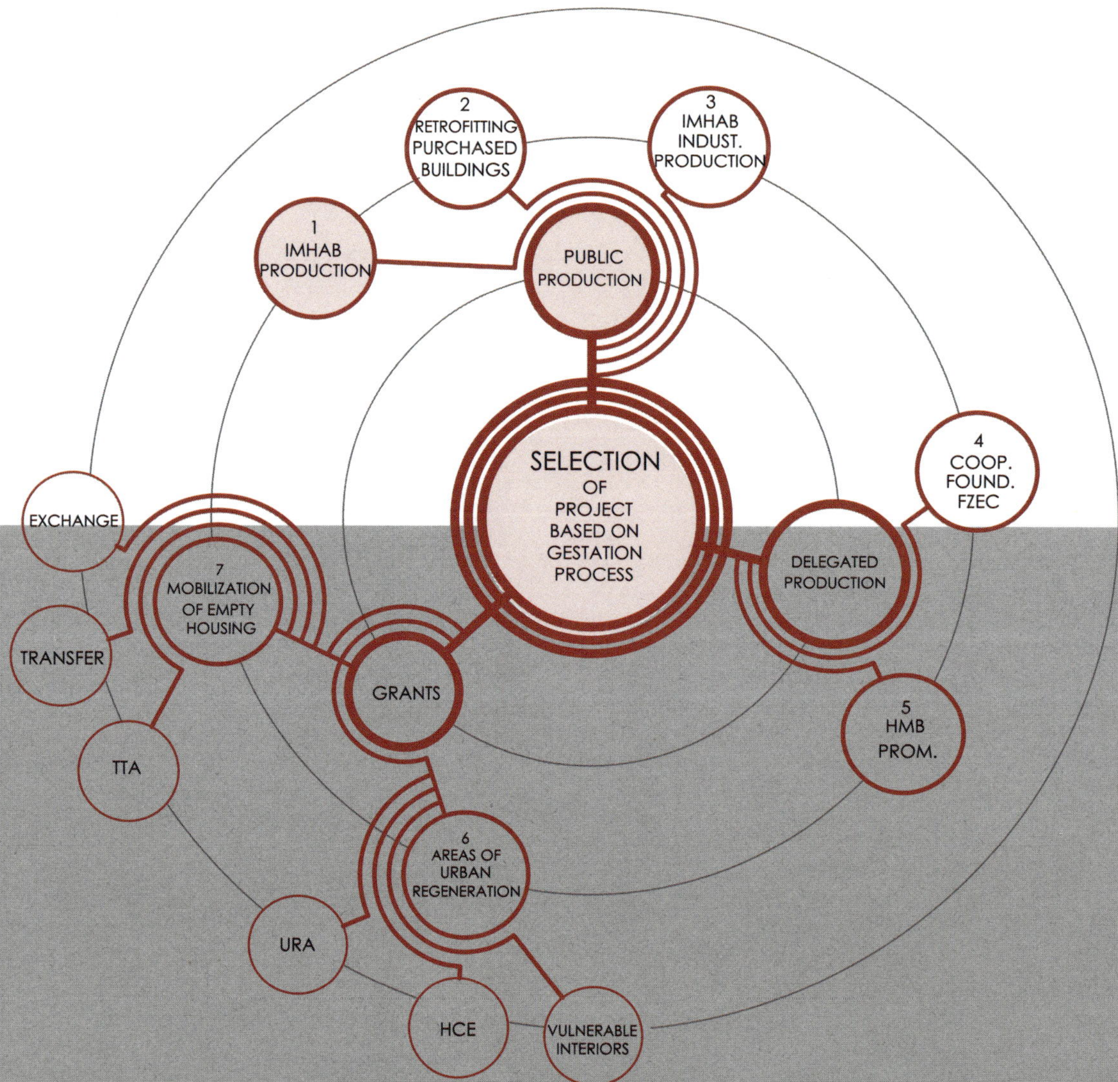
SELECTION
OF
PROJECT
BASED ON
GESTATION
PROCESS
PUBLIC
PRODUCTION
1
IMHAB
PRODUCTION
2
RETROFITTING
PURCHASED
BUILDINGS
3
IMHAB
INDUST.
PRODUCTION
DELEGATED
PRODUCTION
4
COOP.
FOUND.
FZEC
5
HMB
PROM.
GRANTS
6
AREAS OF
URBAN
REGENERATION
URA
HCE
VULNERABLE
INTERIORS
7
MOBILIZATION
OF EMPTY
HOUSING
EXCHANGE
TRANSFER
TTA

IMHAB council housing production

01 68 housing units / Sancho de Ávila II **Baas - Jordi Badia** Surface right

02 105 housing units / Glòries **Bonell i Gil / Peris + Toral** Seniors

03 44 housing units / Can Fabra **Roldán + Berengué** Young people

04 81 housing units / Josep Pla **Estudi Massip-Bosch** Seniors + Surface right

05 61 housing units / Bon Pastor **Pascual-Ausió** Affected by urban planning

06 44 housing units / Quatre Camins **Ravetllat-Ribas** Seniors

07 47 housing units + 20 accommodations / Tànger **Coll-Leclerc** Social rent

The need for collaboration between designers and constructors

Juan Carlos Melero
Director of Technical Services of the IMHAB

The habitual model of public procurement

When developing council housing, designing a building in collaboration with the constructors who will carry out the work is almost impossible in the usual public procurement systems.

The application of the Spanish Contracts Act is mandatory in the production of public housing, and the usual contracting systems deriving from it radically separate the work of the designers from that of the constructors responsible for building it, blocking progress in the industrialization of public housing construction.

The designer of the project wins an ideas competition in which a jury chooses the proposal with the most architectural quality. This proposal must be materialized by foreseeing the construction of the building using materials and systems that guarantee "the maximum competition" in the future tender for the construction. This is determined by the Spanish Contracts Act, which, with this premise, makes it impossible to draft projects that use construction systems developed by companies that invest in research and develop their own systems.

The contractors participating in the public tender for the construction of the work make a financial offer on a project in the design of which they play no part. They will take risks in the future hope of forcing changes to the project that will allow them to recover a financial loss that, in many cases, is calculated on the basis of statistics of previous tenders.

Once the tender has been awarded to the contractor, work begins and the battle is on. The works management will fiercely defend the soundness of its project. The construction company will question it, looking for a loophole that allows it to introduce modifications to reduce the impact of excessive economic losses. The constructors, who actually build the work, will see their prices forced down in an attempt to adapt to the budgets presented by the contractor to win the tender. Only the good will of the parties and the mediation of representatives of the public housing body will prevent each from fighting its own battle.

The seed of this conflict is the habitual bidding model established in the Spanish Contracts Act, which makes collaboration in the design of the project between works management and constructors impossible. It is an inoperative production model to achieve the IMHAB's objectives for its new production, including:

- Reducing the environmental impact associated with the manufacture of materials used to construct buildings.
- Reducing the deadlines for building work.

Joint contracting of project design and construction

In order to meet these objectives, in February and October 2020 the IMHAB promoted a new type of tender according to which project designers and contractors had to make joint proposals for buildings that, guaranteeing their architectural quality (35% of the score in the tender process), had to be developed with materials that produced the minimum environmental impact in their manufacturing process (25% of the score), using prefabricated construction systems that reduce construction times (25% of the score). The fact that the economic offer represents just 15% of the total score explains why the winning proposals were those with the highest quality, not those with the lowest price.

The consequence of this new type of tender in which the technical project is drafted jointly by planners and construction companies is the production of council housing that replaces reinforced concrete structures, responsible for 8% of global CO_2 emissions, with wooden structures, a material that, during its growth, captures CO_2 present in the atmosphere. With this change in material, buildings become CO_2 sinks, and the emissions associated with the manufacture of construction materials are reduced by more than 30%.

The use of solid wood makes it possible to turn the construction site into the place of assembly of solid panels, previously manufactured in the workshop. Simultaneous production in the workshop of solid wood walls and floor slabs with the on-site construction of the foundation makes it possible to reduce construction times by approximately 35%. Workshop production also reduces accidents, improves the conditions of the workforce, opens up new opportunities for professionalization in the sector and efficiently manages the waste generated during construction.

Work carried out shows that the objectives described can be met, without a significant increase in cost, if planners and constructors work together in a collaborative framework. Unfortunately, the Spanish Contracts Act specifies that this model of joint bidding for design and construction that has produced such good results is exceptional and, therefore, cannot be replicated.

New forms of public procurement

However, this same act opens a small loophole that could allow the collaboration of constructors in the design phase of the technical project without it being exceptional. It involves bidding for construction of the work by defining the object of the contract according to its functionalities rather than limiting it to a single solution. This is a hitherto unexplored approach, an intermediate path between the two previous models.

The objectives of the IMHAB's new building productions have been outlined, and the new procurement model enabling collaboration between planners and constructors in the design phase of the technical project is underway. We trust that the end result will be as hoped.

Inhabiting without owning

Marta Peris
Doctor of Architecture. Lecturer in Architectural Projects, UPC. ETSAB.
Co-founder of Peris+Toral Arquitectes

Inhabiting is the process that brings together all the visible or invisible traces left by the inhabitant on the architectural support during the process of appropriation. By inhabiting, each person adapts to their environment, while making it their place. Appropriation is, then, an appearance. Invisible links appear between the inhabitants, their objects, depositors of memory, and the space in which they are set. Objects that represent the values of those who live there. Objects that do not reveal memories but build intimate atmospheres. Atmospheres made up of thoughts, memories and dreams. Atmospheres that are the result of enveloping materiality, its touch, the way light enters the space, the way this space reverberates, and the inside and outside views that it articulates.

In new-build projects, the challenge of designing these atmospheres without the participation of the end user make the architect the *first inhabitant* and the house, their gift for the future occupant, who will take over the task of inhabiting. In the words of Juhani Pallasmaa, “the architect is always obliged to conceive of the design essentially for himself as a momentary substitute for the real occupant. Without realizing it, the designer becomes a silent actor on the imaginary stage of the project. He is also a director who needs to master the progression, mood, rhythm and perfection of a complex, multisensory whole. At the end of the design process, the architect offers the building to the user as a gift”.[1]

To pick up Pallasmaa’s simile, like a director with the staging, the architect transforms the spatial framework into an environment capable of conveying attitudes, emotions and moods; he designs an experience. With each stroke proposed by the pencil, he visualizes a virtual tour of the house that becomes a *promenade architecturale*, a choreography that places the body and its movements at the centre to connect views, situations and sensations, where architecture is not the objective so much as the frame. As the floor plan unfolds, the future occupation is considered: sufficient space to hold the sofa next to the terrace; the spacious corner to anchor the lamp and the armchair next to the window; the generous setback to support the table next to the kitchen… Closeness and proximity that hint at forms of appropriation. Suggesting without imposing. Inhabiting without owning. This is the invisible footprint of the architect as the *first inhabitant*.

If we accept that every atmosphere influences the inhabitant’s perception and that observation, memory and imagination come together in the perception process, we will also accept that the home is not a mere stage of life, but rather an experience in which mind and space intertwine. The house frames and guides our actions, perceptions, thoughts and feelings. We might say, then, that inhabiting a real house is a creative act.

Given the dizzying advance of new information and communication technologies and their omnipresence in our lives, it is worth asking how they will affect the verb to inhabit. Augmented reality and mixed reality promote immersion in settings in which real and virtual elements interact in real time and in three dimensions, becoming integrated into the real environment, superimposing a layer of digital information that reconfigures the immediate space. Another form of appropriation of space probably appears here, one that no longer falls exclusively to the objects that surround us and that acquire a symbolic value in the process of inhabiting. The home will not only be occupied with real objects, it will also act like a stage that offers and accumulates experiences. On the other hand, technological devices have largely monopolized the private space. The intimacy of the person that we previously associated with the solid privacy of the bedroom now seems more liquid when limited to the immediate vicinity of the body, either to access our personal computer or to hold our mobile in our hands.

As a *dreamer of houses*, faced with this displacement of jealously guarded intimacy from physical to virtual space, faced with this displacement of the forms of appropriation of space from possession to experience, I cannot help wondering whether the home, in spite of or thanks to technological pressure, will continue to stimulate us to feel, think and create while still being “nest and shell”.[2] As an architect, I wonder if these displacements will promote plural living, since sharing will be the key to an environmentally sustainable and responsible life.

1 Pallasmaa, Juhani. *Tocando el mundo*. Barcelona: Ediciones Asimétricas, 2019, p. 85.

2 In the phenomenology of the verb to inhabit, according to Bachelard, there are initial images or archetypes of the refuge, such as nests and shells, which show how humans like to withdraw into their corner: “Only those who know how to withdraw inhabit intensely. We carry within us a whole store of images of withdrawal.” BACHELARD, Gaston and CHAMPOURCIN, Ernestina (trans.). *La poética del espacio*. Mexico: Fondo de Cultura Económica, 1975, p. 30.

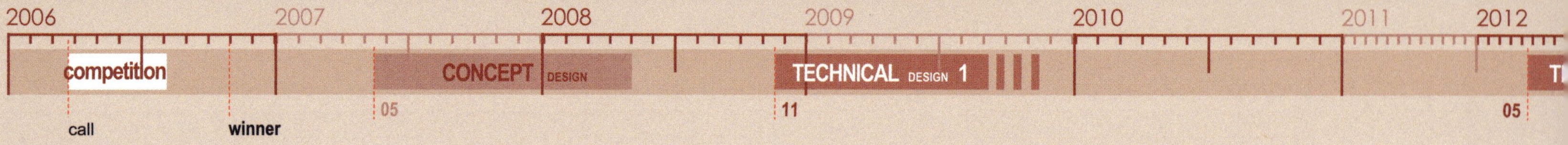

68 housing units / Sancho de Ávila II

BAAS - Jordi Badia

The building is situated in a strange location, in the middle of a landscaped courtyard at the centre of a Poblenou street block with no direct access to the street. This awkward two-part volume, the product of planning, one 11 storeys high and the other six, is nuanced by a strategy of crushing the corners to relate it to the heights of the buildings around it and its wider surroundings. On the ground floor, the building is perforated to allow passage through it and improve connection with the public space.

The project is materialized in rough, solid, dark-coloured brick that contrasts with the building's technological environment and evokes the material used to build most of the industrial architecture in this place. The horizontal windows give the rooms plenty of light and exceptional views for such small homes.

Model - Process

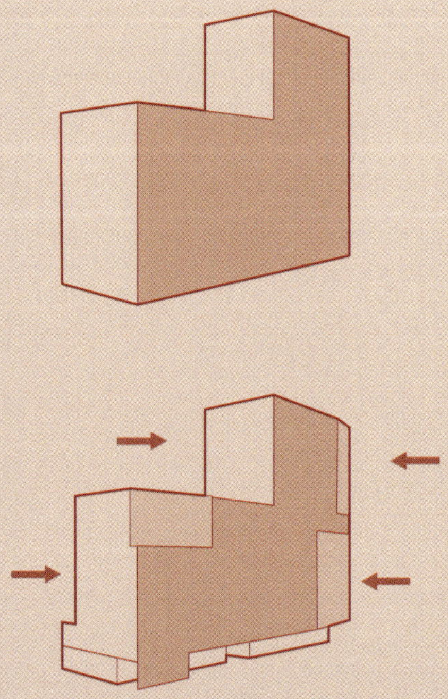

Concept – Competition

Models - Process

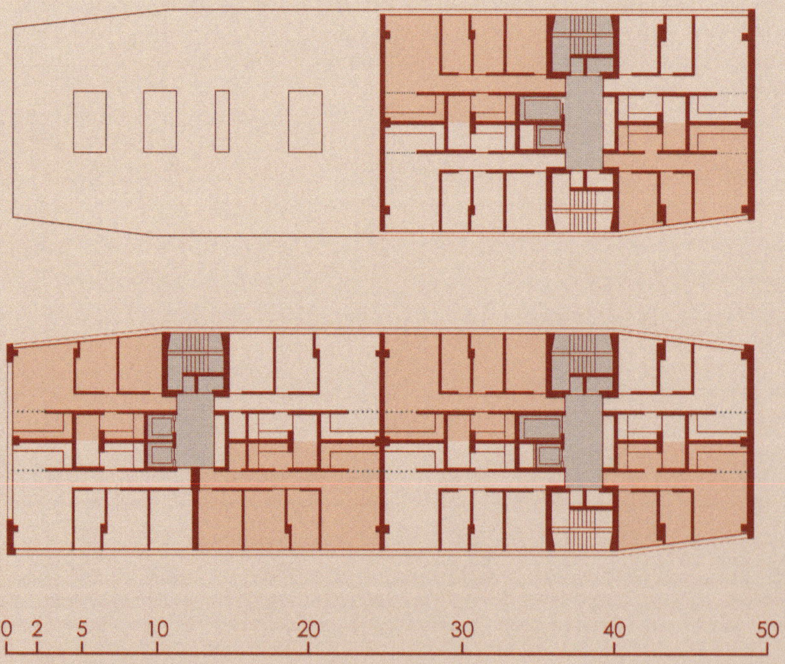

Typical floor plan 1:500

Location: pl. Dolors Piera, 9-11. Barcelona. **Programme:** 68 homes. Surface right. **Surface area:** 15,195.95 m². **Cost:** 7,073,283.35 € (CEB VAT incl.). **Architect:** Jordi Badia. **Collaborations:** Alba Azuara, Andreu Egido, Victoria Llinares. **Contractor:** Sacyr. **Consultancy:** AIA (installations), BOMA (structures), Salvador Arisa (building engineer).

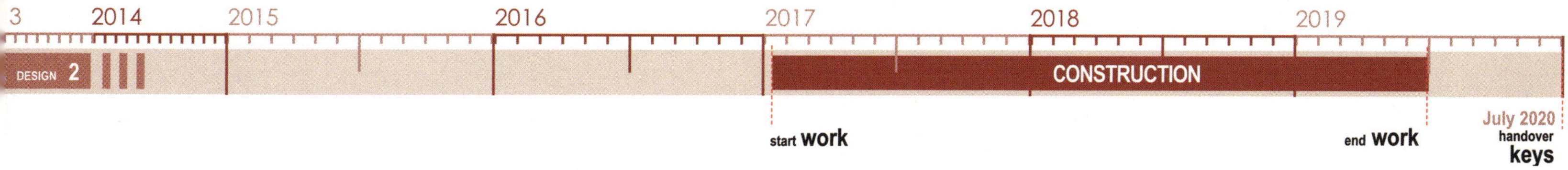

Photographs - Adrià Goula © - 2022

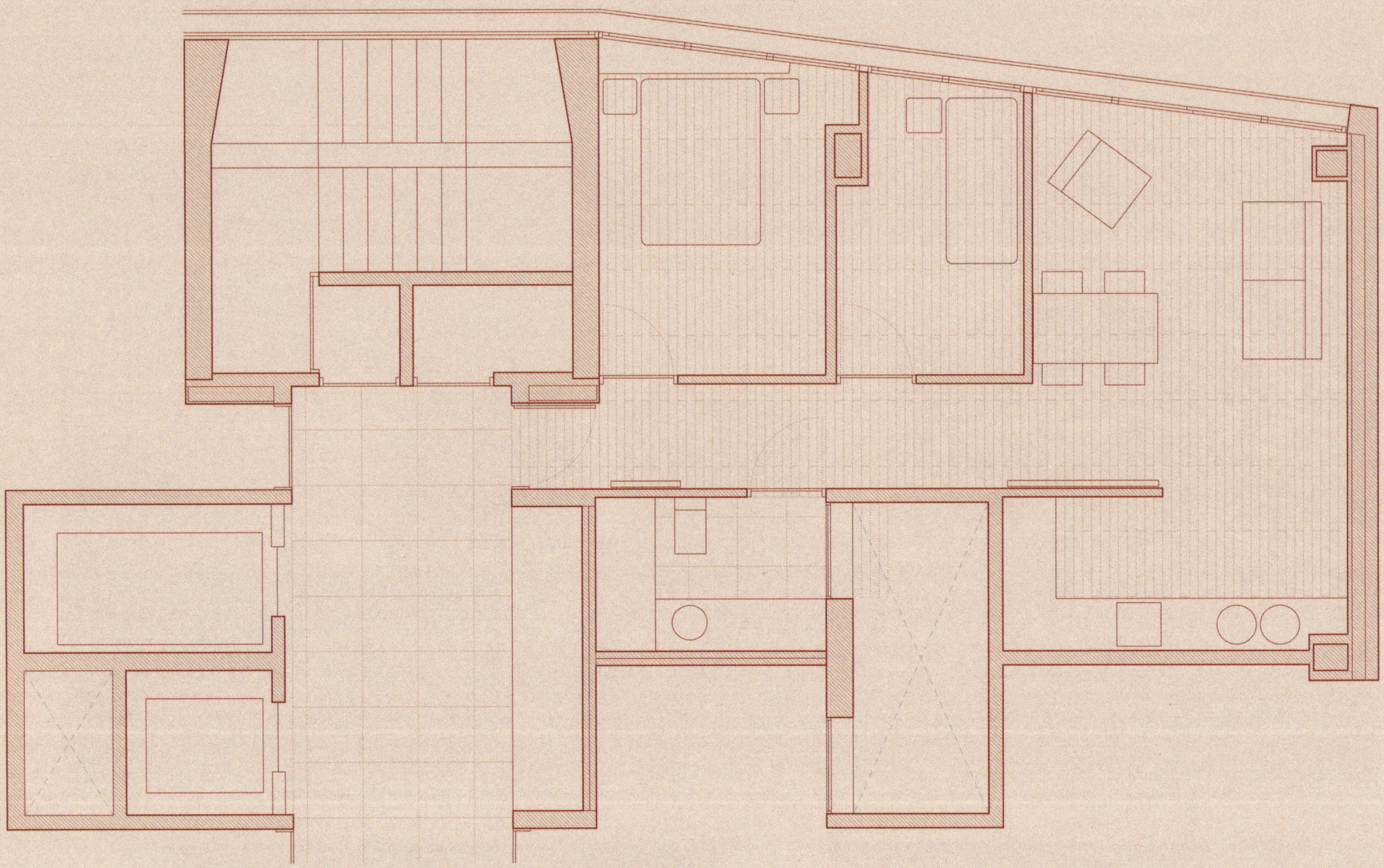

ΓFloor plan of dwelling 1:75

ΓReference image provided by the author

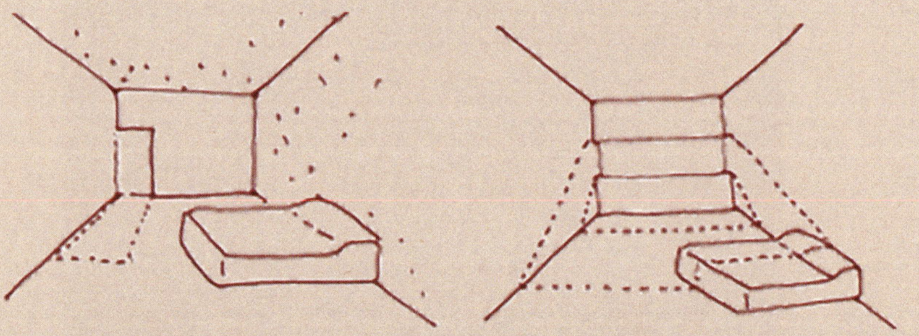

ΓConceptual lighting diagram - Competition phase

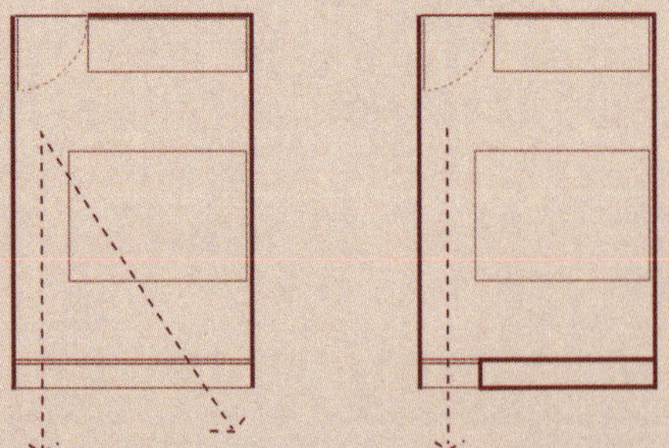

Horizontal window

Vertical window

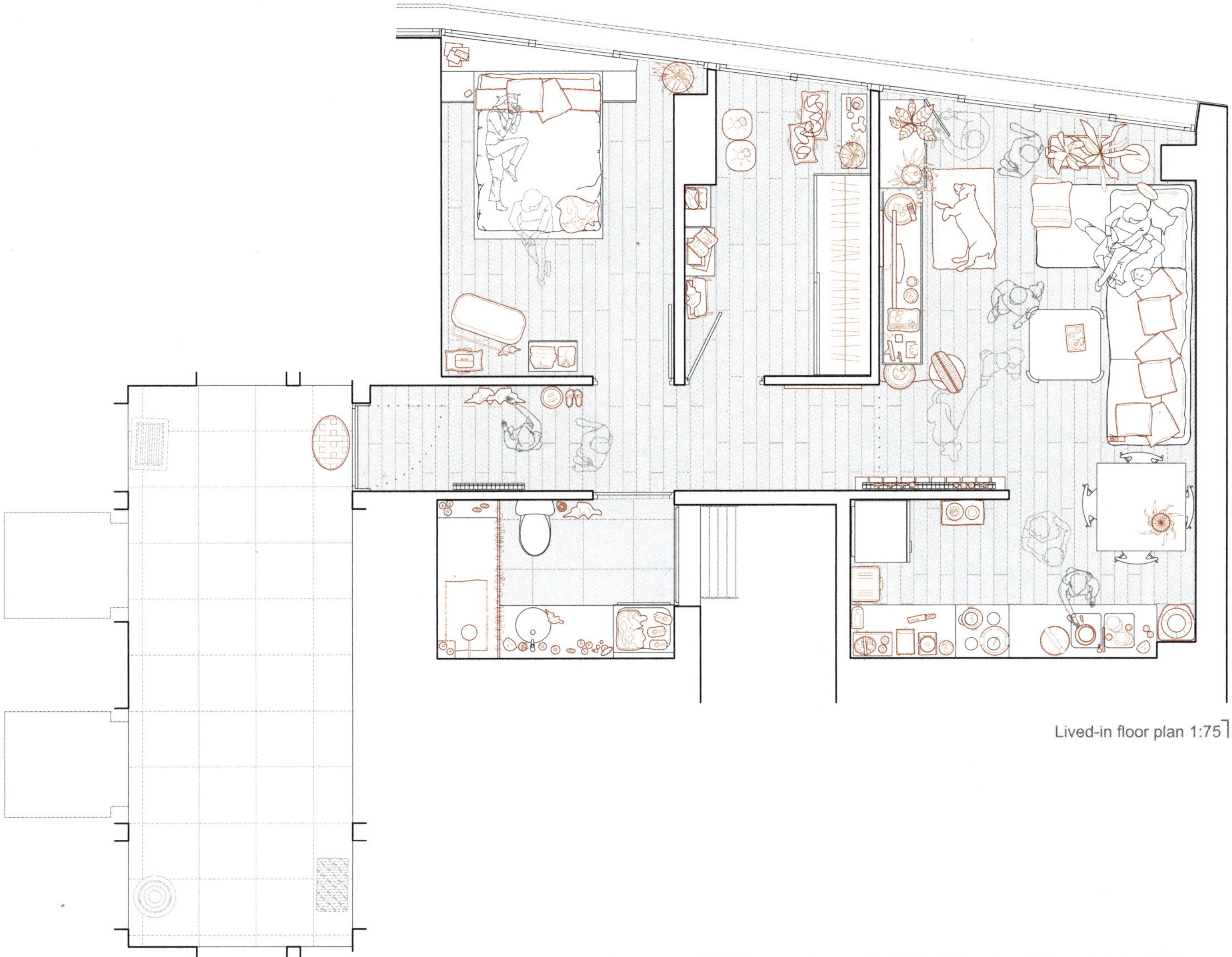

Lived-in floor plan 1:75

"We're living in a prime location, with incredible views and lighting. Considering the market value of the flats, it would be unthinkable to be able to live where we live."

Interview – 2022

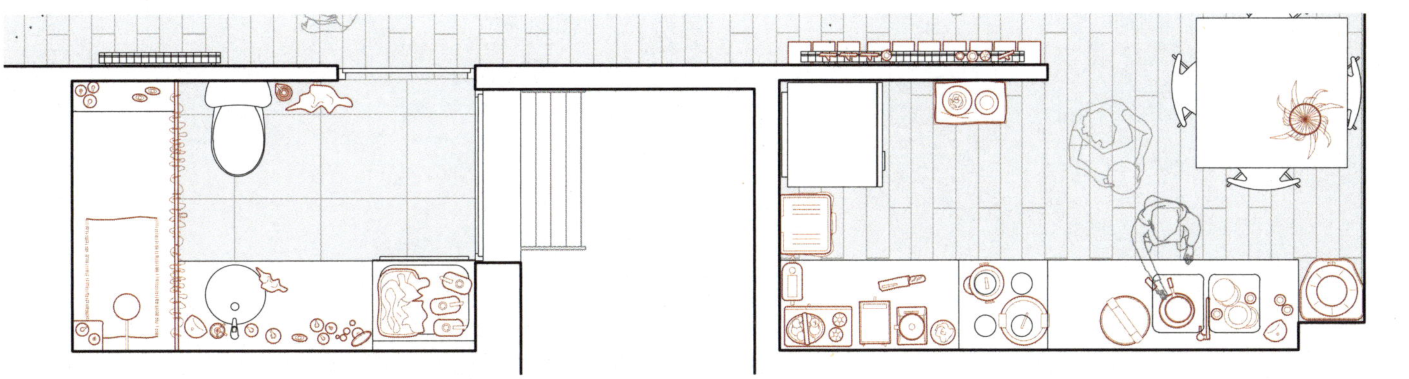

Model - Process

Model - Process

Model - Process

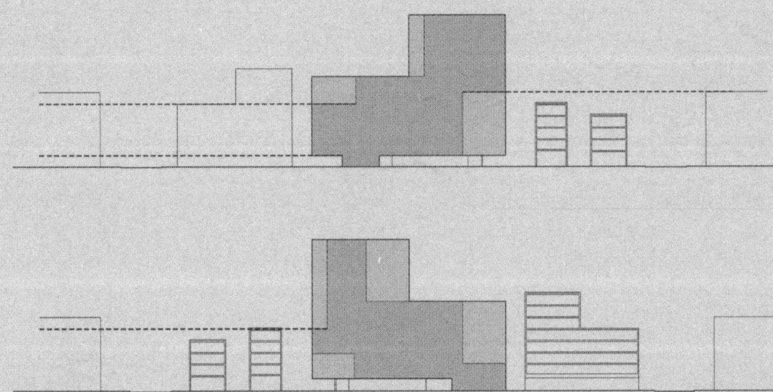

Render of concept project

Elevations

Photographs - Adrià Goula © - 2022

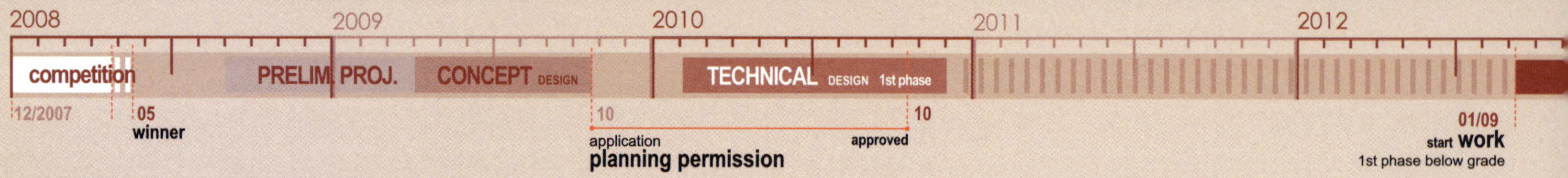

105 housing units / Glòries

Bonell i Gil / Peris + Toral

The project is located on a plot of land close to Plaça de les Glòries that forms part of a block where the urban fabric is cut across by Diagonal. To respond to the complexity of the setting, two different strategies are superimposed. A continuous plinth recognizes the layout of the Eixample grid, while three tall volumes continue the sequence of adjacent freestanding blocks that respond to Diagonal. The two geometries are superposed on the chamfered corner, reinforcing the identity of Cerdà's grid.

A plinth that houses the social and health centres supports three blocks of housing, each with seven or eight homes per landing along a central corridor. On the roof of each block is a laundry, a porch for community clothes lines and a sunroof where urban allotments are planned. The rooftop of the plinth level is turned into a community terrace. Directly connected with this terrace, each block has a multipurpose room to hold activities organized by the social services that manage the building.

The 40 m² of each home are laid out in a sequence of spaces around a central core that houses the bathroom. The use of sliding doors creates rooms that are not permanently enclosed and expands the spatial experience. Doors can be closed or opened to transform the space and allow different degrees of privacy.

Model - Competition

Model – Project

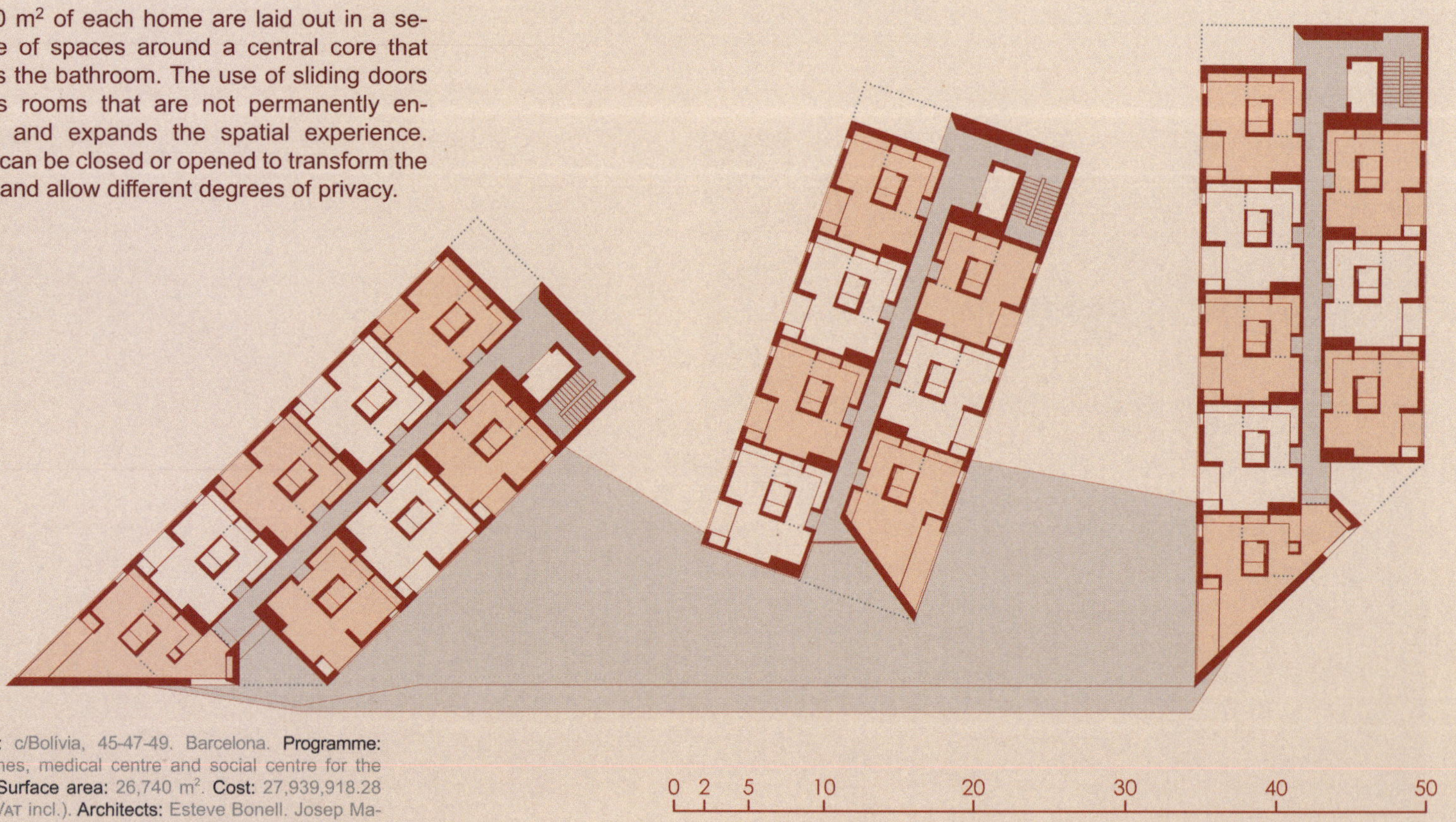

Typical floor plan 1:500

Location: c/Bolívia, 45-47-49. Barcelona. **Programme:** 105 homes, medical centre and social centre for the elderly. **Surface area:** 26,740 m². **Cost:** 27,939,918.28 € (CEB VAT incl.). **Architects:** Esteve Bonell. Josep Maria Gil, Marta Peris, José Manuel Toral. **Collaborations:** Elisabet Aguilar, Ana Espinosa, Genís Fernàndez, Izaskun González, Miguel Ángel Gorrachategui, Roger Parareda, David Pérez Ordeig, Cristina Porta, Cecilia Rodríguez, Albert Rubio, Maria Ubach. **Consultancy:** AIA (installations), Jaume Pastor - Eletresjota Tècnics Associats, Manel Fernández - Bernuz-Fernández, UTE Scrinser & Primur.

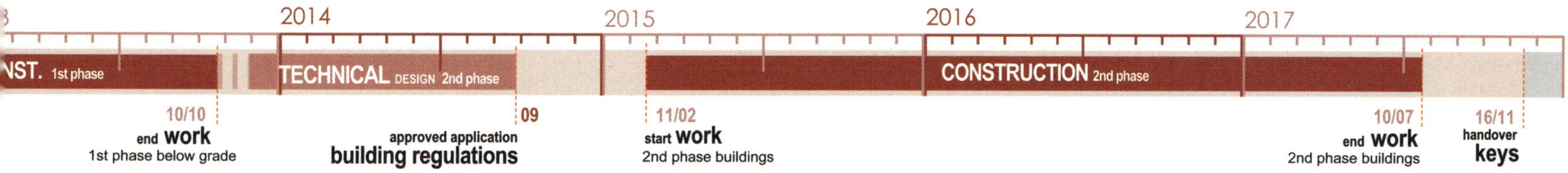

Photographs - Adrià Goula © - 2022

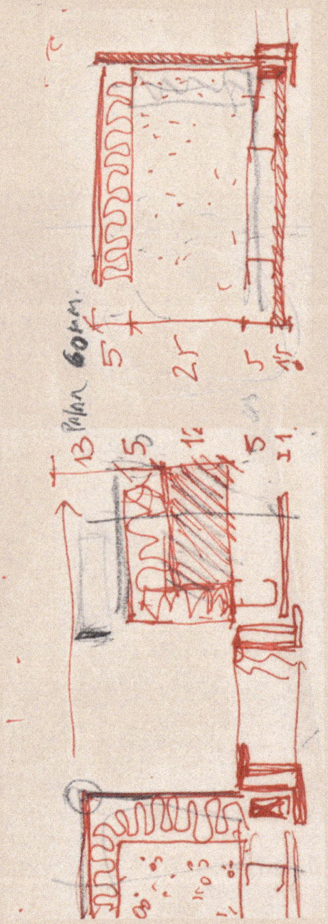

Façade detail sketch

Façade detail sketch

Construction photograph

Photographs - Marta Peris © - 2022

Photographs - Adrià Goula © - 2022

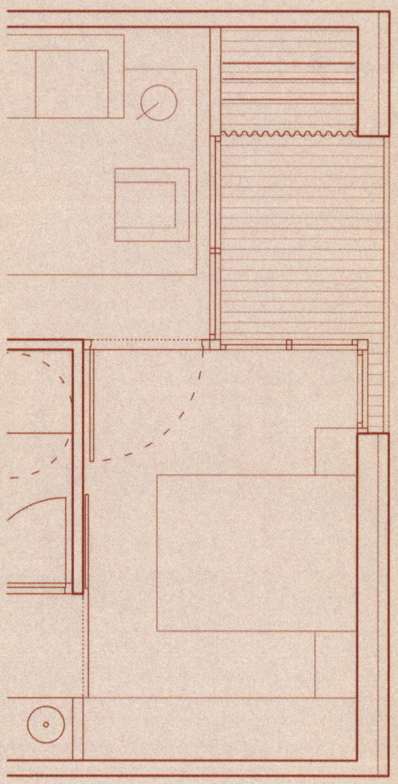

Floor plan of dwelling - Competition

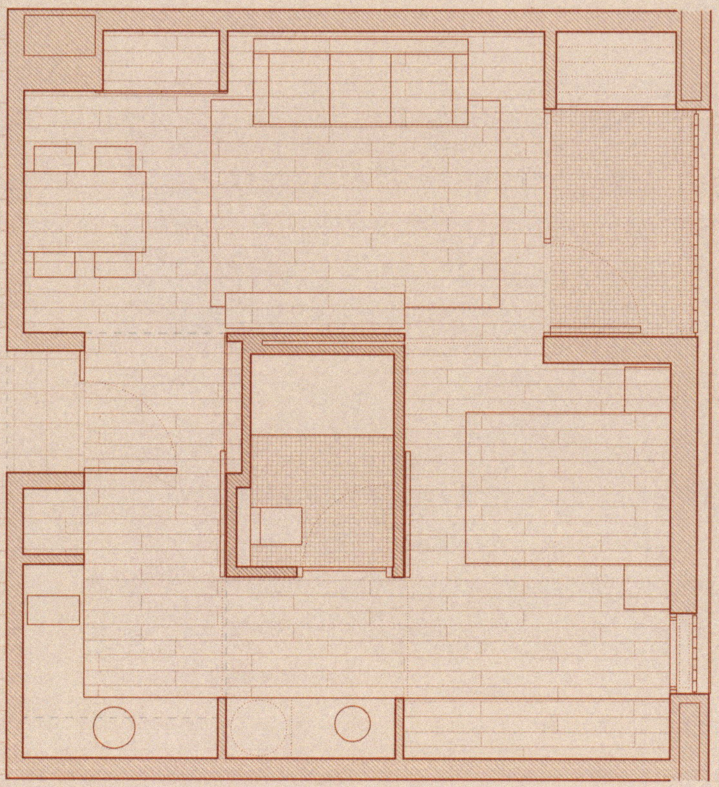

Floor plan of dwelling 1:75

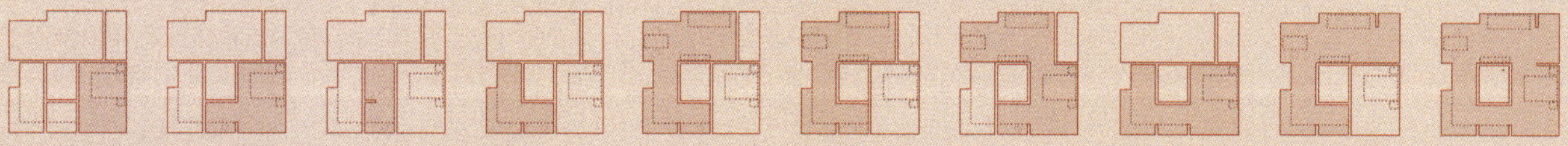

Succession of spaces inside the home

Conceptual view of dwelling

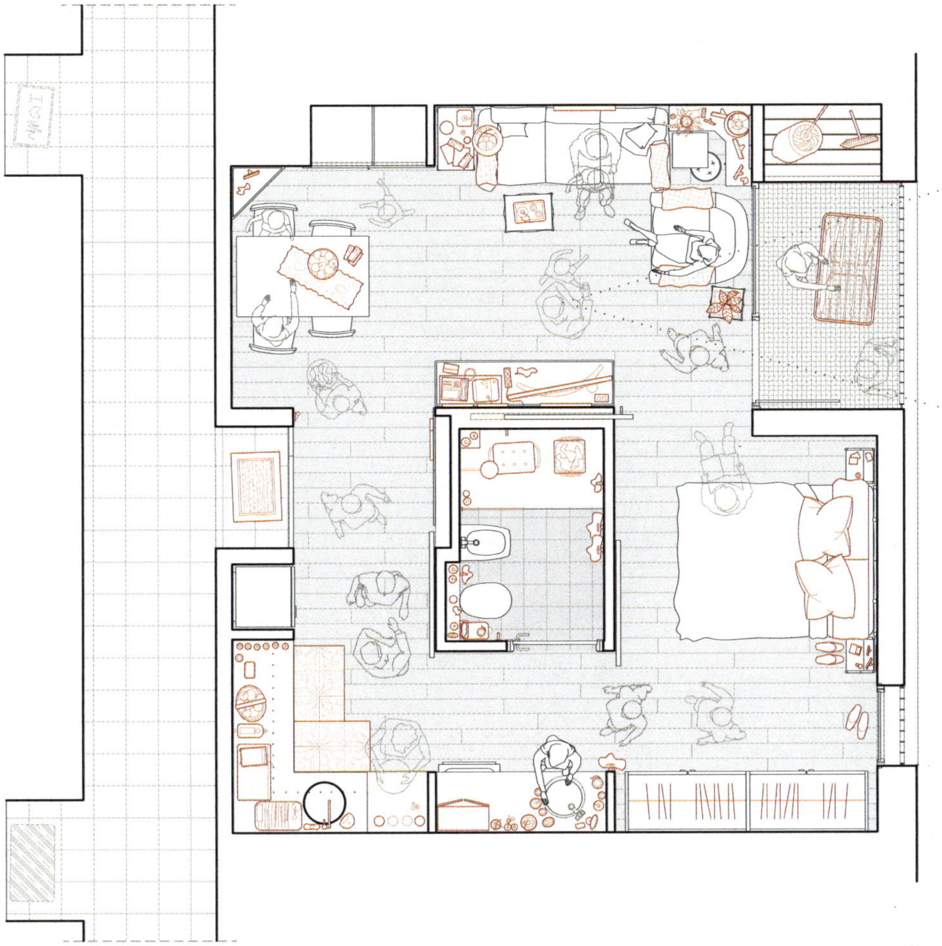

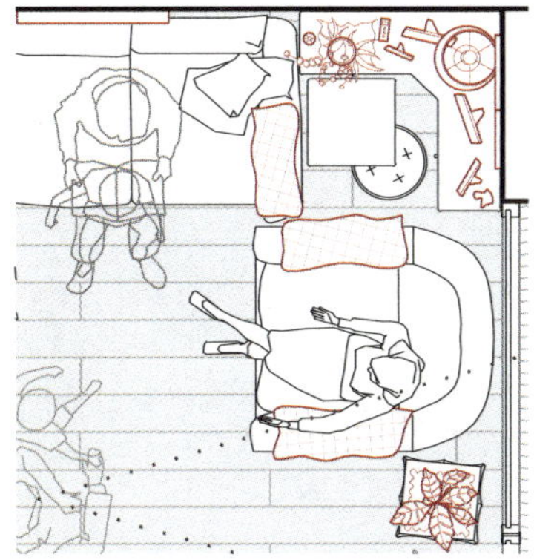

Lived-in floor plan 1:75

Interview – 2022

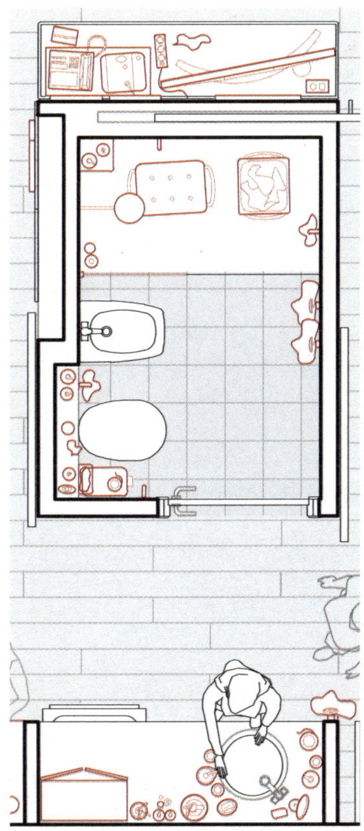

"When we close the door, it's like our kingdom, and I feel really comfortable here. From having had very big houses to now being in this one, which is smaller but with all conveniences, it's really practical to look after (I like it to be clean and well-kept), it doesn't take me that long and I enjoy it. Also, because it's such a bright, airy flat with great views... it's all really easy."

Render – Competition phase

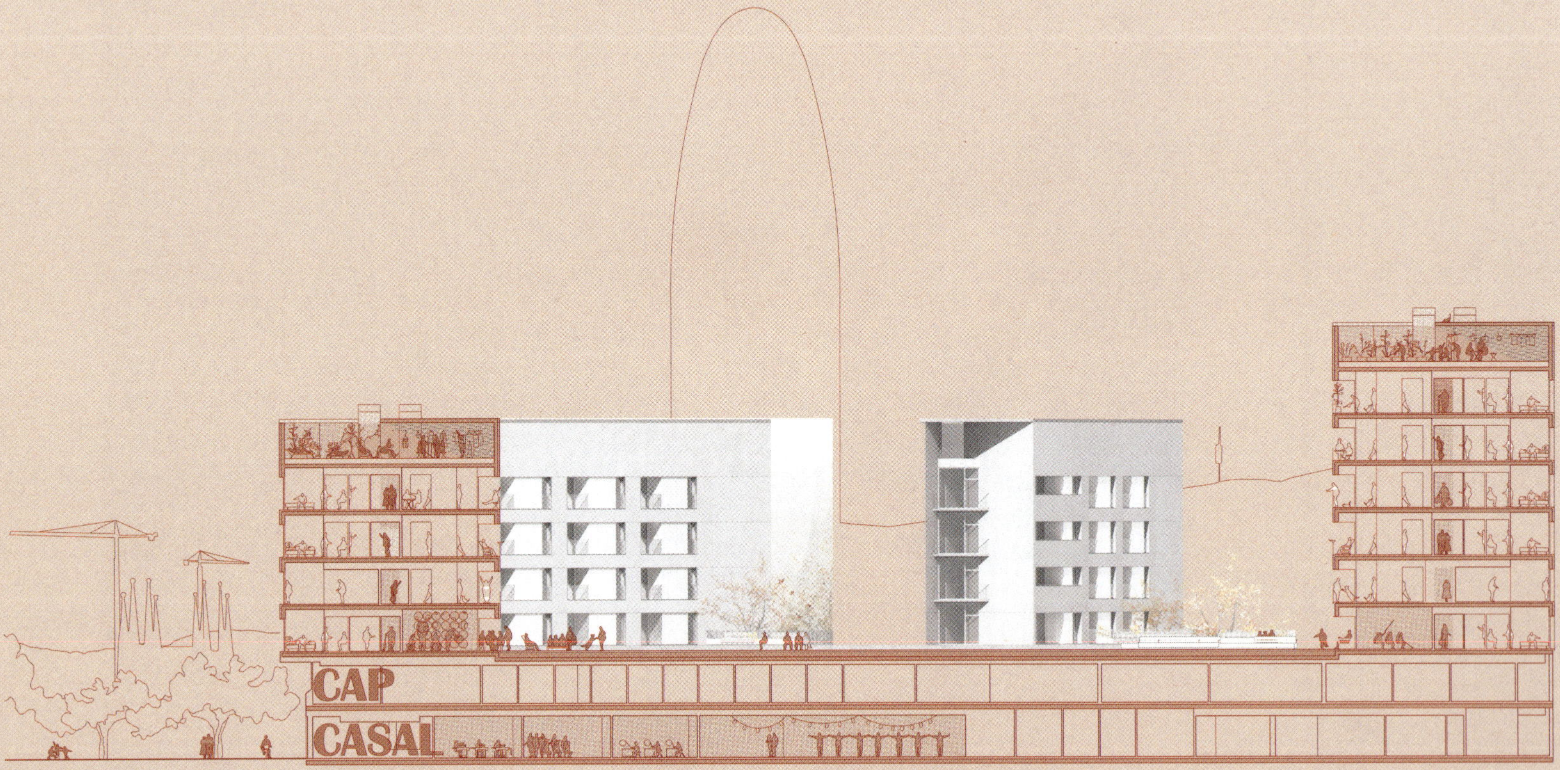

Longitudinal section

Photographs - Maite Caramés © - 2022

Photographs - Marta Peris © - 2022

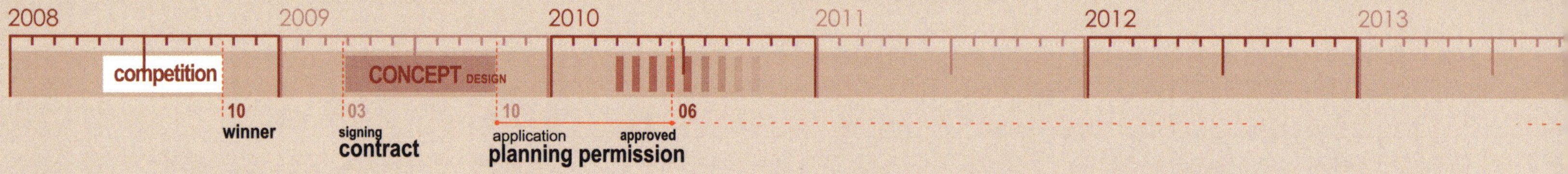

44 housing units / Can Fabra

Roldán + Berengué

Warehouse G was built in 1905 to store yarn. It measures 100 m long by 15 deep and 11 high, and is divided into two floors by a concrete floor slab.

Our intervention in the warehouse activates all the original elements for the new programme and reuses its physical, spatial and historical qualities to make the new construction more efficient and reinforce the nature of the original building.

As it is a 100-m-long warehouse, the first decision was to highlight its largest dimension, its length: we enter through the centre, creating an inner plaza that marks the starting point of the double stairway, where it begins its diagonal ascent. This cascading community space is our structural contribution to the original building.

The new building is "assembled". It is a dry construction, built, like the industrial warehouse, using very few materials.

The existing warehouse acts as a thermal buffer. The new homes are separated from the original façades and roof of the warehouse and have their own wooden façade.

Structurally we reuse the warehouse's two floors. We use them with no type of reinforcement to support the two new levels on each, increasing the original two floors to four floors of homes.

Intervention: industrial heritage + social housing + cultural venue. The community spaces in the lobby can be occupied completely freely, generating a space for neighbourhood relations in which the exchange of ideas and the common use of these areas are part of the daily life of their occupants.

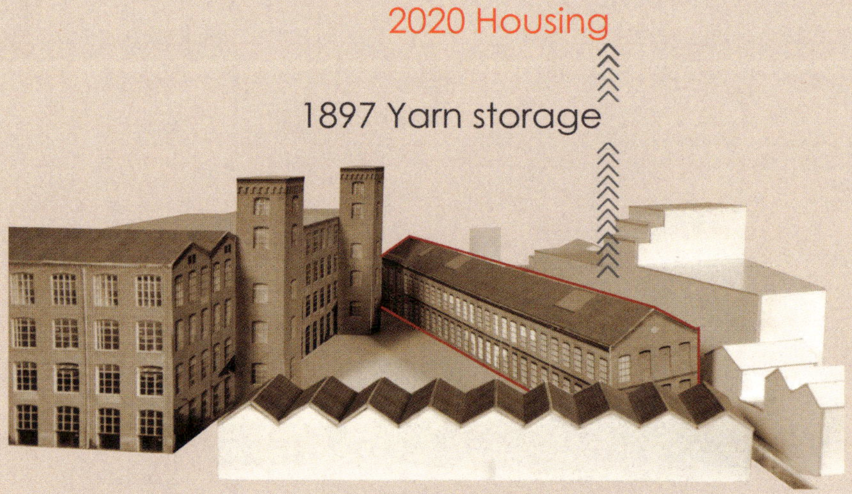

Model – Project

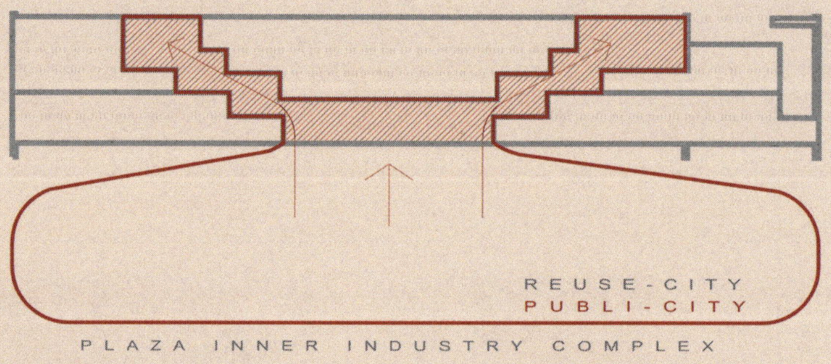

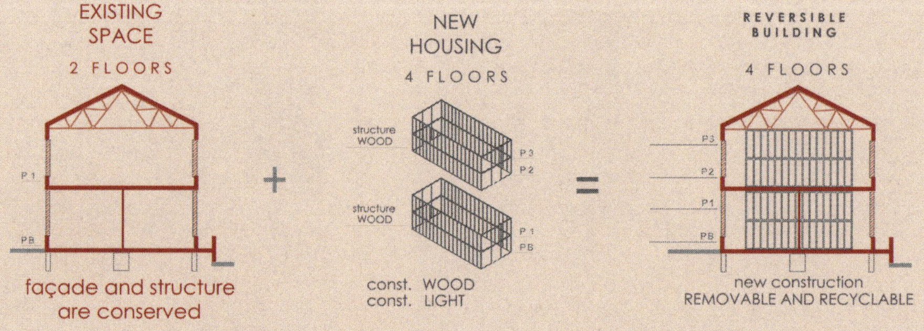

Intervention diagram

Location: c/Parellada, 7-11. Barcelona. **Programme:** 44 homes for young people. **Surface area:** 4,252 m². **Architects:** Mercè Berengué, Miguel Roldán. **Collaborations:** Zana Bosnic, Vicenç Sanz, Juan José Pérez Jarque, Eduard Resina, David Espuña, Martí Pardo. **Contractor:** Sacyr. **Consultancy:** Caba Sostenibilitat, SL (installations), Bernuz-Fernández Arquitectes, SL (structures), Salvador Arisa, Joan Just (building engineers).

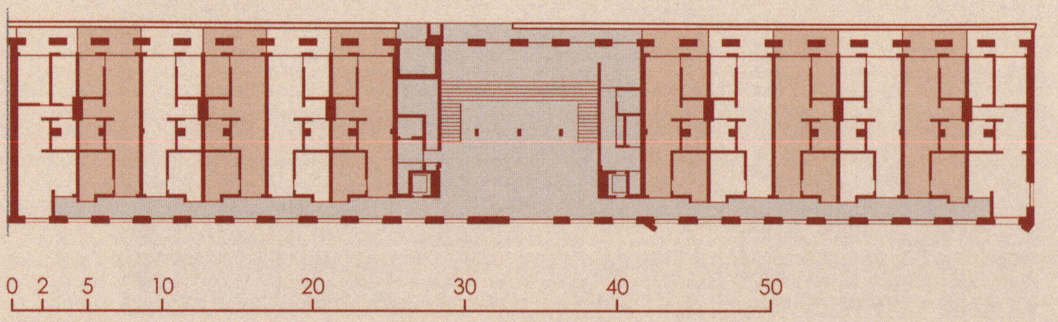

Typical floor plan 1:500

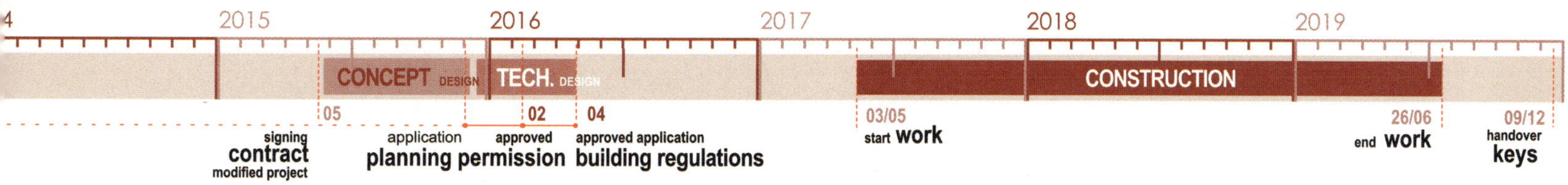

Photographs - Maite Caramés © -]

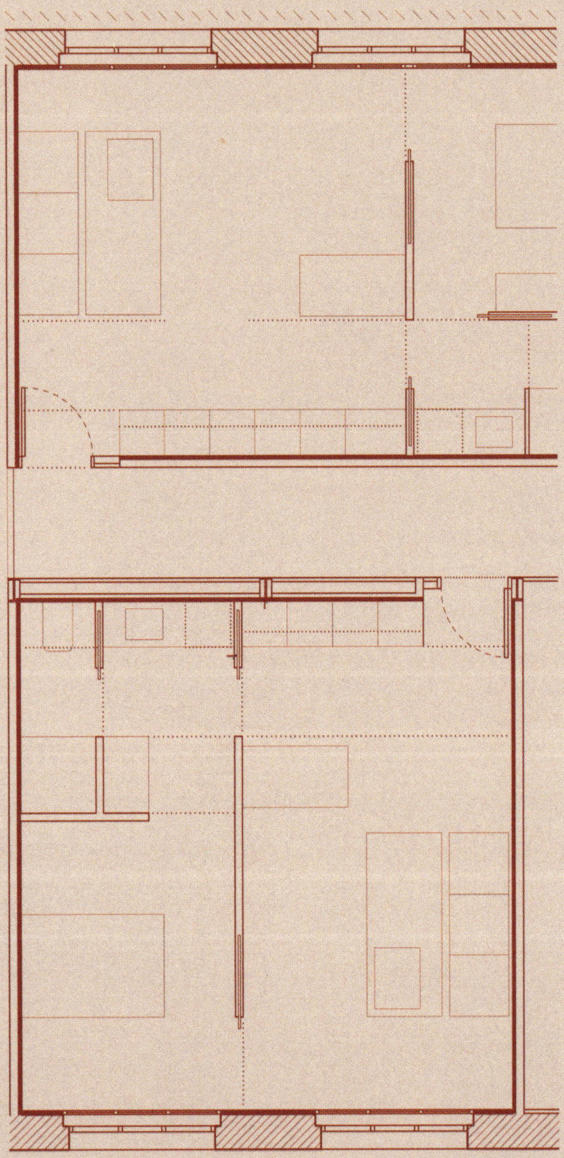

Floor plan of dwelling - Competition phase (without scale)

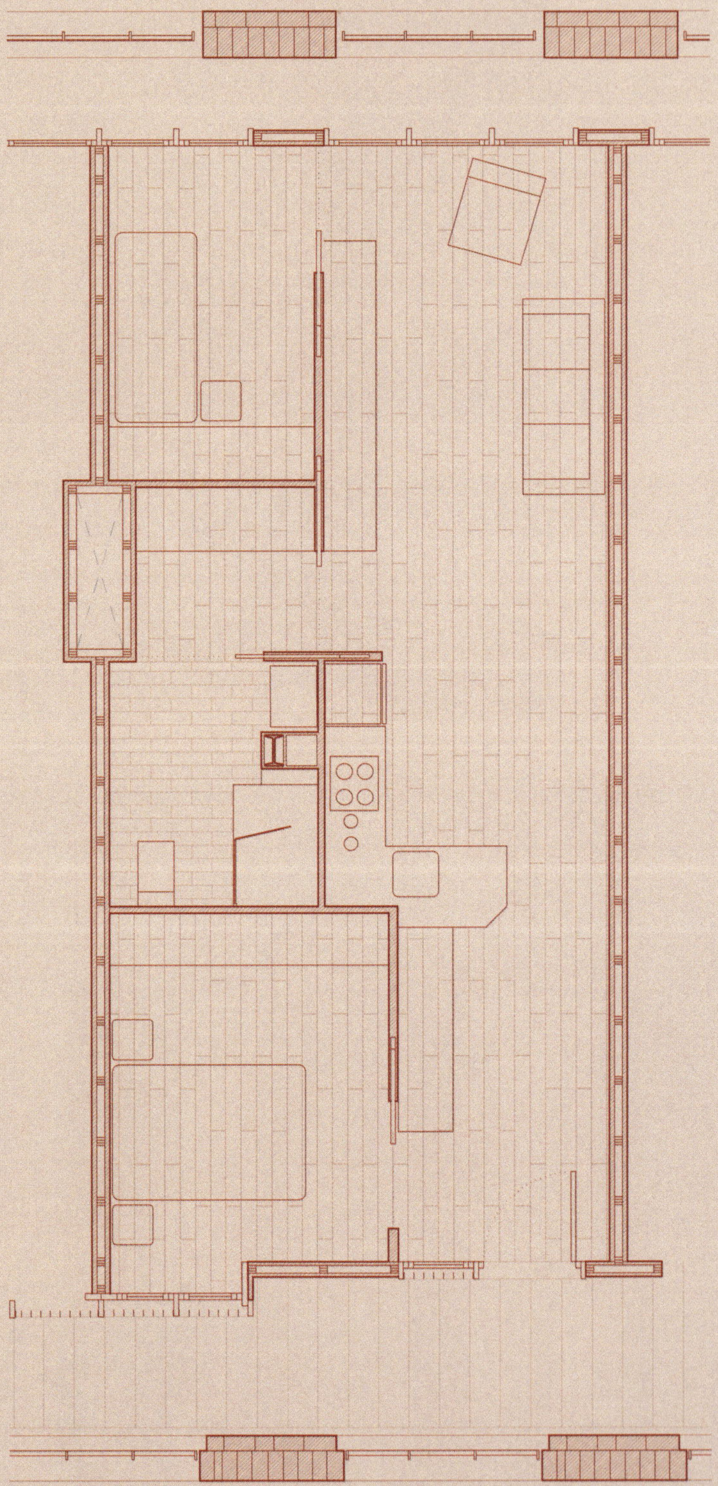

Floor plan of dwelling 1:75

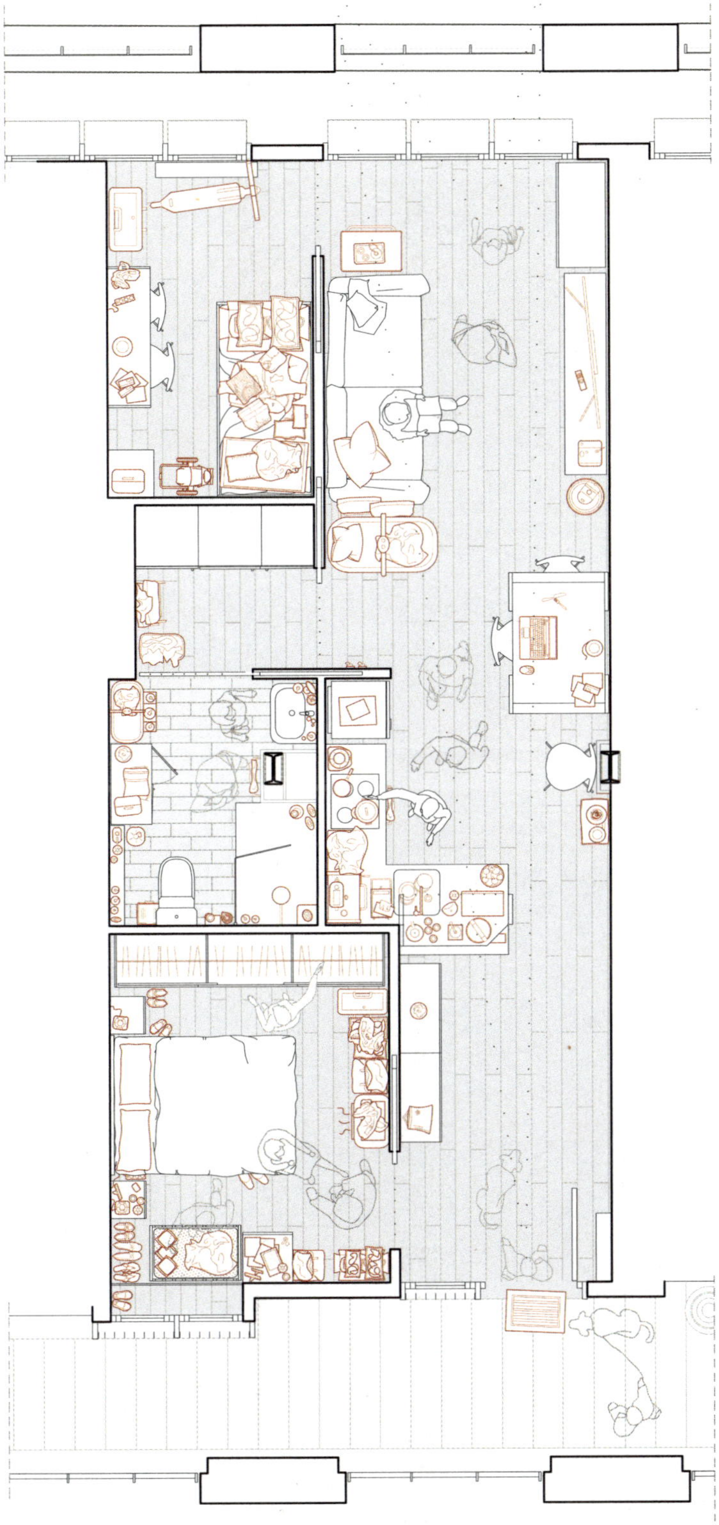

Interview – 2022

"It's a new flat, inside an old factory, which is striking in itself, but it's new, it's well laid out, it makes the most of the space... Well, for two people it's fine. For two adults and a child... as you know, next week we'll find out!"

⌈Photograph of interior space, 1905

⌈Construction photographs - ROLDÁN-BERENGUÉ ©

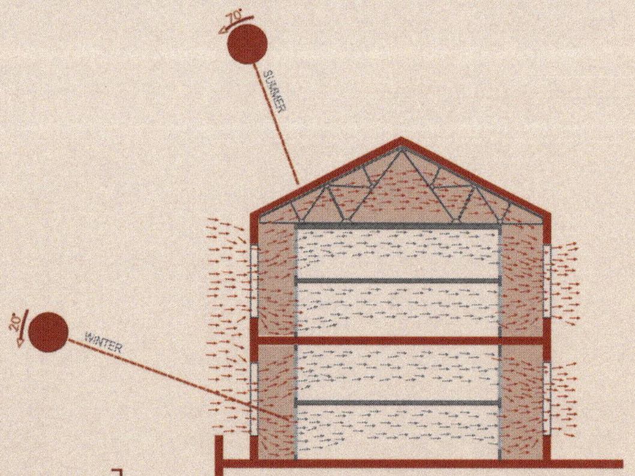

Typical section⌉

cross-ventilation
double solar orientation

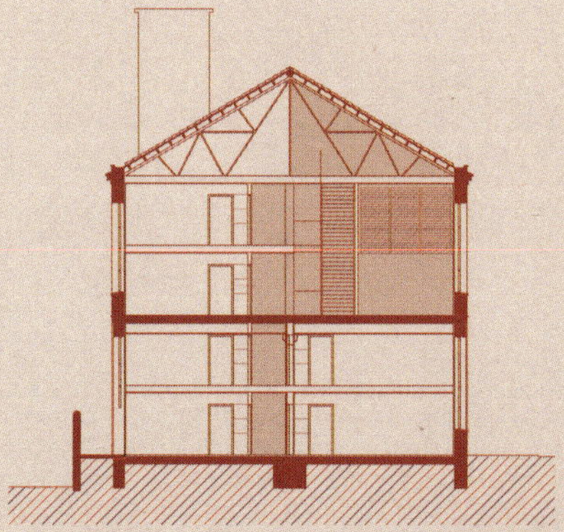

Typical section - Competition phase⌉

[Construction photographs - ROLDÁN-BERENGUÉ ©

Photographs - Maite Caramés © - 2022]

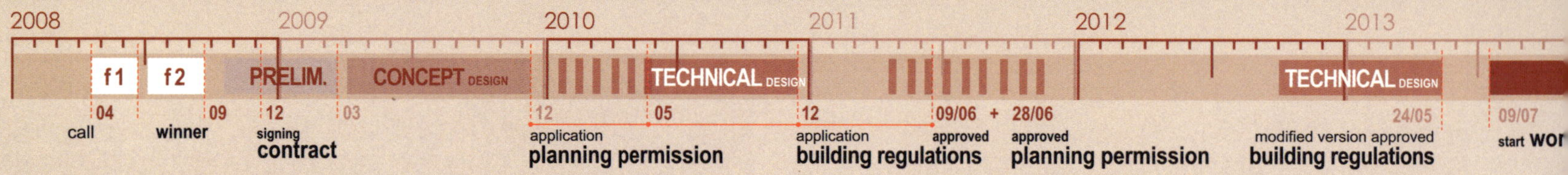

81 housing units / Josep Pla

Estudi Massip-Bosch

The project responds to a complex programme (homes for seniors, social housing, a nursing home, a district social club and a car park) in a volume that is also complex, strictly situated according to the urban transformation project for the 22@ area of Barcelona.

Large residential and industrial buildings coexist in this area. The project takes on these conditions and adds one more: maximum visual unity of the solutions and elements of the various briefs contained within the project. The result is a volume of similar scale to the neighbouring buildings that communicates clearly and forcefully with its surroundings.

Model – Technical phase

Location: c/Pere IV, 455-457. Barcelona. **Programme:** 54 social housing units, 27 homes for seniors, district civic centre, social centre for the elderly. Surface area: 5,050 m² (social housing), 2,312 m² (homes for the elderly), 1,077 m² (social centre for the elderly), 480 m² (district civic centre). TOTAL: 8,919 m². **Cost:** 15,139,000 € (CEB). **Architect:** Enric MASSIP-BOSCH. **Collaborations:** Bet Cases, Jon Ajánguiz, Inma Rodríguez, Juliana Bracchi, Patrícia Gonzàlez Margalef, Cornelia Memm. **Contractor:** Corsan-Corviam - Roser Bigorra. **Consultancy:** Xavi Noya - AE-T Enginyeria (installations), Albert Sagrera - Societat Orgànica (sustainability), Manuel Arguijo (structures), Xavier Aumedes, Cesc de Haro - Aumedes DAP SLP (quantity surveyors, cost control, health and safety), Francesc Sampedro - SiS Consultoria (acoustics).

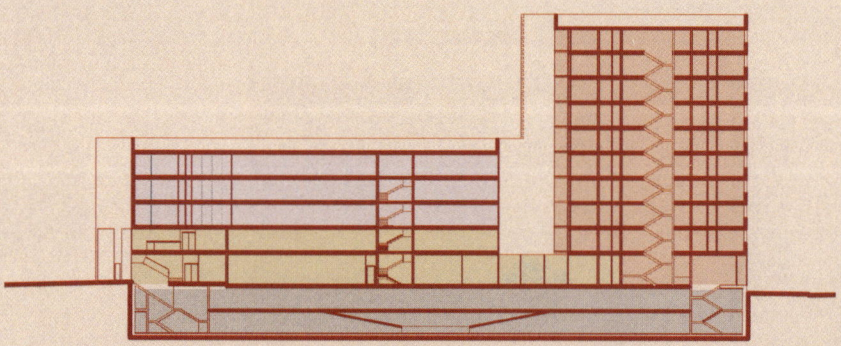

Typical section housing for seniors social centre social housing

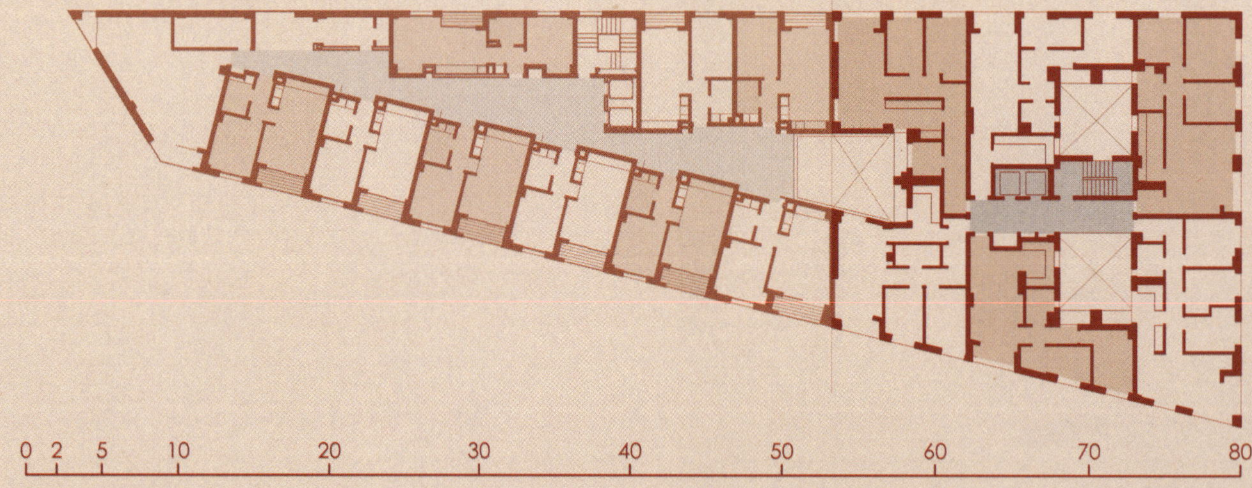

Typical floor plan 1:500

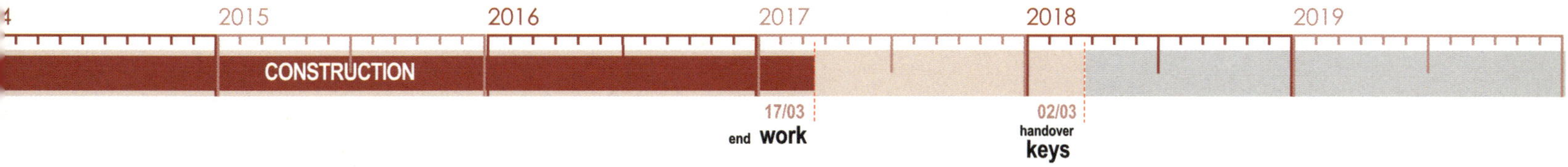

Photographs - Adrià Goula © - 2022

Model - Competition phase

Model – Technical phase

Render – Competition phase

Render – Concept design

Photographs - Josep Maria de Llobet, Jordi Surroca, Gael del Río © - 2018

Construction photograph

Photographs - Josep Maria de Llobet, Jordi Surroca, Gael del Río © - 2018

Floor plan of dwelling 1:75

Interview – 2022

“On New Year’s Eve we all go outside and drink champagne with the neighbours to see the new year in… It’s great, really, I’ve got fantastic neighbours. In the flat I’m really comfortable, great, really at home. And so far I haven’t had any problems.”

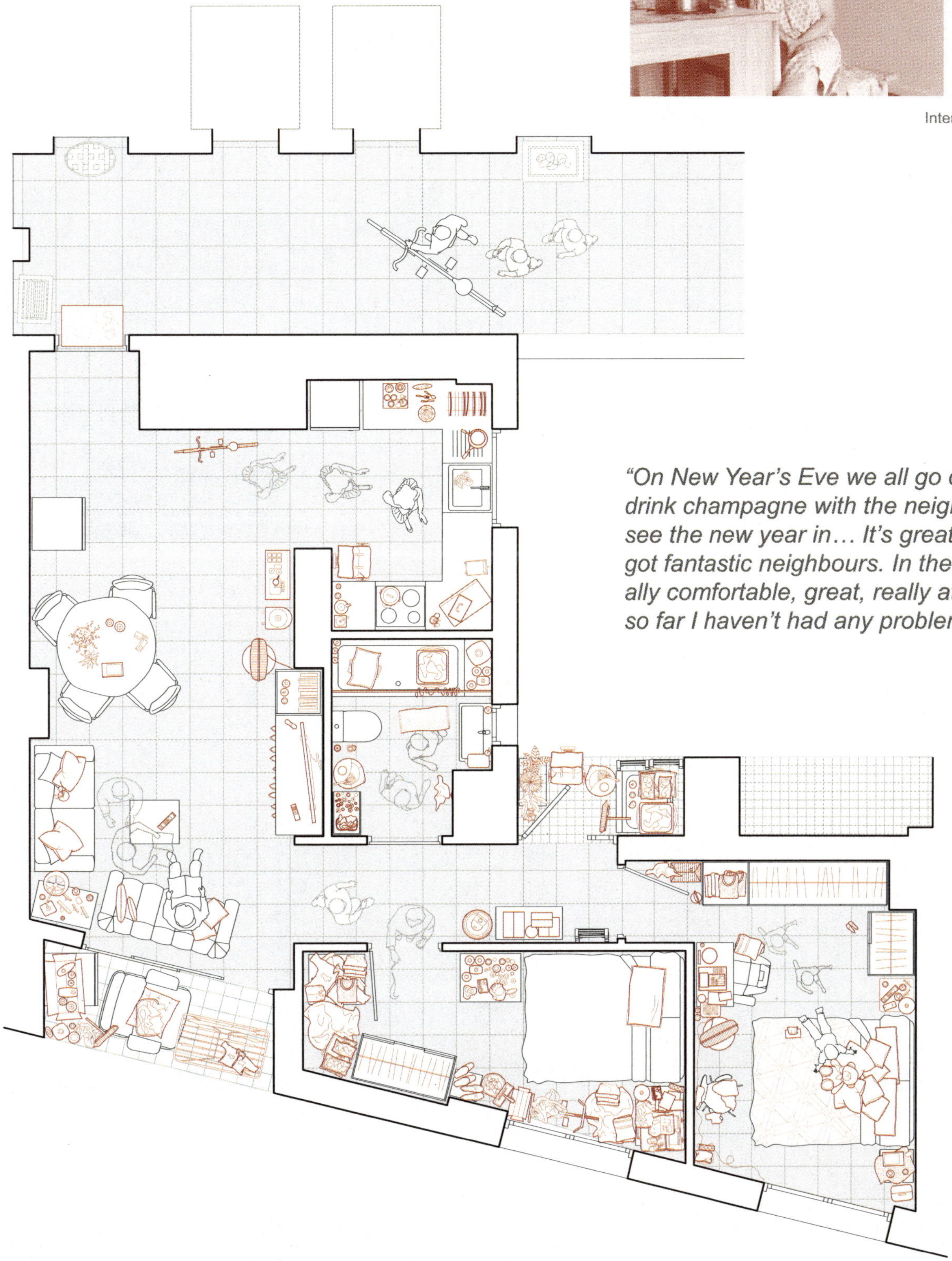

Lived-in floor plan

MI FAMILIA

LA ESPOSA

Prefabricated GRC panels in façade

Construction photograph

Façade render - Competition phase

Sketch of façade concept

Façade detail

Photographs - Adrià Goula © - 2022

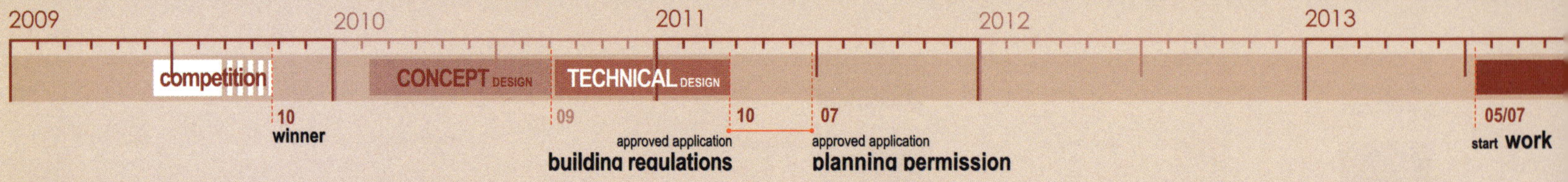

61 housing units / Bon Pastor III

Pascual-Ausió

The *cases barates* or cheap housing district in Bon Pastor are a series of small, very modest single-storey houses, built during the hardest moments of migration in the 1920s.

The redevelopment plan will involve demolishing these 784 houses and replacing them with blocks of flats built in the same place to rehouse all the tenants. Barcelona Municipal Housing Board has taken into consideration the opinions of the future-former users as to their rehousing.

The project is conditioned by what these people think an appropriate, lasting construction should be: cross-ventilated homes. Outer facings of bare brick. Brick cavity-wall partitions. Terrazzo. Varnished beech woodwork inside. Exterior window frames of aluminium.

This 61-home building is part of the third phase of remodelling. The four buildings that define the large central plaza are arranged according to planning in a north-south direction, perpendicular to c/Sant Adrià and c/Mollerussa. With a maximum depth of 15 m and a typological cross-ventilation design.

The daytime spaces face west, with the night-time areas facing the morning sun. The living room-diner, kitchen and terrace overlook the central plaza.The greater depth of the commercial premises creates space for patios in the first floor homes.

A degree of leeway in the parameters regulating volumes generates varying heights in different sections of the building.

Render – Competition phase

Location: c/Biosca, 17-19-21-23-25. Barcelona. **Programme:** 61 homes. **Surface area:** 11,540.91 m^2. **Cost:** 8,649,554.33 € (CEB VAT incl.). **Architects:** Joan Pascual Argenté, Ramón Ausió Mateu. **Collaborations:** Carolina Araneda Avelló, Pilar Enjuanes Quintillà, Rafael Bayarre. **Contractor:** Construcciones Rubau, SA. **Site supervisor:** Xavier Queralt Rius. **Consultancy:** JSS Enginyeria i Arquitectura, SLP / Measurements: Francesc García / Works management: David Morros (Dalmau+Morros Tècnics, SLP), Arnau Ricart (renders).

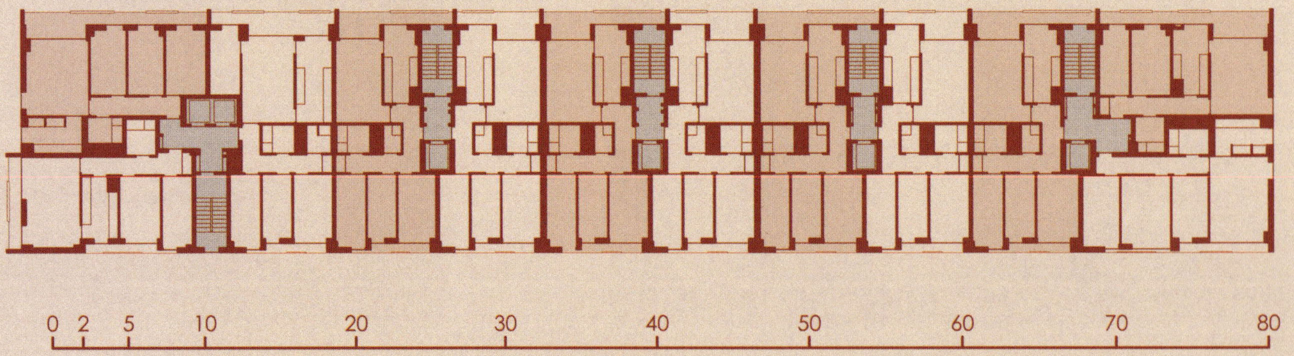

Typical floor plan 1:500

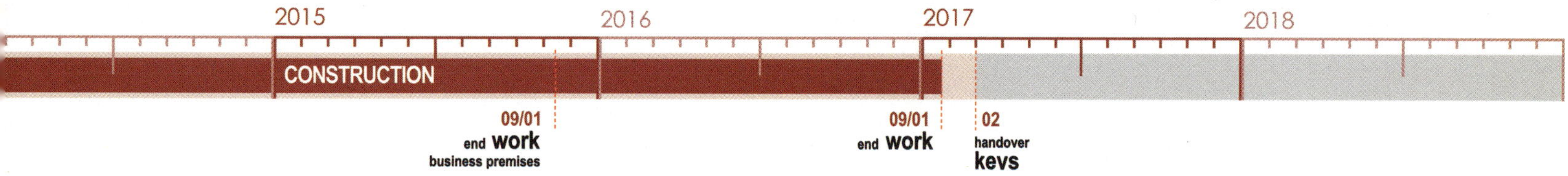

Photographs - Adrià Goula © - 2022

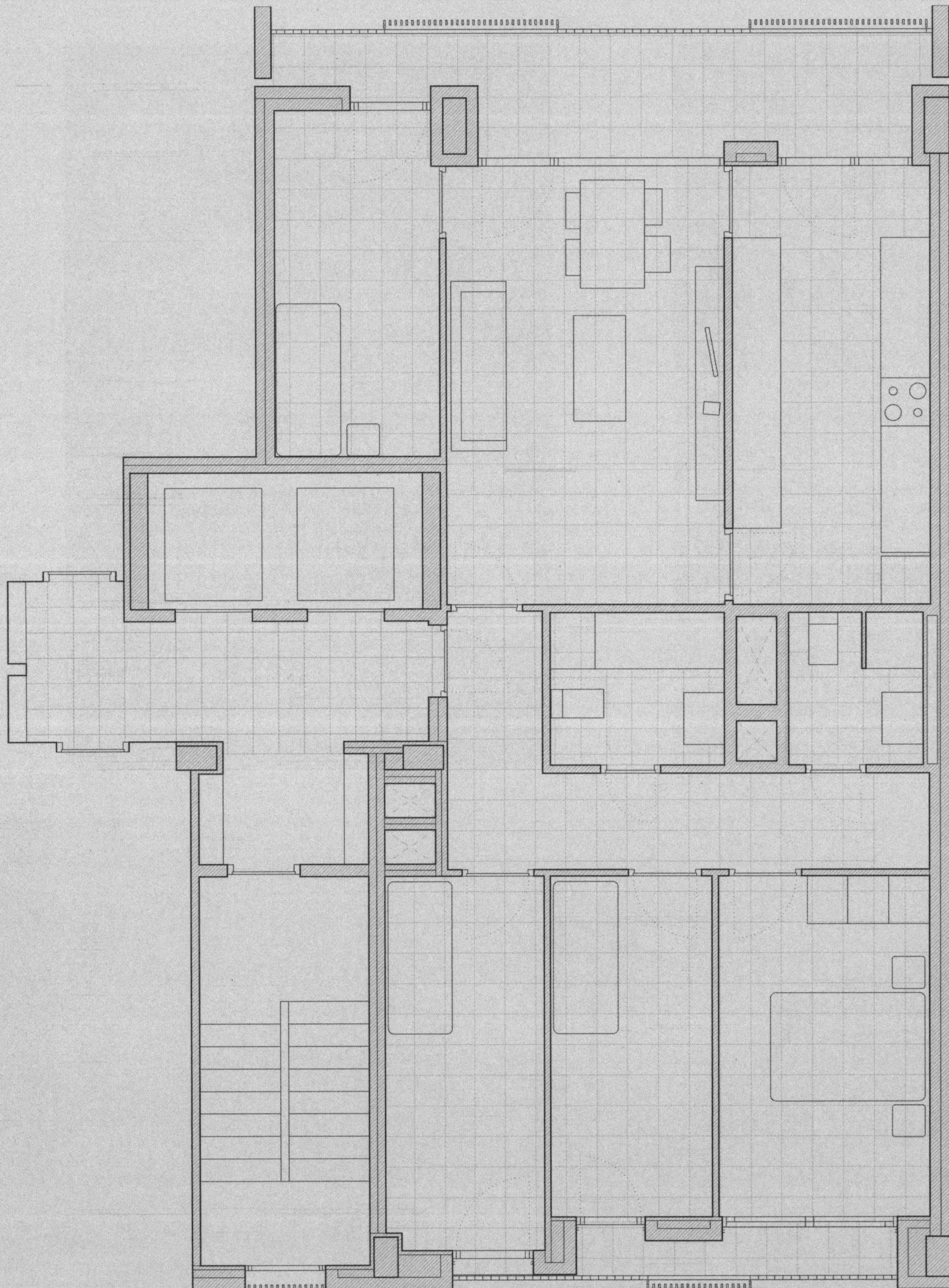

Floor plan of dwelling 1:75

"Compared to where we were before, this is a palace. Our house was so small. On top of that, you'd go out and bump into someone from three streets away, or the neighbour across the road... and you were always out and about, there was always something going on. But here, once you get in, it's a real pain to have to go out and buy a load of bread... Either you spend all afternoon outside, walking around, shopping or whatever, or you get settled down and don't want to go out again."*

Interview – 2022

Lived-in floor plan 1:75

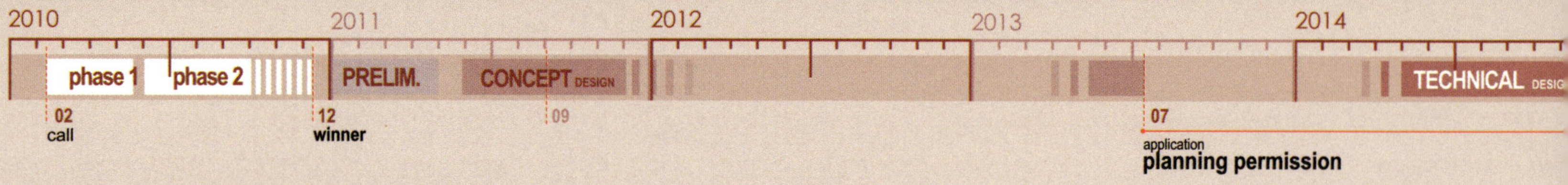

44 housing units / Quatre Camins

Ravetllat-Ribas

The small scale of the neighbouring domestic buildings mixes with larger teaching and care facilities, combining low density with exceptional views and orientation. The aim of this proposal was to find a scale of implementation in keeping with its setting. It seems logical that a social housing block like this should choose to alternate the domesticity of the existing single-family residential fabric with the larger dimension and scale of the other elements around it.

The building presents a compact volume onto the street, with a north façade in which the corridors to the homes are arranged, generating an energy filter. On the other side, it is broken down in steps towards the interior of the site, addressing orientation and creating a more domestic contact with the courtyards of the neighbouring homes.

The homes, with a useful surface area of some 40 m², have a protected outdoor area, especially those on the lower level, since their location offers more space. All the spaces –open, semi-open and closed– have protected and controlled openings for good energy performance. The Passivhaus system is incorporated to improve energy efficiency, reducing total consumption by 75%.

Render – Competition phase

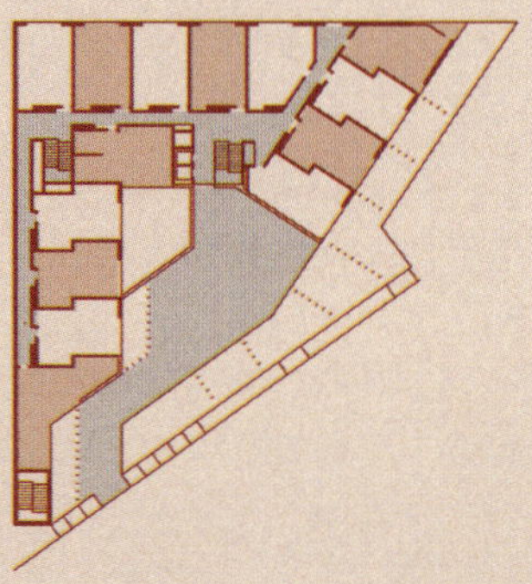

Typical floor plan – Competition phase

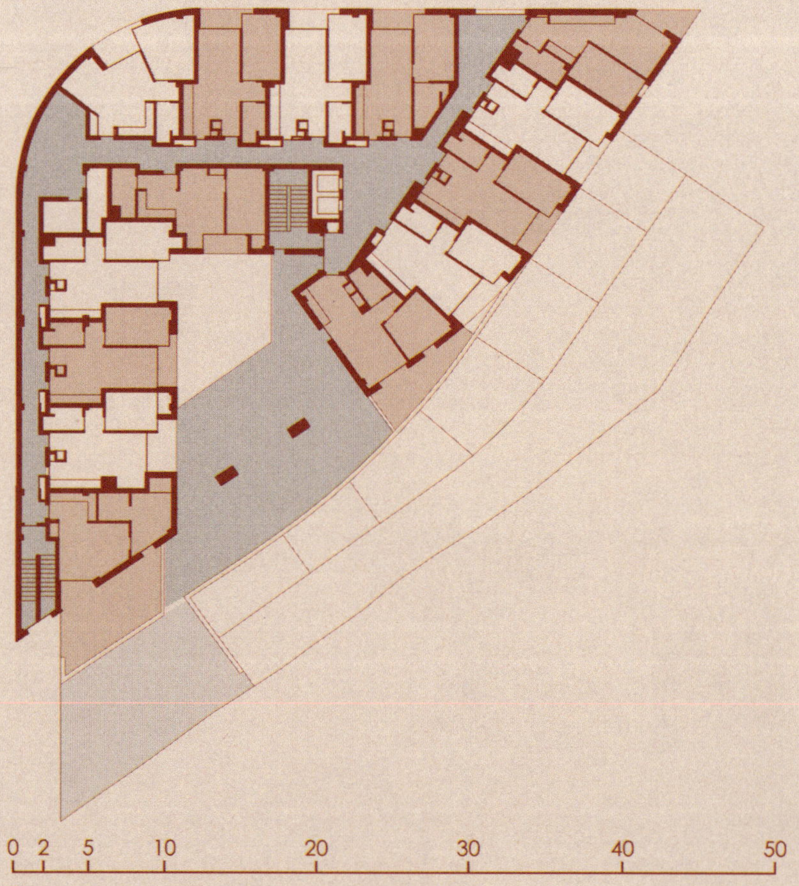

Typical floor plan 1:500

Location: c/Infanta Isabel, 9-11. Barcelona. **Programme:** 44 homes for seniors. **Surface area:** 4,833.90 m². **Cost:** 4,842,565.55 (CEB VAT incl.). **Architects:** Pere Joan Ravetllat, Carme Ribas, Nicolás Markuerkiaga (+6 collaborating practice members). **Contractor:** CALER - Jordi Cárdenas, Jordi González, Eusebio Pérez. **Consultancy:** JG Ingenieros (installations), Micheel Wassouf (Passivhaus), STATIC Ingeniería (structures), Ángel Gil (quantity surveyor).

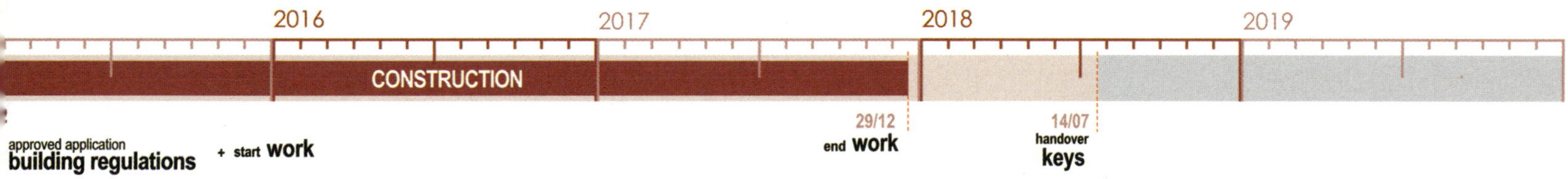

Photographs - Adrià Goula © - 2022

Render - Concept design phase

Render - Concept design phase

Photographs - Adrià Goula / Jordi Surroca © - 2022

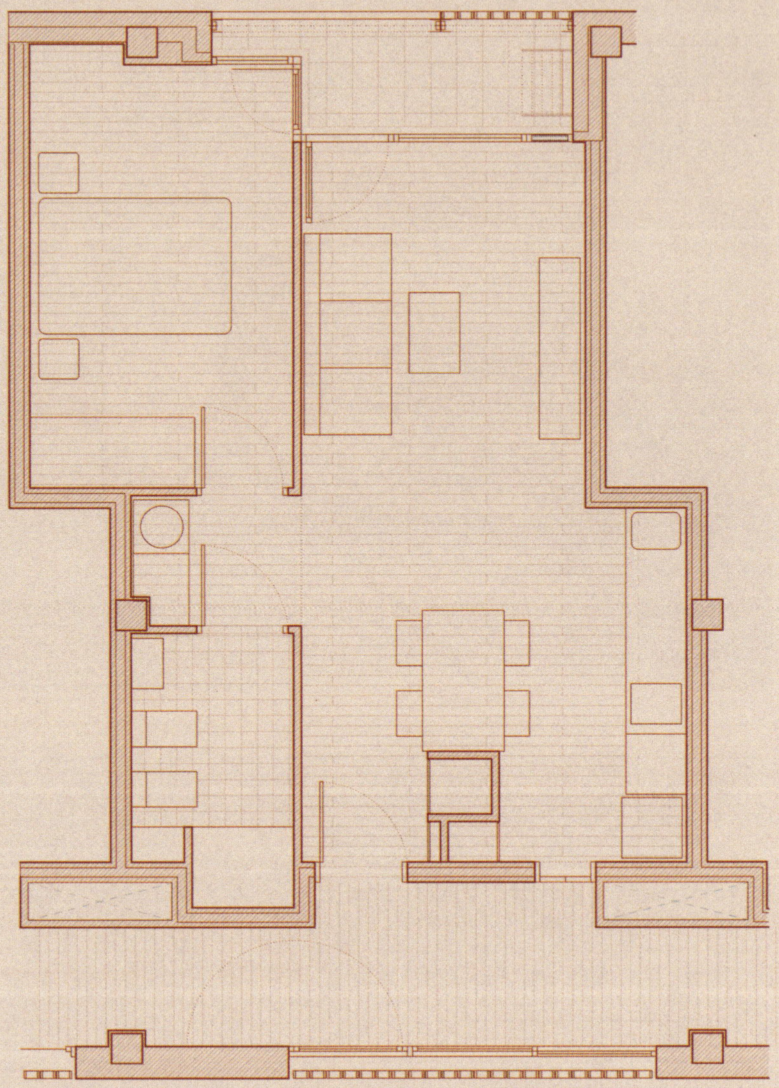

⌈Floor plan of dwelling 1:75

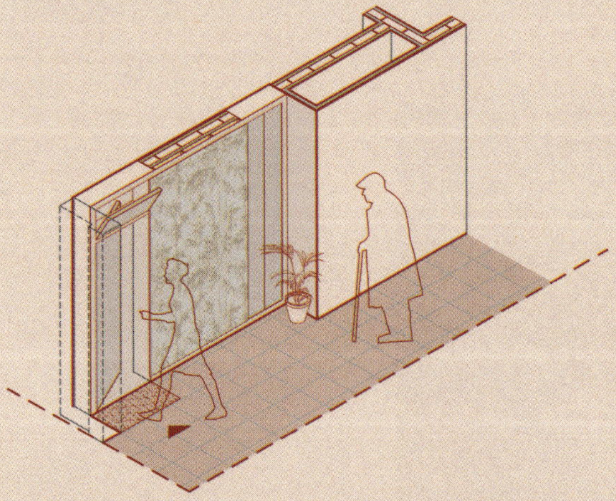

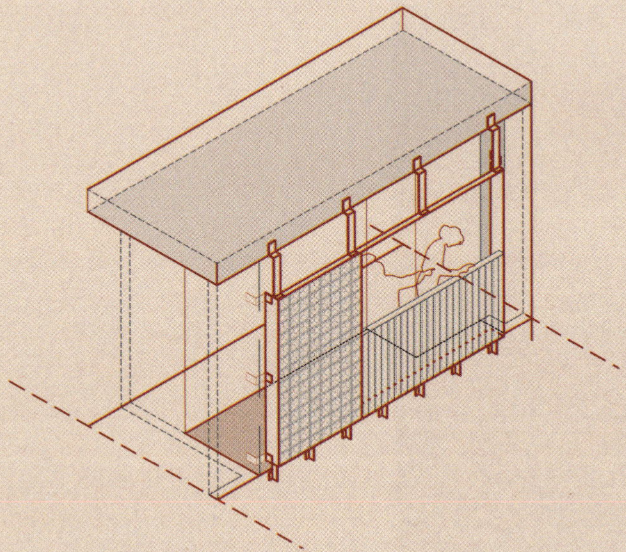

⌈Details of entrance and balcony

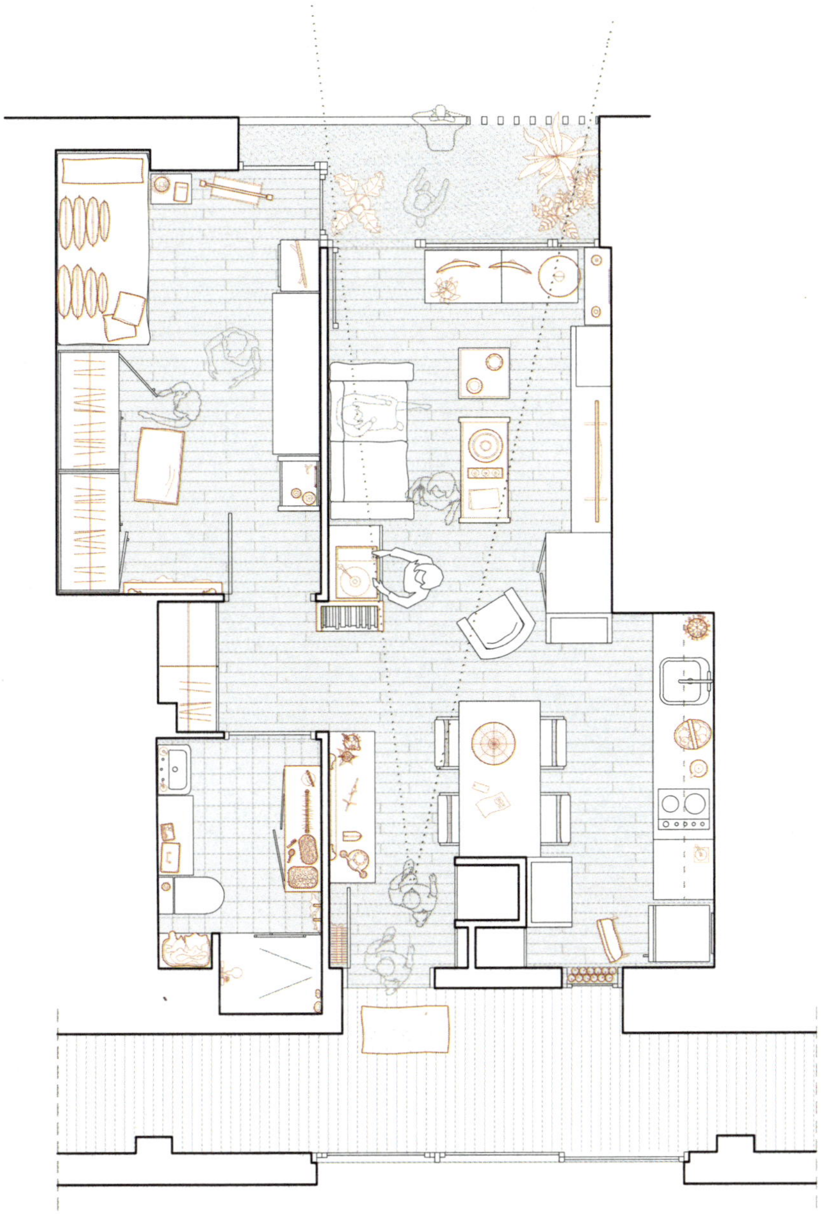

Lived-in floor plan 1:75

“The building’s fine. The communal spaces, perfect. Some time back, over a year ago, an assistant, a helper started, she’s called Adriana, and she’s great, she great with us. She brings us all together... Really great. She helps us a lot. She helps us a lot and she helps people who’ve got problems, she’s great. The director helps, too. And the architecture of the building is really nice. I think it’s really attractive, and very functional.”

Interview – 2022

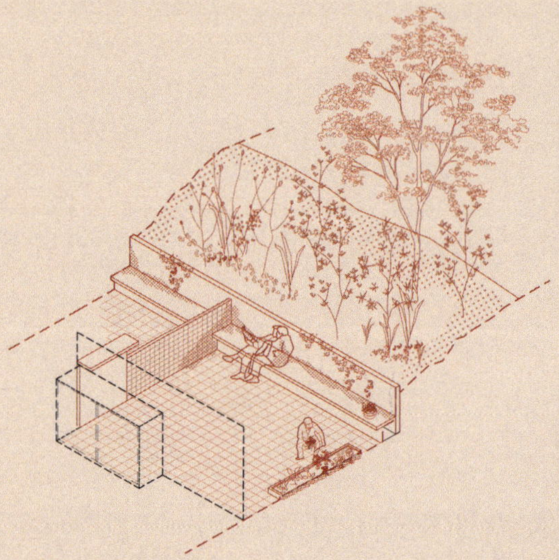

Γ Details of limits

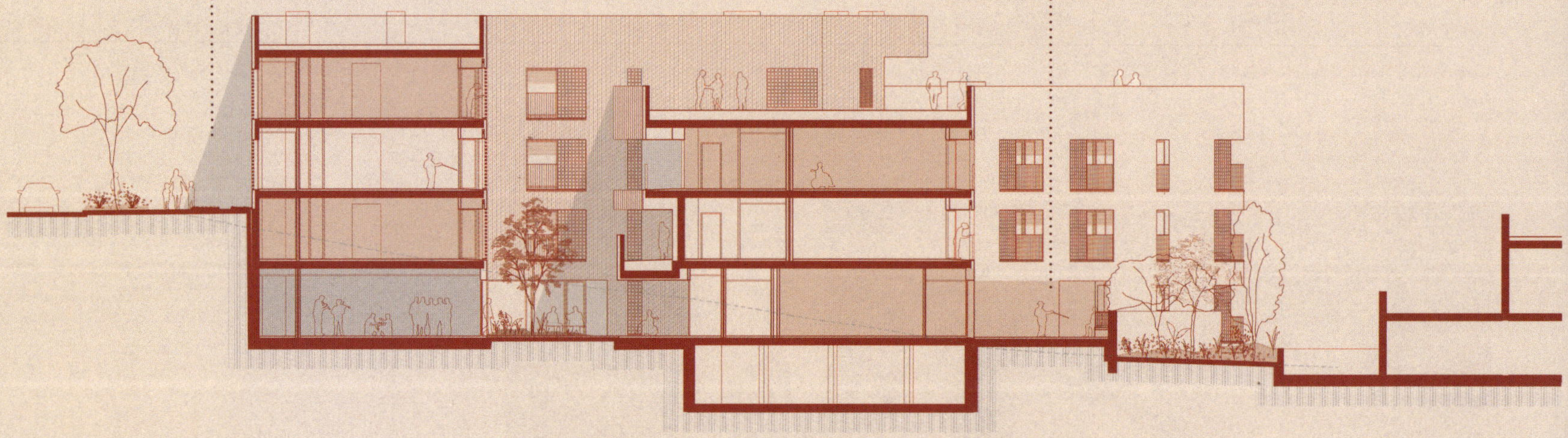

Γ Typical section

Γ Model – Project

Photographs - Adrià Goula © - 2018

Photographs - Maite Caramés © - 2022

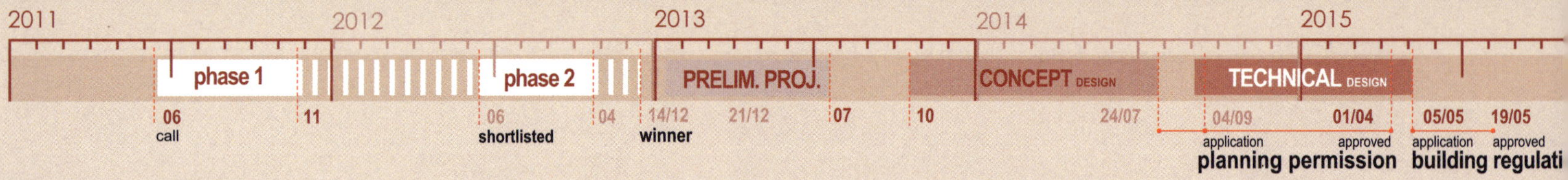

47 housing units + 20 accommodations / Tànger

Coll-Leclerc

For the first time in Barcelona, two programmes that are usually separate are combined in the same building: social rental housing and temporary accommodation for the inclusion of the most vulnerable groups. The design of the building responds to three basic criteria:

1. Urban responsibility: we create city, generate public space and equip the ground floor with collective services. We organize the programme in three vertical blocks, generating public space with an interior street that both separates and connects the accommodations with the homes, organizes access and communication, and allows good cross-ventilation throughout.

2. Social responsibility: the programme addresses the inclusion and accessibility of marginalized people in the broadest sense. The conditions of the different parts of the programme are the same or compensated, offering decent accommodation without increasing the cost. It will be possible to reuse the temporary accommodation building for another purpose, and we strike a balance between the parts of the programme. All the homes have the same qualities, and there are no differences in orientation or sunlighting.

3. Energy responsibility: we bring a passive environmental attitude to the site and the programme that reduces energy demand: good ventilation and good solar capture to save energy. All the homes have sunlighting. This allows us to create the passive solar energy harvesting device of conservatories, which cover 23% of the heating demand in winter. In summer, night-time cross-ventilation of the conservatory and daytime solar protection with shutters cover 43% of the cooling demand. All this is complemented by high-efficiency aerothermal and heat-recovery systems using double-flow ventilation that give the finished building an A-rating for energy performance.

Render – Competition phase

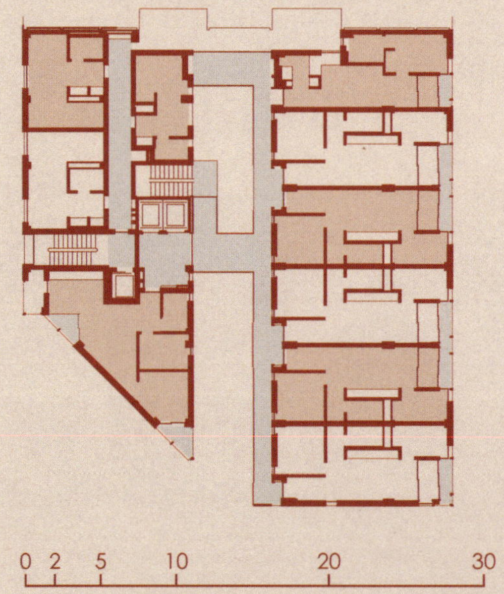

Typical floor plan 1:500

Sketch - Competition phase

Location: c/Tànger, 38-40-42. Barcelona. **Programme:** 47 homes, 20 accommodations. **Surface area:** 1,137 m² (accommodations) / 3.472 m² (homes). Total: 5,570 m². **Cost:** 5,995,631 € (CEB VAT incl.). **Architects:** COLL-LECLERC. **Collaborations:** Guillem Villalta i Narcís Font (competition), Inés Alomar (preliminary project), Marina Povedano and Albert Sabas, Anna Sala, Noemi Martínez (concept and technical), Carla Blanch (DO). **Contractor:** GUINOVART & OHL. **Consultancy:** JSS (installations), Alex Ivancic (sustainability), Manuel Arguijo (structures), AT3 and Salvador Arisa (budget), Angela Vidal (DE).

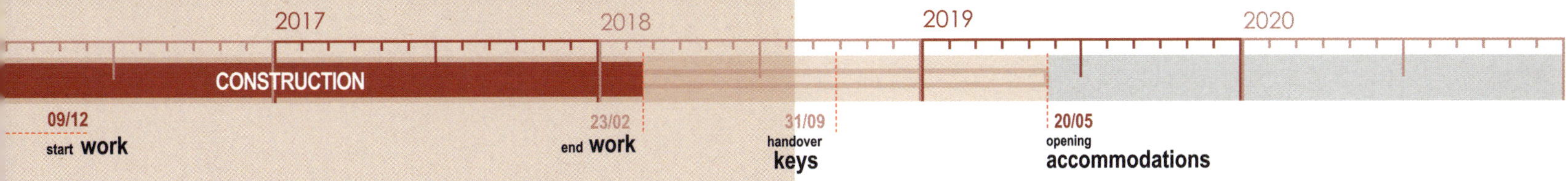

Photographs - Roland Halbe © - 2018

Photographs - Adrià Goula © - 2022

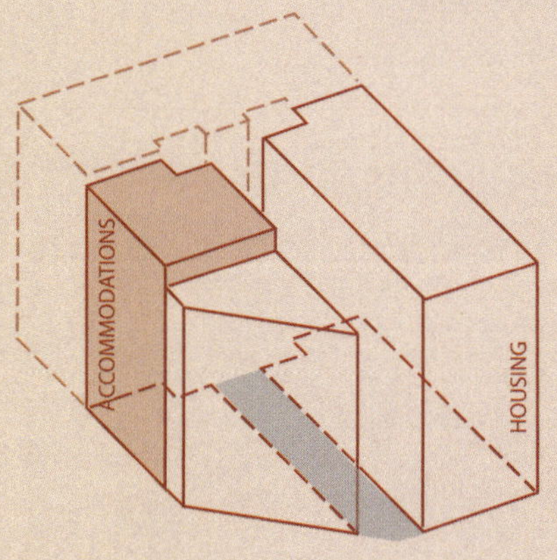

⌈Diagram of volumes

⌈Render – Competition phase

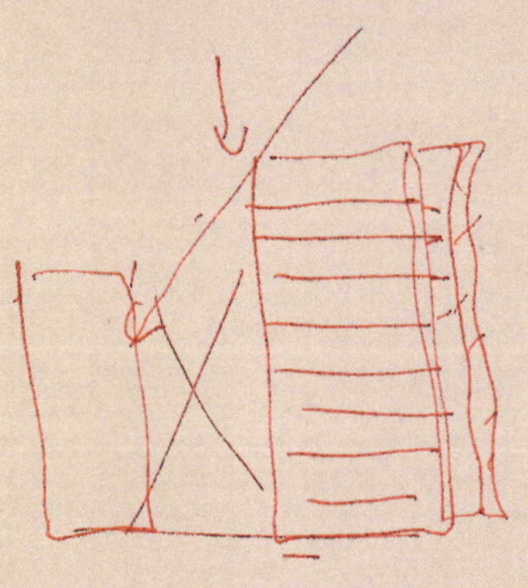

⌈Sketch – Competition phase section

⌈Sketch – Competition phase section

⌈Photographs - Roland Halbe © - 2018

Photographs - Adrià Goula © - 2022

Photographs - Maite Caramés © - 2022

ESTA CASA
Somos reales
NOS DIVERTIMOS
"gracias" y "lo siento"
COMETEMOS ERRORES
Damos ABRAZOS y BESOS
Somos felices y sobre todo
NOS QUEREMOS un montón

KAISER

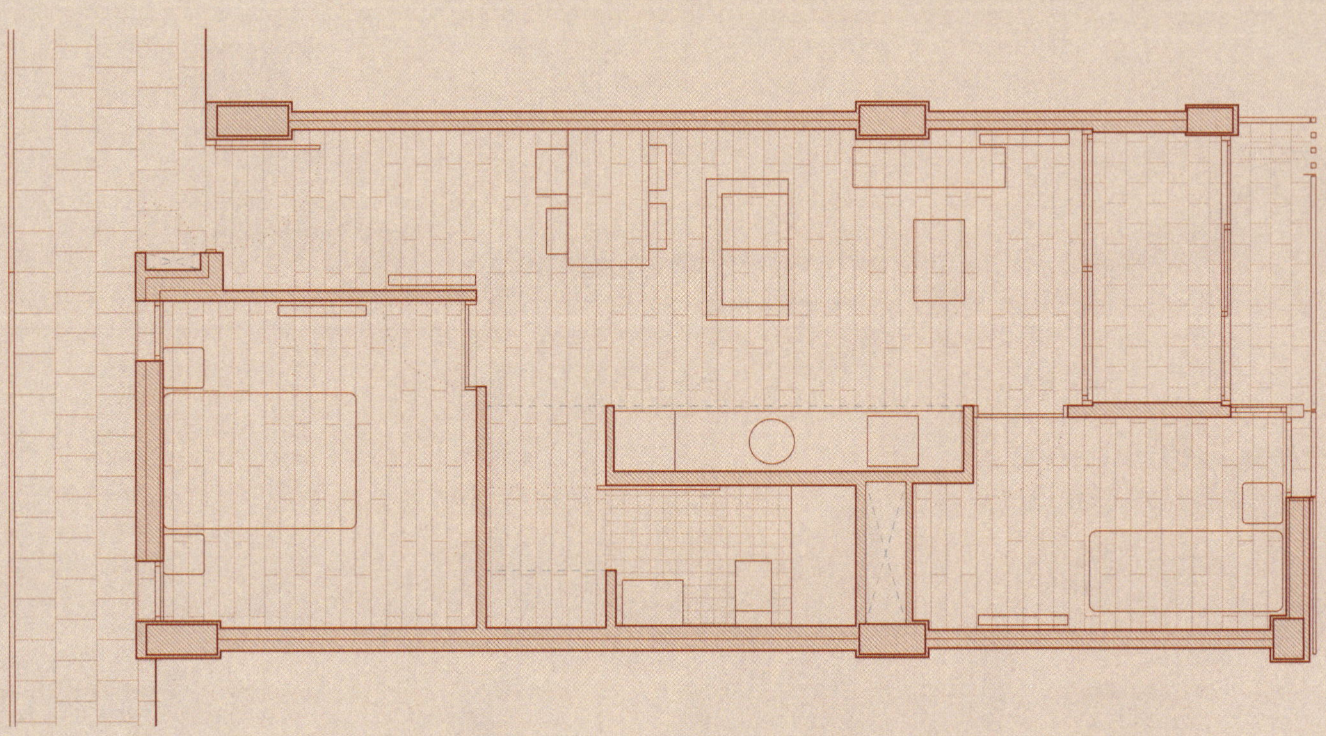

Floor plan of dwelling 1:75

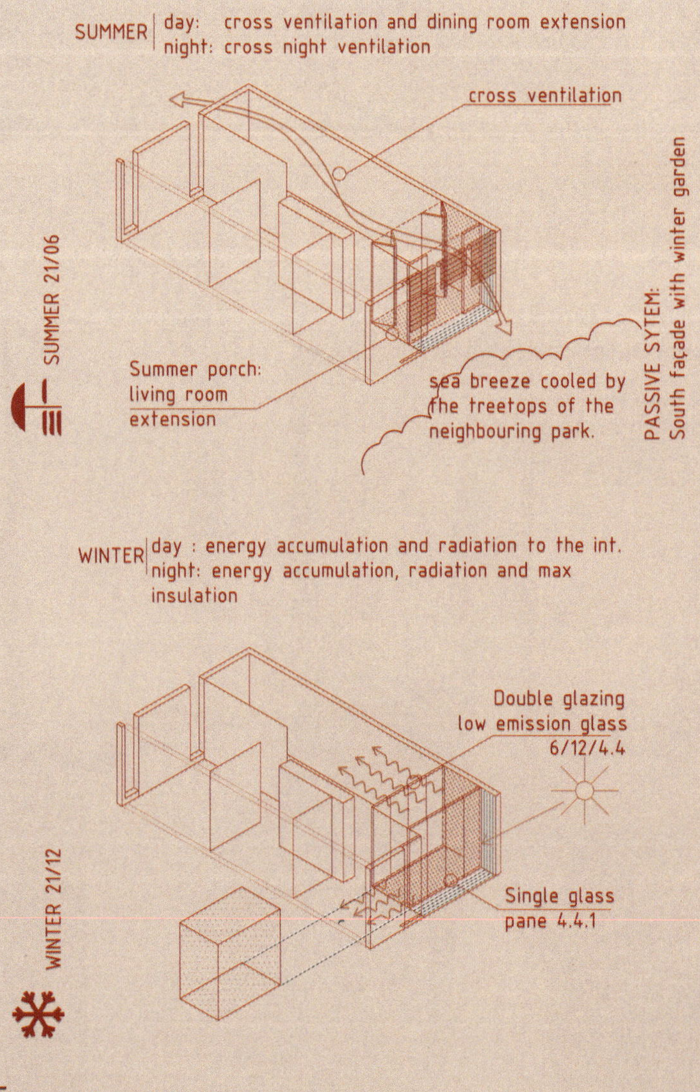

Diagram of climatic functioning

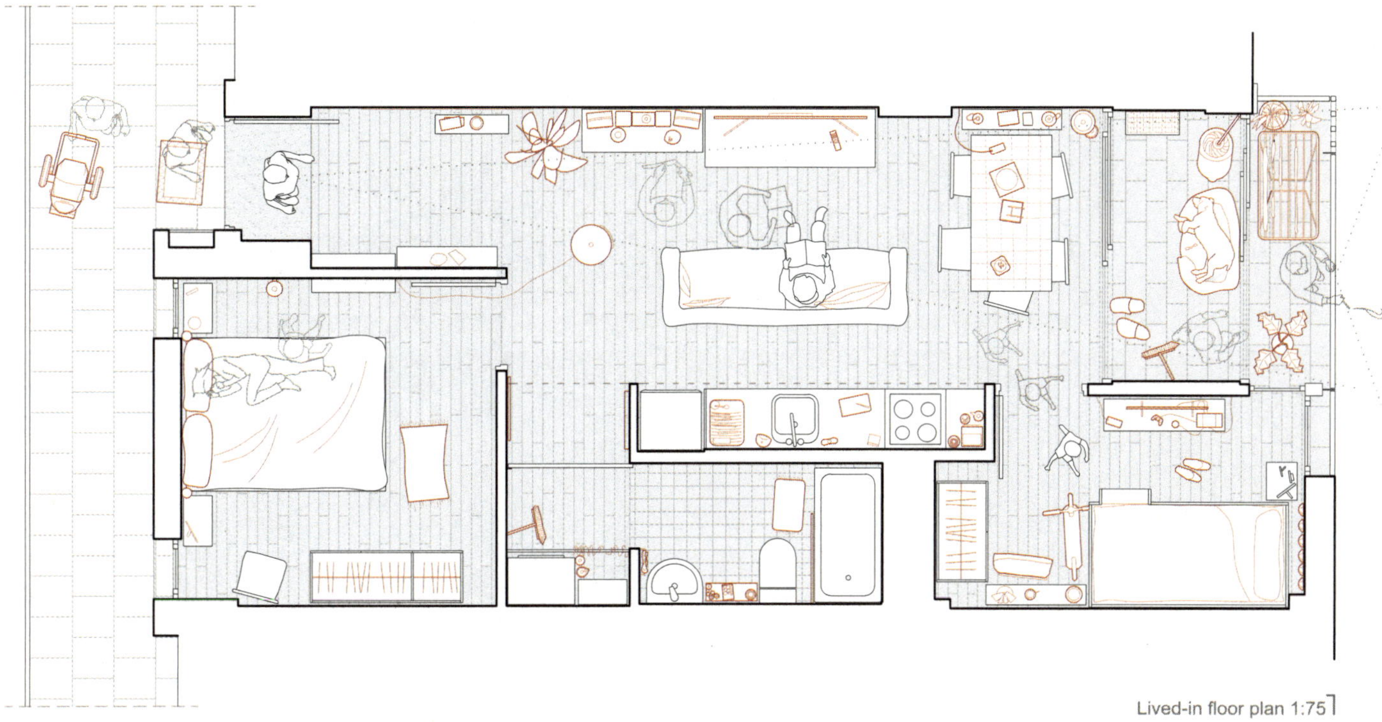

Lived-in floor plan 1:75

Interview – 2022

"It's new but it reminds you of the old times because of the way the stairway's arranged, and the doors that open to the outside, and lots of the people here go outside and stand in the corridors and talk... a lot of people leave the door open because of the heat."

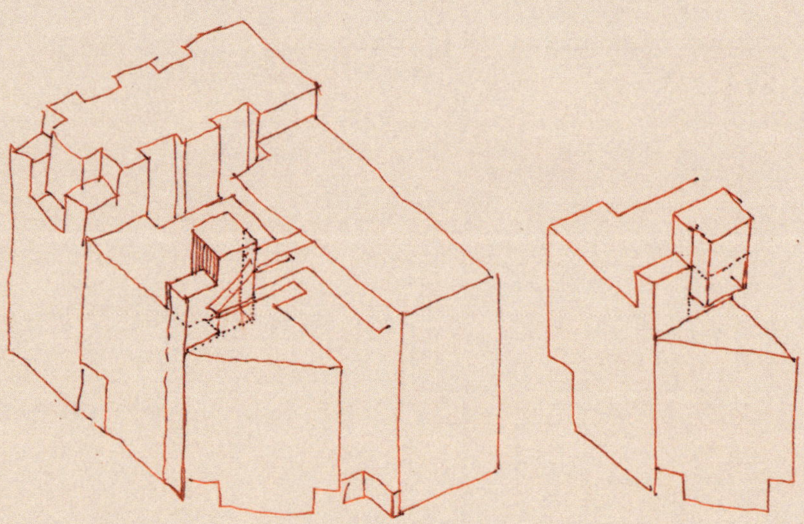

Diagram of volumes - Competition phase

Model – Technical phase

Render – Competition phase

Photographs - Roland Halbe © - 2018

Photographs - Adrià Goula © - 2022

Photographs - Adrià Goula © - 2022

Photographs - Maite Caramés © - 2022

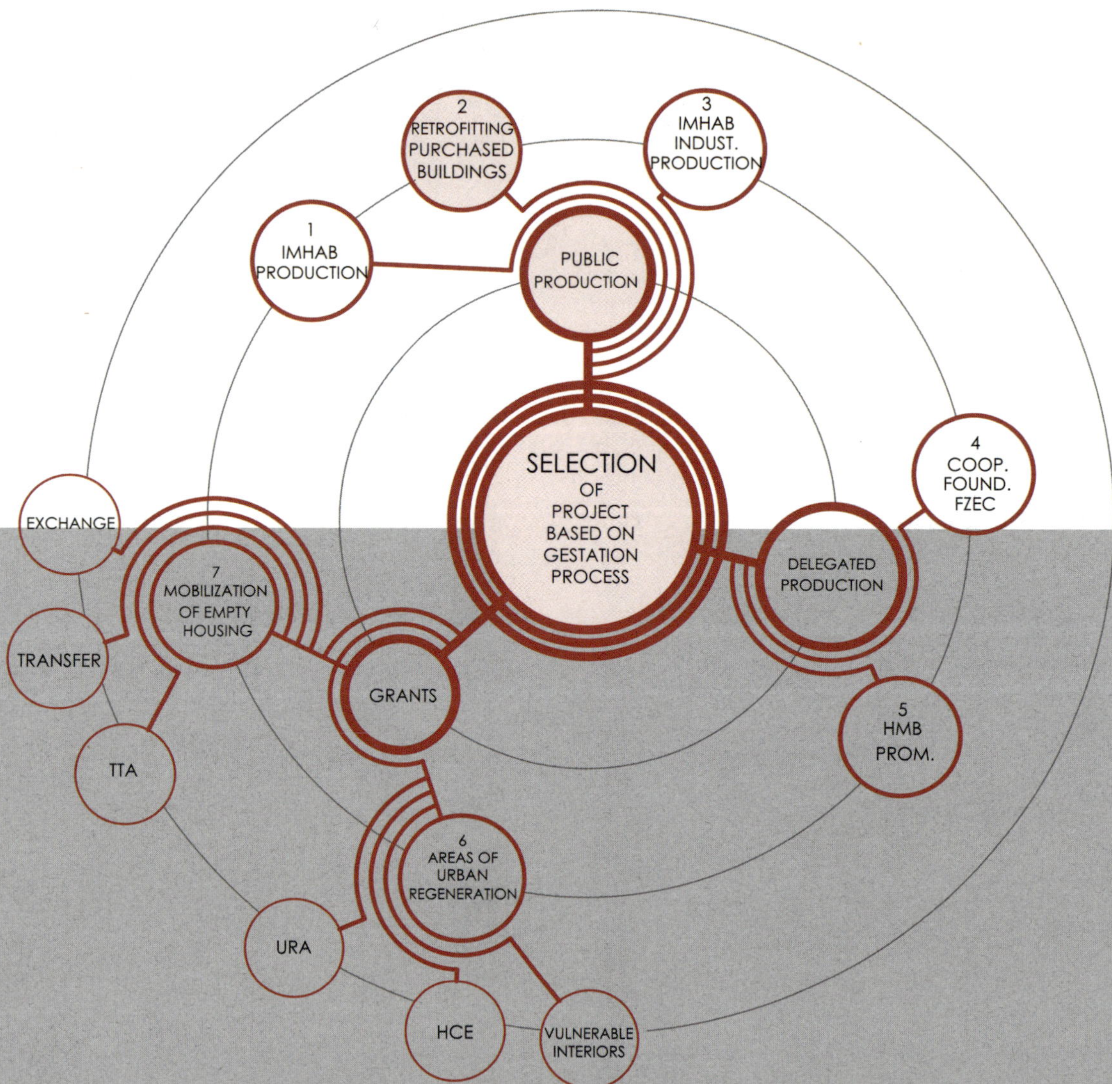
SELECTION
OF
PROJECT
BASED ON
GESTATION
PROCESS
PUBLIC
PRODUCTION
1
IMHAB
PRODUCTION
2
RETROFITTING
PURCHASED
BUILDINGS
3
IMHAB
INDUST.
PRODUCTION
DELEGATED
PRODUCTION
4
COOP.
FOUND.
FZEC
5
HMB
PROM.
GRANTS
6
AREAS OF
URBAN
REGENERATION
URA
HCE
VULNERABLE
INTERIORS
7
MOBILIZATION
OF EMPTY
HOUSING
EXCHANGE
TRANSFER
TTA

Retrofitting purchased buildings

Housing acquisition strategy and its contribution to sustainability by retrofitting

gestating

Isidre Costa

Director of Legal Services, Contracting and Patrimony of the IMHAB

In 2016 Barcelona City Council began a specific housing acquisition policy, taking advantage of the existing legal instruments of right of first refusal and generating new ones. This was set within the framework of the Plan for the Right to Housing in Barcelona, of the same year, with the aim of increasing council housing stock, also provided for in the Charter of Rights and Duties of Citizens of Barcelona. It aims to help to meet the objective of urban solidarity, a cardinal principle of Article 73 of the Right to Housing Act, which calls for 15% of housing in the city to be allocated to social policies by 2027.

The purpose was, then, to include the policy of buying existing homes in the scope of action of the municipal council housing service, and to promote the rehabilitation of residential fabric in the consolidated city that was purchased to improve the living conditions of citizens, increase energy efficiency and reduce CO_2 emissions to help mitigate climate change and adapt to it.

This was carried out under the umbrella of the IMHAB, which, in its statutes, is assigned, among others, "the function of promoting the processing of housing acquisitions by Barcelona City Council, to expand affordable housing stock intended for social policies".

Accordingly, alongside the production of new buildings, historically the IMHAB's main means of increasing council housing stock, it took on this new role, which involves promoting the purchase and subsequent retrofitting of properties and homes. To this end, public tenders are promoted to draft technical projects and carry out construction.

Decree 1/2015, of 24 March, on extraordinary urgent measures to mobilize homes resulting from mortgage foreclosure processes, was initially adopted to this end, allowing the Generalitat Government to purchase these homes by right of first refusal, for its own use or that of the municipalities. Subsequently, Barcelona City Council became co-owner of this right and was able to purchase individual homes as well as multi-family residential buildings. In this framework, the Director of Housing issued an instruction that established maximum purchase prices in relation to the average market prices for buildings and for protected housing in the case of individual homes. In 2021, the average purchase price of buildings was 34.5% below the market price.

As of 2018, the Council was able to benefit from Catalan Finance Institute financing to purchase homes, which the Generalitat instrumentalized by passing a framework agreement, making 10 million euros available through the IMHAB.

Simultaneously, in accordance with article 172 of the revised text of the Urban Planning Act and article 15 of the Right to Housing Act, the City Council passed a modification of the Metropolitan Master Plan to make the entire area of Barcelona a right of first refusal area, for an initial period of six years, extendable for a further six, directly subjecting multi-family buildings with vertical ownership to it.

Other objectives of the area were to increase municipal patrimony of land and housing; conserve and retrofit buildings, especially in areas with conditions of economic and social vulnerability; avoid the eviction of occupants, given the high incidence of gentrification processes in many parts of the city, and, in general, deal with speculative processes that make housing more expensive and make it difficult for citizens to access it.

The Modification of the Metropolitan Master Plan calls for market values to be taken into account and sets out a number of prioritizing circumstances for purchase, such as being in an "abnormal situation or use; in a poor state of conservation, especially those subject to conservation enforcement orders that affect the building as a whole; with occupiers, especially considering leases subject to forced extension; in areas of economic and social vulnerability, and in areas with processes of gentrification or replacement of residents".[1]

From 2015 to the present, using these two instruments, Barcelona City Council has acquired 1,316 homes with a rehabilitation cost of 30,052 million euros, having made available for this purchase the sum of 162.49 million euros, mostly from its municipal budget.

These two right of first refusal instruments serve to generalize the purchase of homes and, due to their scope and effect, make other mechanisms, such as direct purchase and public purchase by tender, unnecessary.

After seven years of experience buying land, the future of housing purchase policy will also involve public-private collaboration, in order to scale the programme and reach all districts in the city.

1 Modification of the Metropolitan Master Plan (https://docplayer.es/131234562-Modificacio-del-pla-general-metropolita-per-declarar-la-ciutat-de-barcelona-area-de-tanteig-i-retracte-i-definir-els-terminis-d-edificacio-juny-2018.html).

Built city, future city

Magda Mària

Doctor of Architecture. Lecturer in Architecture Projects, UPC
Joint head of HABITAR Grup de Recerca

We are living through crucial times that call for energy saving, management of materials and care for the environment. This is the direction that architecture and urban planning proposals have to take. Rather than continuing to build or demolish underutilized or disused buildings or spaces, with the environmental footprint this entails, a paradigm shift is needed that prioritizes their maintenance and reuse.

Reusing buildings is nothing new. The "Atlas del aprovechamiento arquitectónico" (Atlas of architectural use, MINECO-UPC, 2018), a study carried out by our research group, HABITAR, about the reuse of buildings in Barcelona, identifies 1,463 cases of one or more changes in use from the first century to the present day. All survived their initial programme because, fundamentally, the new uses adapted to the properties rather than the other way around. These precedents of adaptive reuse offer us a series of valuable lessons for the sustainable programming of the city's future.

One of these lessons affects the use of housing, a priority in the municipality, since its urban fabric is mainly made up of housing and because, at present, the need is paramount. The Atlas identifies 810 homes that have changed use and 89 buildings with various functions that have become homes. In this "two-way direction of housing use", houses, mostly built with load-bearing walls, have served practically all functions. And offices, factories, warehouses and sports facilities, many with isotropic structures or large bays, have become homes.

All of these cases demonstrate the ability of architectural typologies to accommodate a variety of uses and question the modern movement's dictate that "form follows function". In many, the regularity of rooms, structural rhythms or façade elements has played a decisive role in adapting to the new use and, therefore, preserving the morphological and constructive characteristics of the host building. There are also cases of minimum operations to adapt to a new brief, such as removing obsolete spaces, incorporating services or installing vertical communication elements. This fine-tuning of the habitability requirements of reused buildings prevents them from becoming museums or, in the worst case, disappearing.

At the same time, present-day lifestyles, subject to major changes, have transformed and simplified domestic habits, questioning conventional domestic layouts. Barcelona has seen an increase in shared flats, people living alone and people who spend much of their time away from home. At the same time, the city offers a series of services that allow some traditional functions associated with the home to be outsourced.

This reality opens up a wide range of possibilities to recycle and adapt building stock. This is why strategic planning policies are required when accommodating new uses in the adopted buildings, in order to preserve their morphological integrity and avoid the destruction of their contained energy. There is also a need for changes in regulations that evaluate existing spaces to assess their habitability and value the possibility of reassigning them to much-needed housing.

A sustainable city is one that considers the entirety of its built fabric as its reserve of land, that extends its protection beyond heritage lists and thereby avoids occupying more territory. A city that does not forget that its future has already, to a large extent, been built.

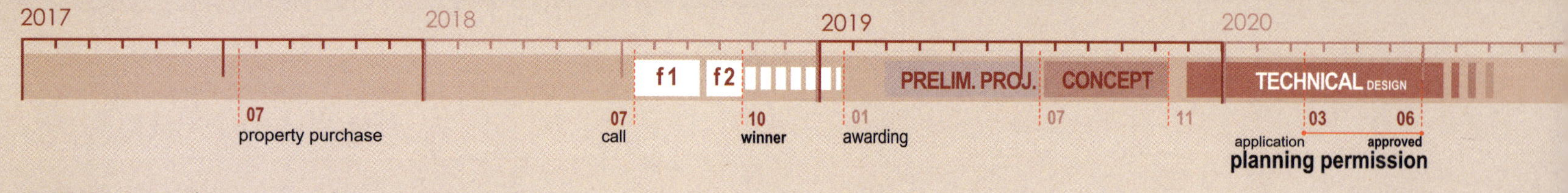

17 housing units / Raval

MIAS Arquitectes

The aim of this proposal, involving a process of microsurgery, is to rehabilitate the entire building to adapt it to present-day regulations on accessibility and habitability, and recover the maximum number of homes possible without modifying the general configuration of the property. The resulting number of homes is 17.

The project will be carried out in phases to avoid emptying the entire building during work. Four construction phases are proposed: the first two address the part of the building corresponding to stairway A (outdoor stairs), and the others concentrate on the part of the building corresponding to stairway B (inside stairs).

In this microsurgical rehabilitation, the communication shafts are seen as elements that serve to promote natural ventilation and lighting of the building, as well as accessibility with the construction of two lifts. The outdoor stairs (A) are maintained and opened up to the existing courtyard via railings. The inside stairs (B) are rebuilt, taking this intervention as an opportunity to strip the most damaged area of the existing building, also the most complicated in terms of habitability. Intervention in this volume is like a prosthetic operation: the existing structure requires a new, almost robotic, lightweight metal part to make the whole building function properly.

We see the courtyard on the site as an important place not just for access, but also to create space for social interaction. We think that the integration of this new communication shaft that opens onto the courtyard will encourage this. The project also proposes to treat the façades of the courtyard with coloured claddings that will bring added quality to this space.

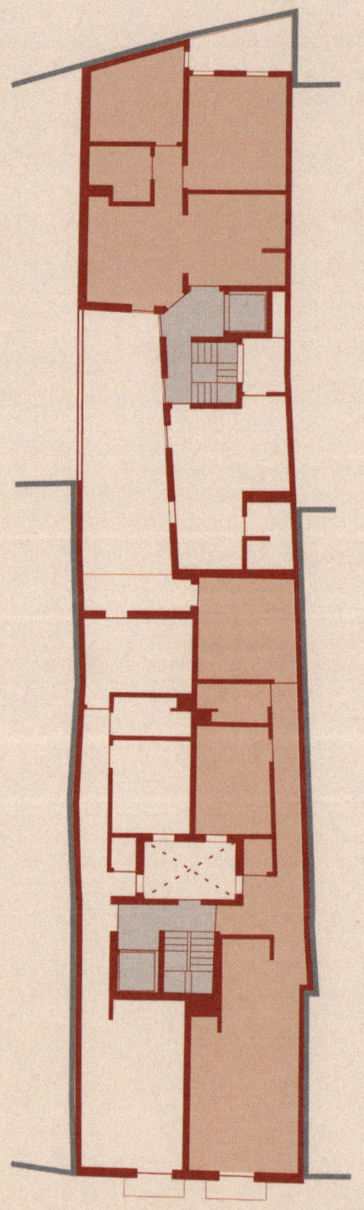

Proposed floor plan 1:250

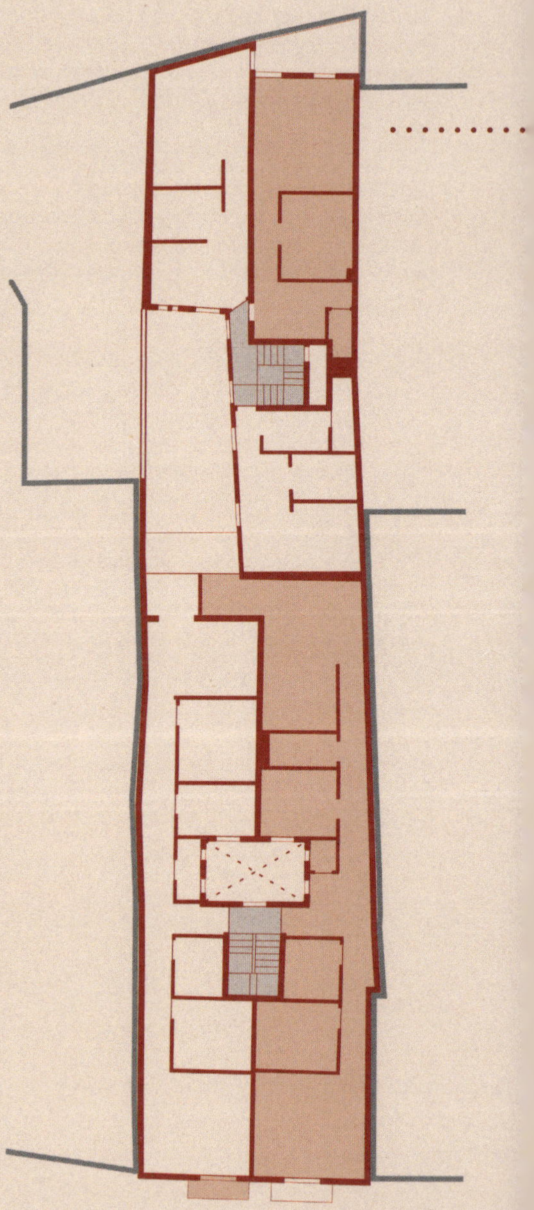

Previous state of floor plan 1:250

Location: c/Hospital, 116. Barcelona. **Programme:** 17 homes. **Surface area:** 1,371 m². **Cost:** €2,067,011.39 (CEB VAT incl.). **Architects:** MIAS Arquitectes. **Collaborations:** Maria Chiara Ziliani, Marta Cases, Marc Subirana, Mireia Simó. **Consultancy:** Josep Domènech - EDDOM (surveyor), IDP INGENIERÍA Y ARQUITECTURA IBERIA, SL (structures/installations).

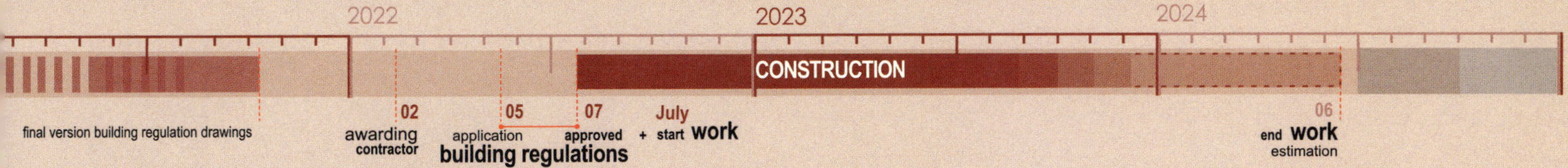

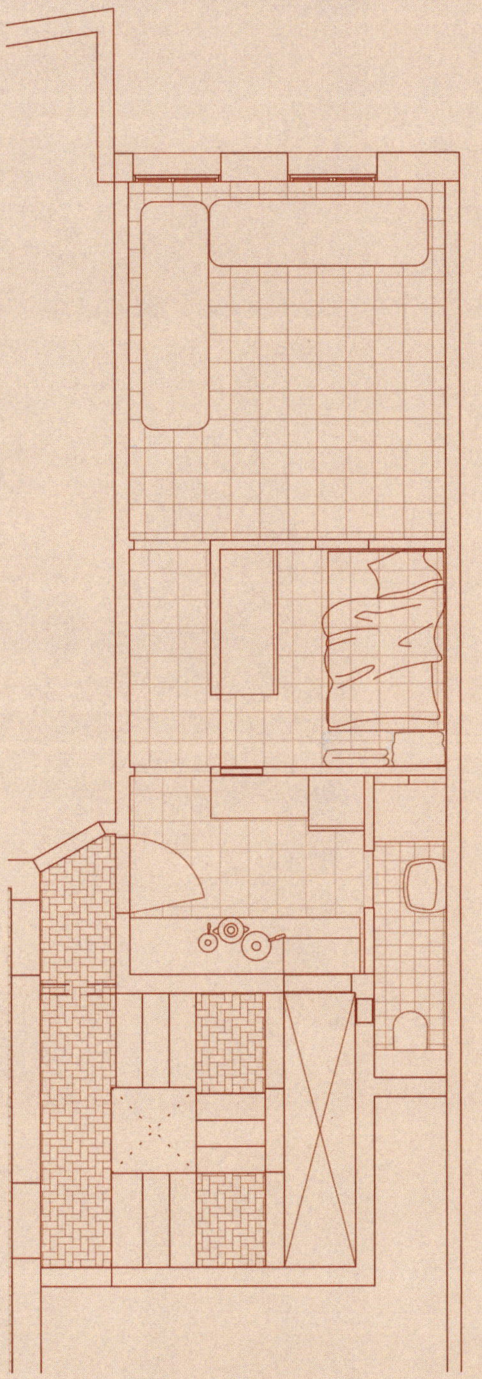

Γ Previous state of floor plan / not to scale

Γ Users

Associació Oasiurbà worked on one of the apartments in the building at the same time as the overall retrofitting project was underway. We think it is a good example to include in order to understand the complexity of this type of operation, where there are often already residents in the purchased building, with urgent needs that have to be taken into account.

In this case, it was a family made up of two adults and four minors who had been living for six years in an apartment on Carrer Hospital that did not meet basic standards of habitability. The building in which the apartment is located, in a terrible state of conservation for many years, was owned by Sareb until 2017, when Barcelona City Council purchased it to avoid the imminent eviction from the block of several families.

In 2018, Oasiurbà began its technical and legal intervention with two very clear aims: in the short term, to improve living conditions in the apartment, in order to improve the family's situation; and, in the long term, to support the family and get them resettled in a dwelling that met their needs, with suitable living conditions.

In the process of rehousing the family, during retrofitting of the building, the City Council assigned them a dwelling outside the Raval district. Thanks to the pressure of Oasiurbà's legal team, however, it was possible to rehouse them in an apartment of 60 m^2 in the same neighbourhood.

1 housing unit / Raval Associació Oasiurbà

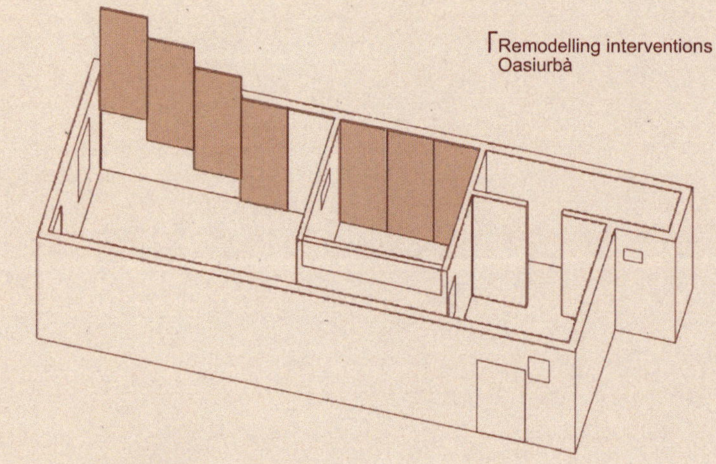

Remodelling interventions
Oasiurbà

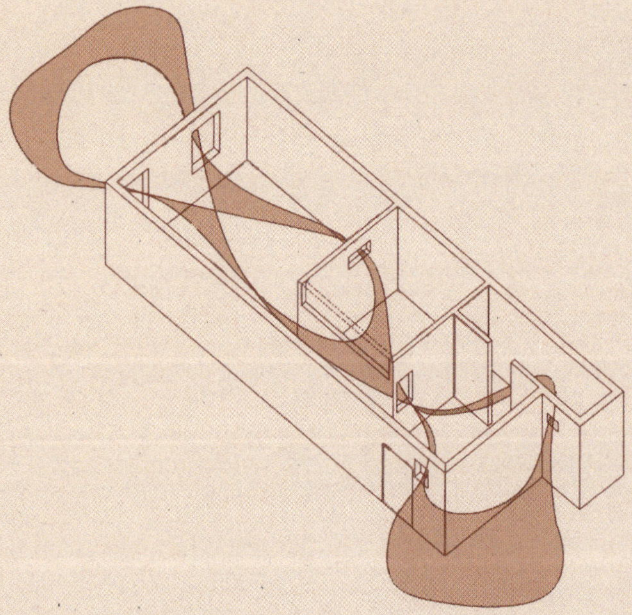

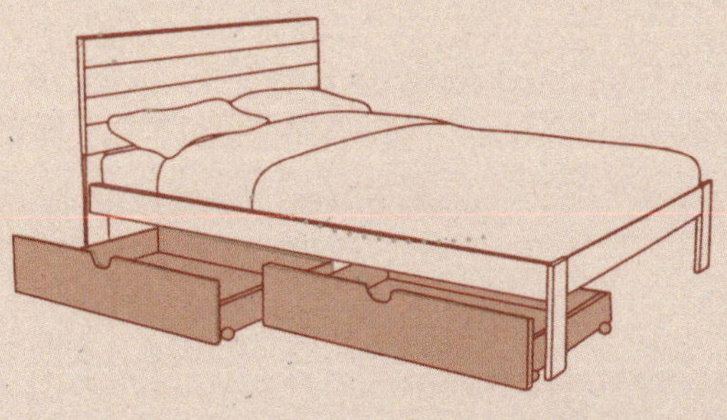

Photographs of the remodelling process

Previous state: Building courtyard

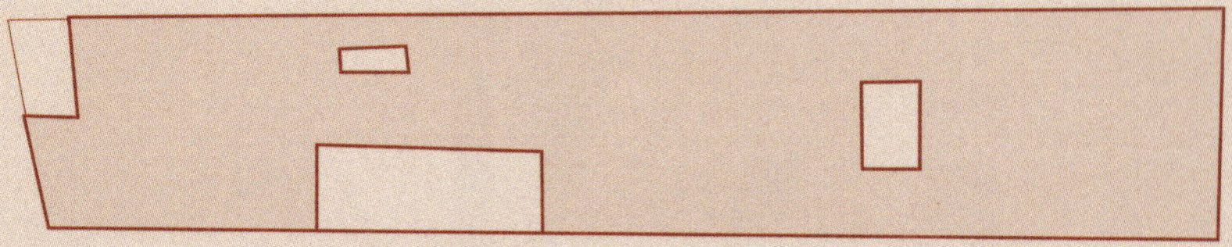

Diagram of courtyards before

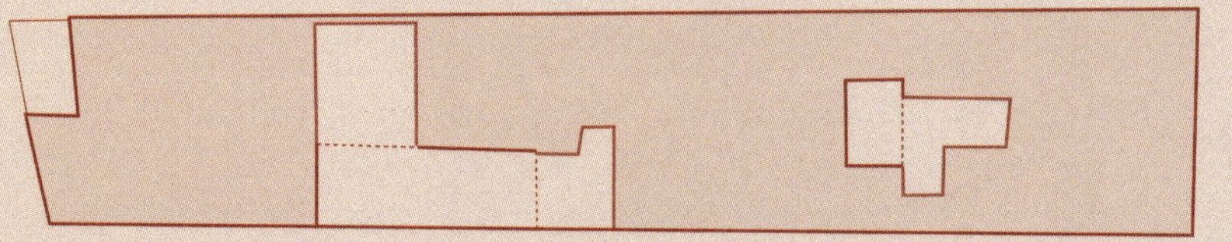

Diagram of proposed courtyards

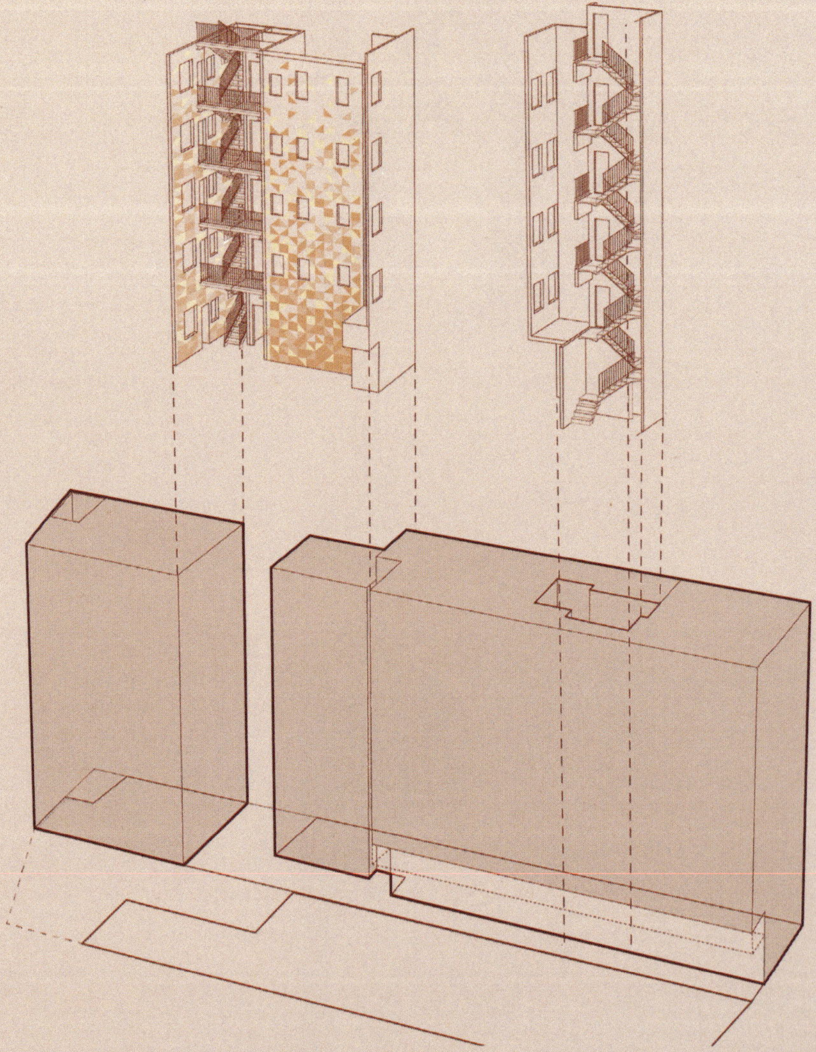

Proposed courtyard intervention

Renders of proposal

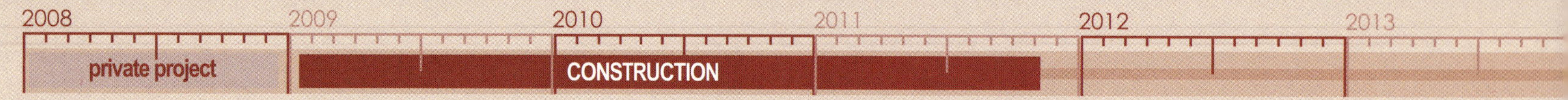

114 housing units / Encuny

MSA+A

The project, intended for public rental housing for young people, is located on a plot of land in Barcelona's Zona Franca, in an old industrial block transformed into a tertiary complex, District 38 Barcelona Business Area.

A 12-storey building with a folded L-shaped floor plan is proposed, laid out around two perpendicular corridors with light and views at either end. These circulation spaces provide access to the homes and facilitate the installation of services and facilities without the need to access the buildings. The stair and lift shaft, in a central position coinciding with the intersection of the two corridors, occupies the only space in the floor plan that does not have a façade. The fold of the building creates a south-facing outdoor entrance court.

It is a compact building from which some corner apartments on the top floors are removed, so that the volume is progressively reduced and the edges are shortened, helping to generate a more slender, complex building. The singularity of this volume is appreciable from distant vantage points, which are many, since the building overlooks Carrer de l'Encuny, Passeig de la Zona Franca and the Ronda del Litoral orbital, as well as numerous sites on the neighbouring mountain of Montjuïc. The roofs that are formed at different heights as a result of reducing the built volume are turned into community terraces.

The façades are tense, comprising three independent facings of dry-construction ventilated façade technology. They are fitted out with a single model of window frame and arranged according to a strict modular mesh of full and empty space. Three compositional resources are used to highlight the svelteness of the building: the windows are grouped vertically every two floors, arranged by height, and some are removed irregularly in alternate columns near the top of the façades.

Location: c/Encuny, 7. Barcelona.
Cost: 5,818,676.89 € (purchase price; the land was already municipal property). **Programme:** 114 homes. **Surface area:** 8,000 m^2. **Architects:** Adolf Martínez, Josep Lluís Sisternas. **Collaborations:** Milena Ibáñez, Yolanda Boto, Juan Pablo Rodríguez / Ignacio Vallet (structures). **Contractor:** Copisa. **Consultancy:** Josep Boltaina (installations).

Photograph 28/01/2020 Barcelona City Council
Encuny 7 neighbourhood welcome ceremony

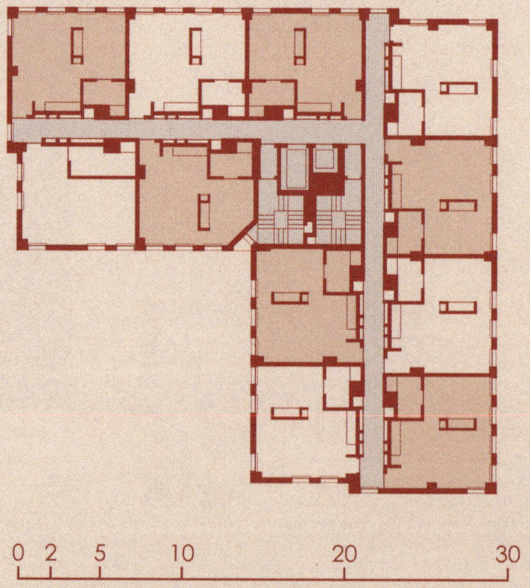

Typical floor plan 1:500

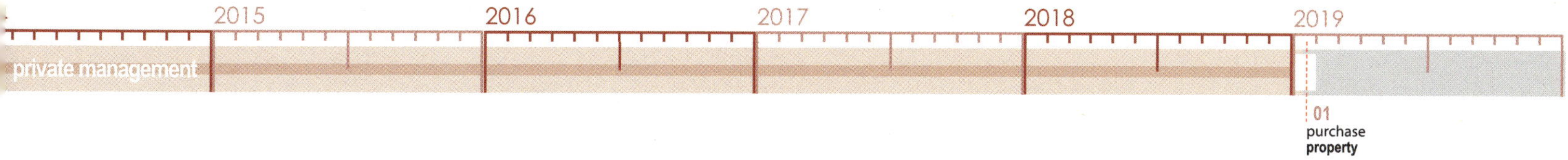

Photographs - Adrià Goula © - 2022

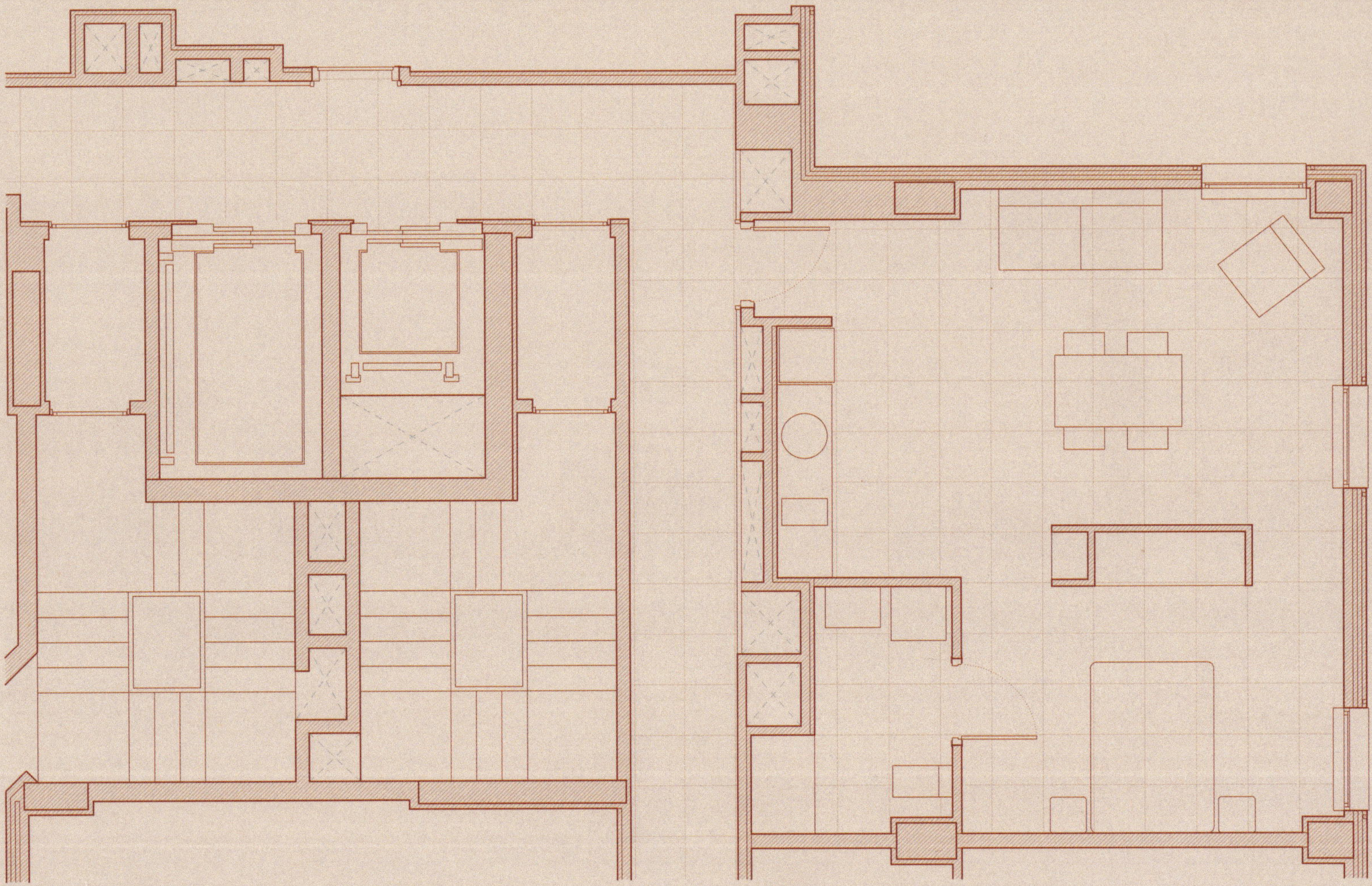

Floor plan of dwelling 1:75

Photographs - Adrià Goula © - 2022

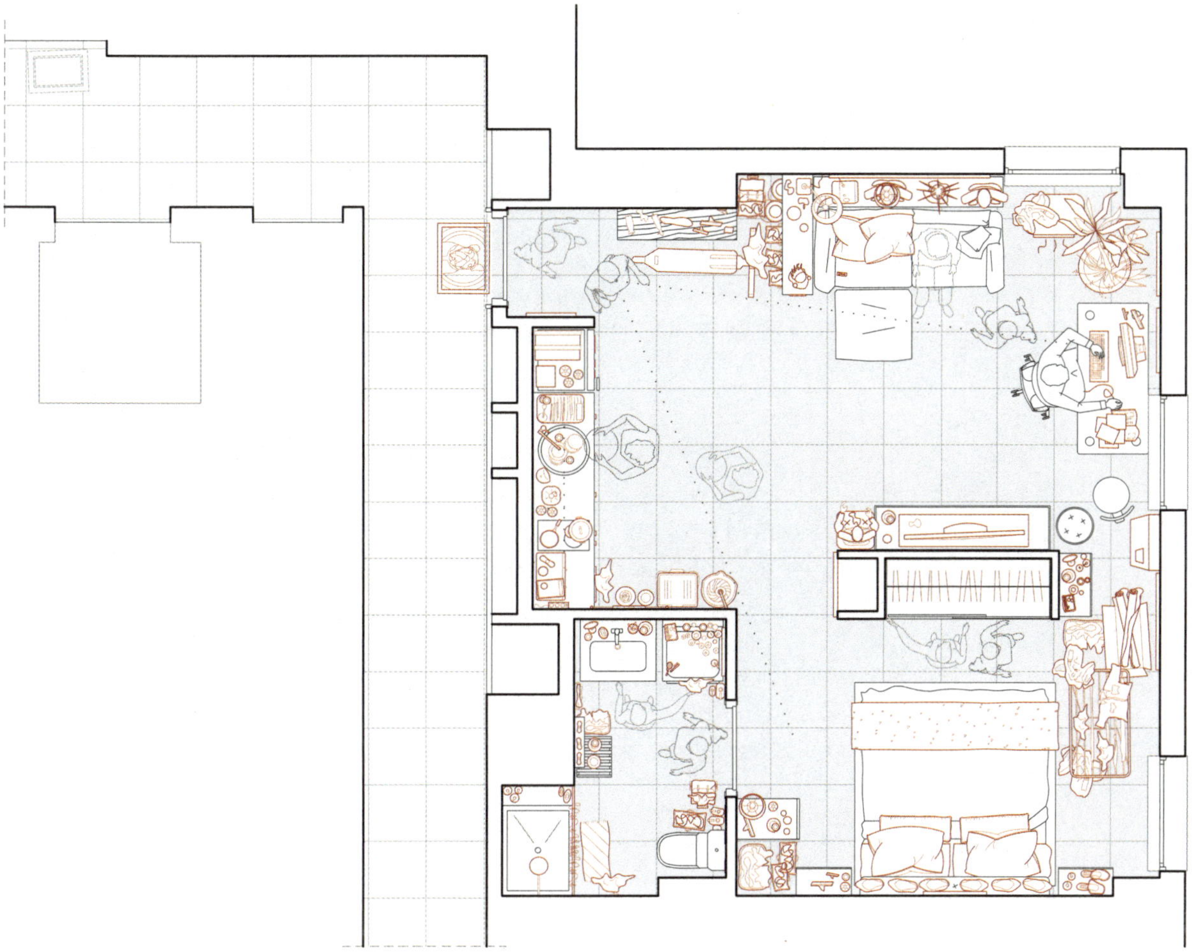

Lived-in floor plan 1:75

Interview – 2022

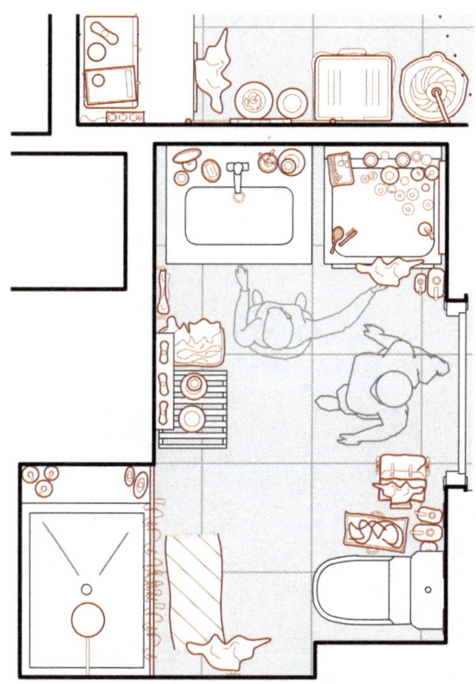

"It's all so open... you just can't heat it... A couple of doors wouldn't be bad to separate the bedroom from the living room..."

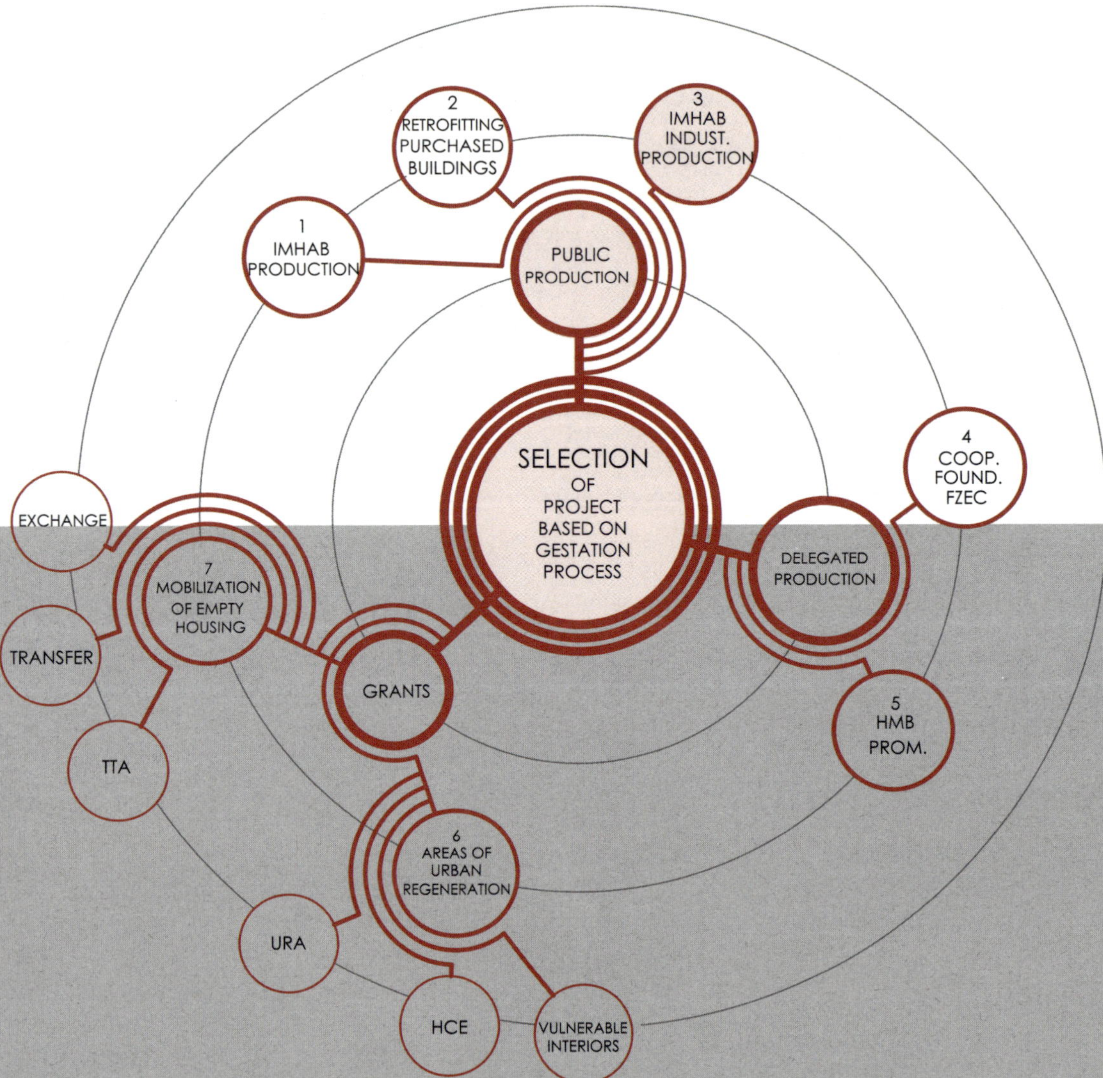

SELECTION OF PROJECT BASED ON GESTATION PROCESS
PUBLIC PRODUCTION
1 IMHAB PRODUCTION
2 RETROFITTING PURCHASED BUILDINGS
3 IMHAB INDUST. PRODUCTION
DELEGATED PRODUCTION
4 COOP. FOUND. FZEC
5 HMB PROM.
GRANTS
6 AREAS OF URBAN REGENERATION
URA
HCE
VULNERABLE INTERIORS
7 MOBILIZATION OF EMPTY HOUSING
EXCHANGE
TRANSFER
TTA

MHAB industrialized production

01 12 temporary local accommodations / Ciutat Vella **Straddle3 / Eulia Arkitektura / Yaiza Terré**

02 42 temporary local accommodations / Glòries **Bestraten-Hormias / Ramos+Roig**

03 40 housing units / Arriassa LOT 4 **Guallart Architects**

The role of industrialized construction in tackling the housing emergency

Tonet Font

Architect. Professor of Architecture Projects, ETSAB-UPC and ETSALS-URL

Industrial construction is known to reduce construction times, emissions, waste and, under certain conditions, costs. In periods of major housing emergency, it is common for it to appear as a recurring solution to speed up the production of new homes, with the resulting prototypes that rarely go beyond the exception to become common solutions. Nonetheless, conventional construction is gradually becoming industrialized, though not so much as a whole as in each of its parts.

In Barcelona, the mortgage crisis that began in 2008 and the unprecedented increase in rental prices are constantly bringing evicted residents to the Emergency Desk: in 2015, as many as 600 families were staying in rooms in pensions with all their belongings, waiting for a decent housing solution. This wait can last for years; apart from the fact that the city has one of the smallest public housing stocks in Europe –less than 2%, a far cry from the European average of 9.1%–, public housing production had practically come to a standstill. Despite the increase in investment since then, the number of completed homes is far from being able to meet accumulated emergency needs, and even further from being able to respond to the bulk of the population with incomes that are too low to be able to pay what are still very high rents.

Apart from the big numbers, losing your home is a traumatic, mutilating experience. Housing people in rooms in pensions or, at best, in homes away from their usual surroundings, is a very expensive solution for the Administration that does not make it any easier for the people evicted to get over the shock; with the loss of their home, they often also lose much of their network of social relations when they need it most.

For Barcelona Council's Social Innovation team, what interested us was not so much the advantages of industrial over conventional construction as the opportunities it could offer for the production of new housing solutions: activating land beyond the scope of public housing, deploying administrative procedures to reduce the five to eight years of conventional operations, and promoting sustainability by means of reuse.

Can we intervene in the housing emergency locally, in the neighbourhoods where evictions occur? And, more particularly, can we do it in city-centre neighbourhoods, where gentrification is most present and where the Administration rarely has residential land? To complement the purchase of homes and buildings in poor condition and their subsequent rehabilitation, we propose using unoccupied sites designated for facilities (which are more numerous) to provide a faster response to the housing emergency. The use of these sites, however, imposes two conditions: provisional construction, as at a future date they will have to accommodate the facility for which they have been earmarked; and the use of a little-explored urban housing figure –accommodation– since housing is not permitted on land designated for facilities, with the exception of social housing.

Potential sites call for nomadic solutions that can temporarily occupy designated land to provide a provisional but local response to urgent needs until a definitive solution is found. This explains our interest in industrial construction, not just to cut construction times, but for easy dismantling and fast relocation, as we learned from temporary modules for schools.

Temporary school modules also open the door to shorter administrative procedures than those usual in housing, which allowed us to carry out the whole operation in one year (from getting the plot to handing over the keys), less than the five to eight years involved in a conventional operation.

The choice of the shipping container for accommodation modules is based on its suitability for sequential assembly and disassembly without becoming deformed, and its condition as a non-patentable universal platform, indispensable for a project of projects that plans to assemble modules from different locations in a new location. Last-trip containers, discarded for maritime operations, get a new lease of life instead of being considered waste and can be recycled, promoting sustainability in construction.

These keys to urban planning, administrative and technological innovation make up APROP (*allotjaments de proximitat provisionals*, or provisional local accommodations): ground-floor modular buildings of amenities that go some way to meeting local demands, stacked accommodation modules connected by walkways, with green roofs and double skins to adapt the buildings to their urban environment and improve comfort and energy efficiency, offering an economical alternative (including transfer) to the huge expense of housing families in pensions.

APROP adds one more housing solution to the many we need to prevent the loss of neighbourhood communities, and it does so by placing the opportunities offered by industrial construction at the service of improved attention to the housing emergency.

The possible industrialization of housing

Sandra Bestraten - Emili Hormias
President of the Barcelona Branch of the COAC
Architects at BH Arquitectura
Lecturers at UPC. ETSAB. EPSEB

The provisional local accommodations, APROP, address the concern with responding to the housing emergency through innovation. This strategy once again focuses on industrial architecture as a means to reduce production costs and deadlines.

To prevent occupants feeling stigmatized by living in an industrial element, the typological optimized-space solutions specific to this architecture incorporate added values such as sustainability and comfort. Accordingly, the contribution of this project is not only to recycle shipping containers as a solution with a very low environmental impact, but to adapt them to low energy consumption. This is achieved by wrapping the metal container in a double layer of insulation that protects the building against fire risk and adverse weather conditions, and giving the indoor spaces warm finishes.

The user does not simply enter the long narrow housing typology produced by using shipping containers, since this is counteracted by cross-ventilation, improving the perception of transparency in the space, guaranteeing the connection between the two end façades, and transforming possible corridors into functional living spaces, as in the case of the kitchen.

The minimum façade area corresponds to the ends of the container. These ends open completely to the outside with large windows that allow the incorporation of balconies in the main façade and walkways leading to the rear. These external elements added to the container are scaled to act as passive protectors against direct summer sunlight by generating a shadow, while letting the lower winter sun shine into the home.

The large balcony doors make these balconies and walkways part of the useful and visual space of the interior. They also increase the perception of spaciousness by appropriating communal space to extend the home with plants and other personal effects. This is an added value with positive effects for emotional health that we saw during the confinement imposed by the COVID pandemic.

The walkways leading to the homes, the community areas for each floor linked to the vertical communication shaft and the green roofs with self-managed vegetable plots encourage interrelation between the users. This is a way of understanding the act of dwelling based on an awareness of community and mutual enrichment through cohabitation, strengthening the bonds of friendship and building a supportive cooperative housing culture. This approach to social housing helps prevent loneliness, one of the consequences of individualistic modern society, and one of Barcelona City Council's challenges for the decade 2020-2030.

This principle of community social integration makes it important that most accommodations are accessible. APROP accommodation guarantees barrier-free spaces in all communal areas and in all two-container homes, which are the majority. The homes are barrier-free, with particular attention to the kitchen and bathroom. This is important not just to facilitate access to social housing for people with functional diversity, but also to improve social inclusion, allowing the occupants to invite friends or family members with reduced mobility to their home.

These accommodations are designed to respond to urgent housing needs, including those redirected from the Emergency Desk. Care has therefore been taken to include storage spaces and cupboards that free up living space to the maximum. This new space attached to the bedrooms provides a diversity of users, from single people to families, with sufficient space to store their belongings while they are in transit.

APROP accommodations are a bold step in innovation in social housing, an intrinsic value of the first social housing projects of the 20th century that were later abandoned in favour of conventional free-market housing. This is a first step towards mixed prefabrication solutions, with combinations of industrialized solutions that optimize construction costs and produce more flexible housing typologies that encourage the diversity of social and cohabitation units.

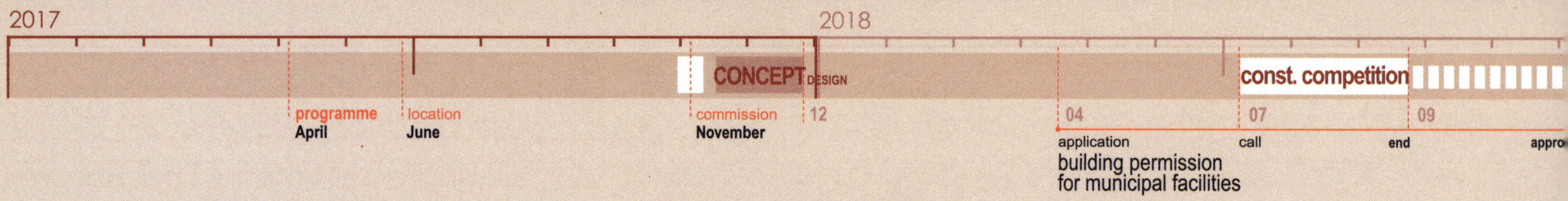

12 temporary local accommodations / Ciutat Vella

Straddle3 + Eulia Arkitektura + Yaiza Terré

These housing facilities are characterized by being modular, transportable and dismountable, which makes it possible to quickly mobilize empty spaces in the city for periods of five or more years. The buildings can also incorporate public facilities and spaces for neighbourhood use.

In the case developed in the Ciutat Vella district of Barcelona, the project is situated between c/Nou de Sant Francesc and c/Josep Pijoan.

The site currently has a provisional use as a public space for the neighbourhood. A five-storey building with a green roof is planned.

The building is made up of prefabricated modules that are combined to create a compact volume. It consists of 12 accommodations: eight individual and four double. All of them are cross-ventilated, in this case facing northeast and southwest, which also promotes solar collection in cold weather.

Designed around this compact volume is a polycarbonate façade that adapts to the plot layout. This double skin serves as a separator between the external environment and the containers, generating a conservatory effect with many climatic and spatial benefits. The communication shaft is strategically positioned against the party wall, thereby addressing contact with the adjacent building and guaranteeing access to all the homes via walkways that are large enough to allow other uses.

The ground floor is reserved for communal uses and local services. A very transparent, open-plan place is designed with direct access to the plaza, enabling different uses. The spaces related to facility management are also located on this level.

Model – Project phase

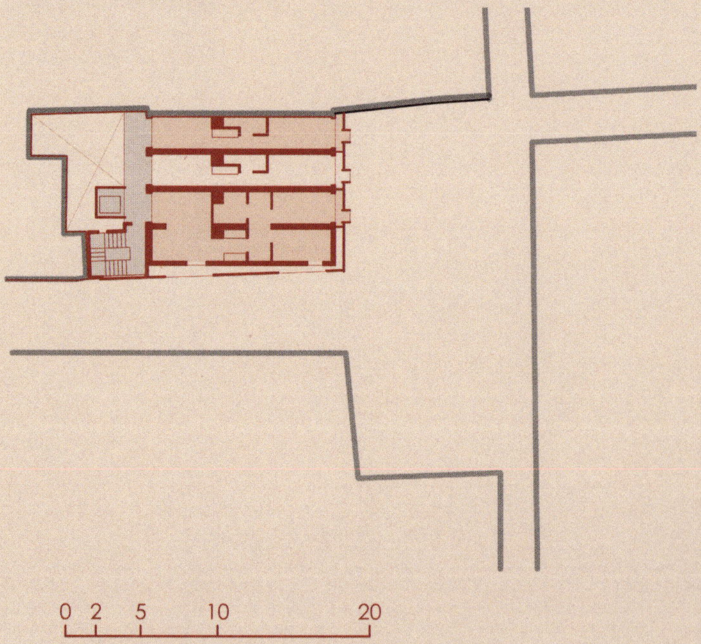

Typical floor plan 1:500

Developed by the Municipal Social Services Institute

Location: c/ Nou de Sant Francesc, 10. Barcelona. **Programme:** 12 accommodations. **Surface area:** 816 m^2. **Cost:** 1,042,402.89 € (CEB VAT incl.). **Architects:** Straddle3 + Eulia Arkitektura + Yaiza Terré. **Collaborations:** Oihana García, Paula Kobeaga, Ibai Lamarca, Pere Estévez. **Contractor:** Constècnia3 + Eurocatalana. **Consultancy:** Ordeic Enginyeria i Consultoria (installations), Societat Orgànica (sustainability).

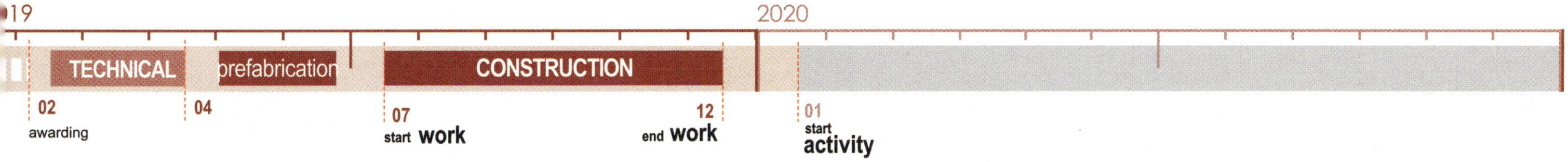

Photographs - Adrià Goula © - 2022

⌈Photograph of prefabrication

⌈Photographs of on-site assembly

Render of concept design

Photographs - Adrià Goula © - 2020

Photograph of work

Photographs of prefabrication and assembly of containers

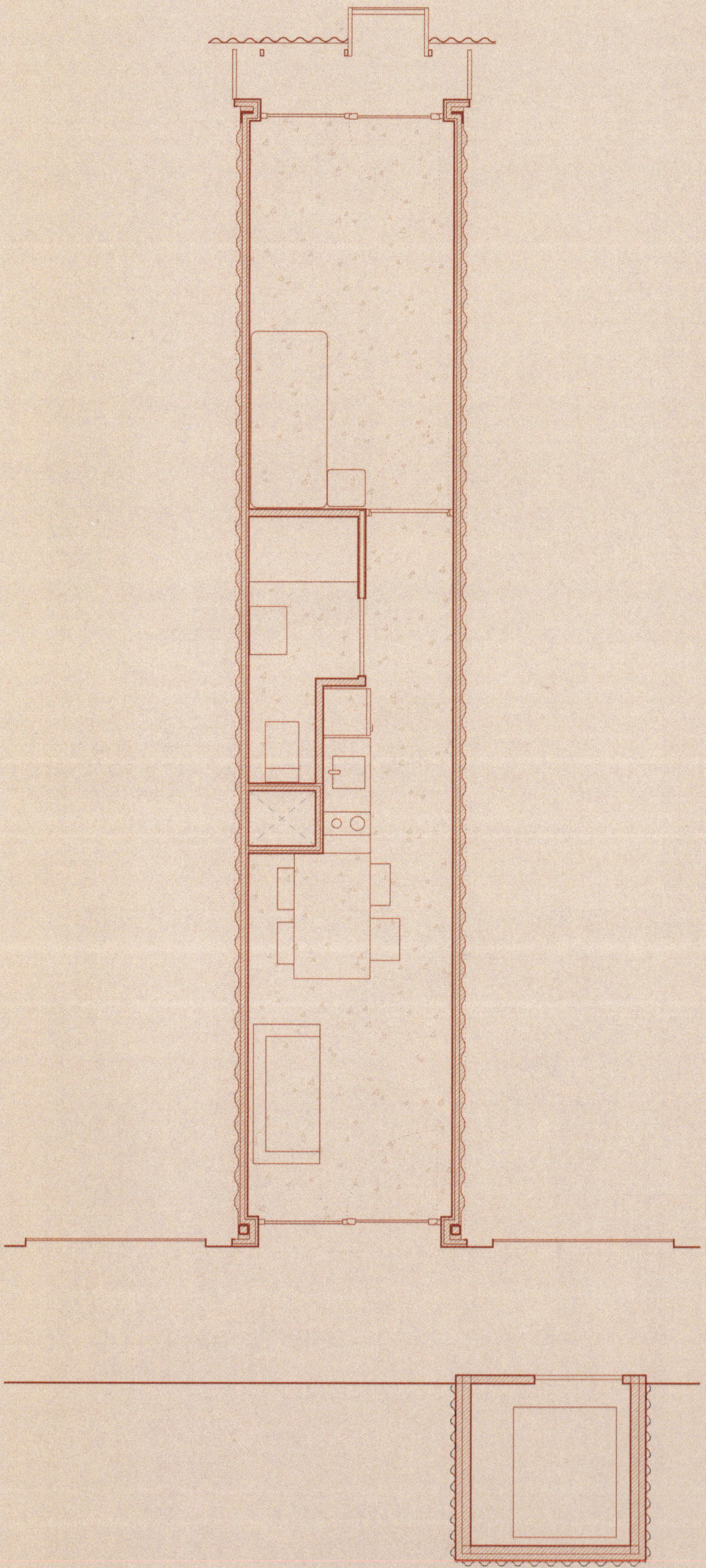

Floor plan of dwelling 1:75

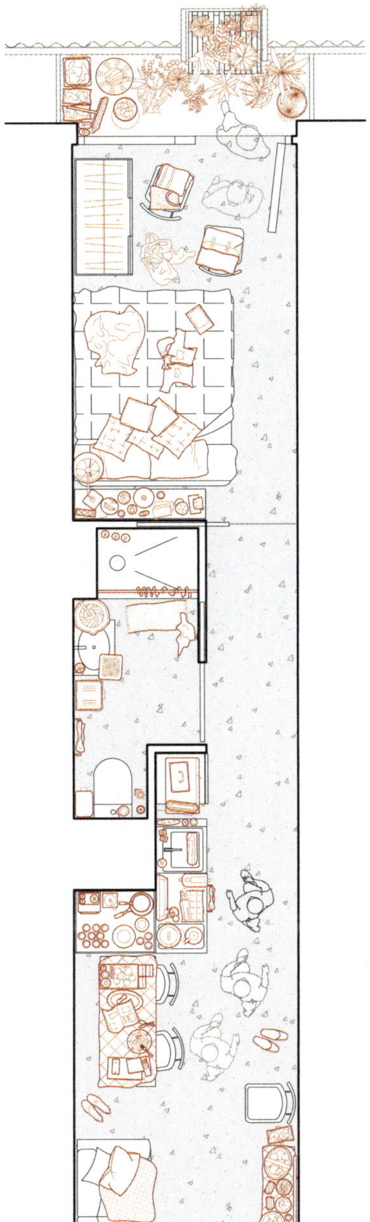

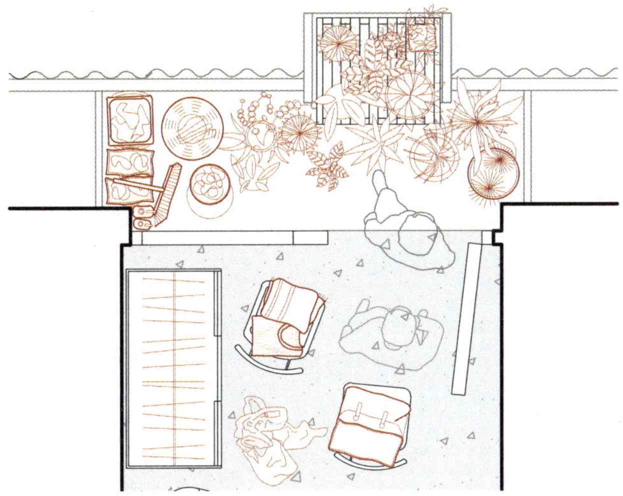

Interview – 2022

"Very quiet. Just for me, this house is fine for me. Great neighbours."

Lived-in floor plan 1:75

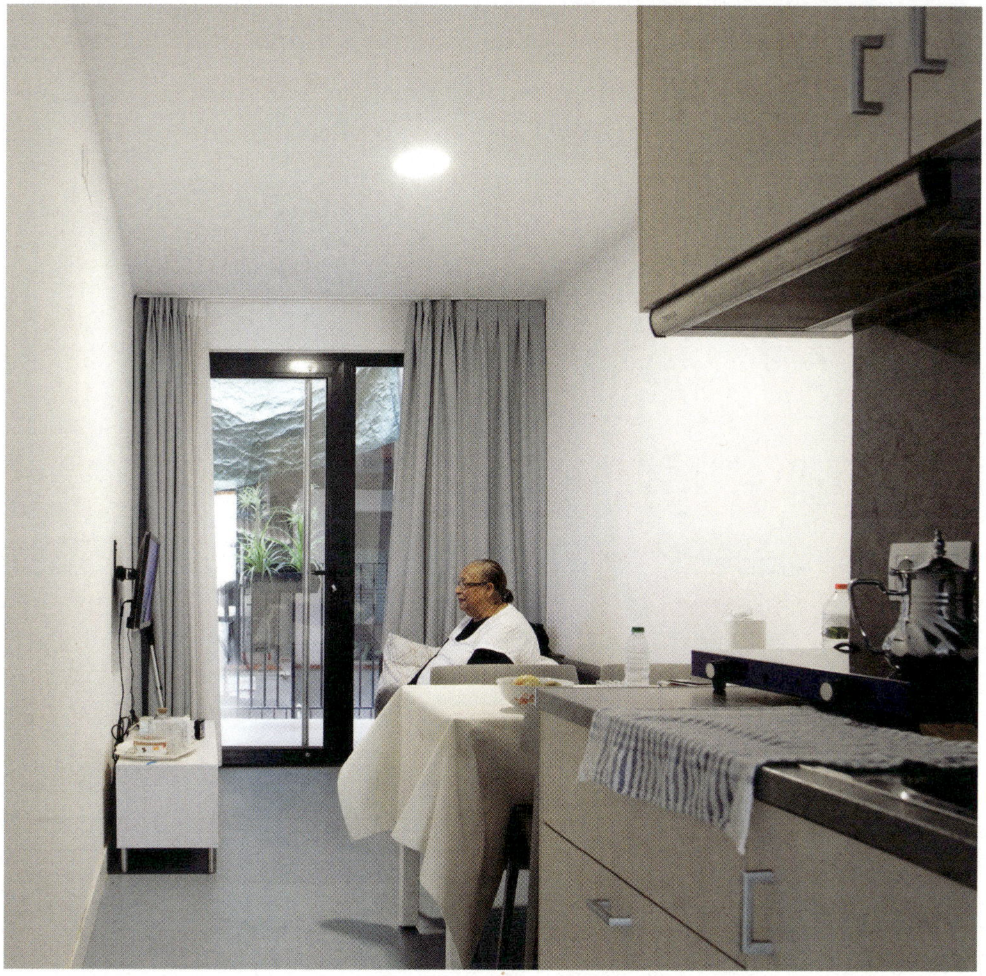

Render - Project phase

Façade material project

Render - Project phase

Photographs - Adrià Goula © - 2020

Photographs - Maite Caramés © - 2022

Photographs - Adrià Goula © - 2020

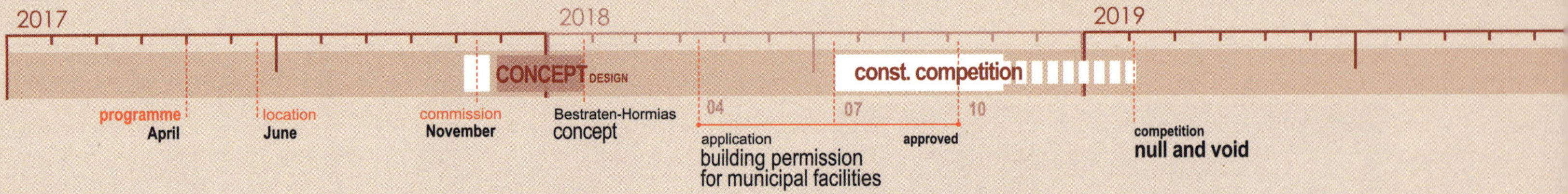

42 temporary local accommodations / Glòries

Bestraten-Hormias / Javier Ramos + Lluís Roig

The project adapts shipping containers for use as emergency accommodation. In the space at the centre of the street block, an urban allotment is planned with therapeutic activities for people with autistic spectrum disorders. All the rainwater from the building is collected in the façade of the inner courtyard of the block and collected in a cistern to be used to water the garden.

The maximum number of containers that can be stacked is seven, which will be the number of floors of the building, with a ground floor for municipal offices and administration. The roof is given over exclusively to installations: photovoltaic panels, and heating and cooling devices.

The containers are load bearing in themselves. The rest of the structure is made up of vertical and horizontal communication spaces, which interlock the structure of the whole. Vertical communication is provided by a staircase and two lifts, and horizontal communication comprises porches. These walkways, as well as being a space for interaction between people staying in the building, are the distribution area for the facilities on each floor for each of the homes.

Each floor has 11 containers. There are two types of home: a single container (one per floor), which is equivalent to one home, and two containers joined by their long sides through perforations (10 per floor), equivalent to five homes. This makes a total of six homes per floor. In total, 77 shipping containers that form 42 accommodations, two of which are adapted.

Prefabrication workshop

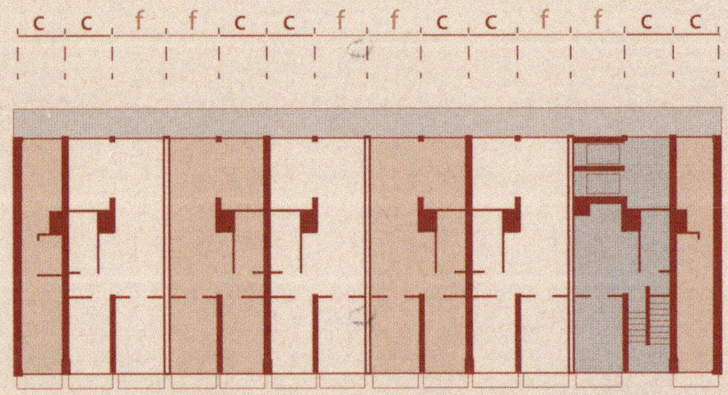

Typical floor plan version 1 1:500
Concept design

In the first version of the concept design, a three-dimensional structure of containers alternated with a two-dimensional structure of cross-laminated timber beams and floor slabs. In the end, the entire proposal was built with containers alone.

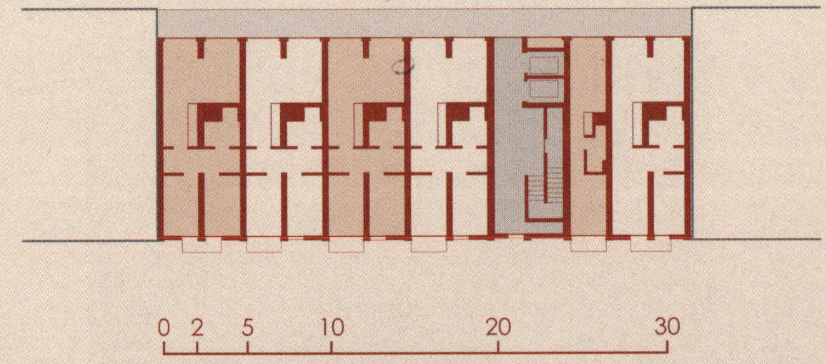

Typical floor plan 1:500

Developed by the Municipal Social Services Institute

Location: c/Irena Sendler, 22. **Programme:** 42 accommodations. **Surface area:** 3,650 m². **Cost:** 4,989,394.05 € (CEB + VAT). **Architects:** Bestraten-Hormias (concept), Lluís Roig, Javier Ramos. **Contractor:** CALAF Constructora. **Consultancy:** UrbanProma (management) + PRC Ingeniería Industrial (installations) + Otherstructures (structure).

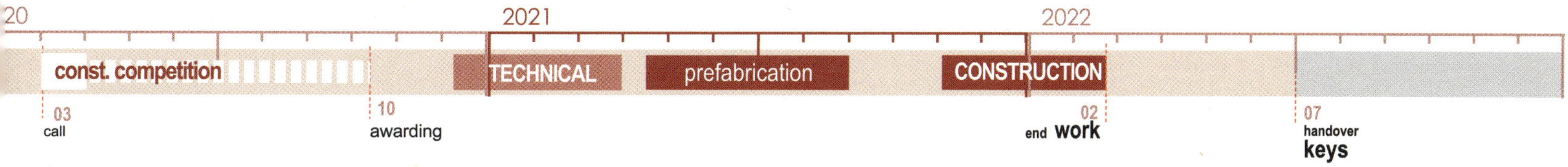

Photographs - Adrià Goula © - 2022

Photograph of work

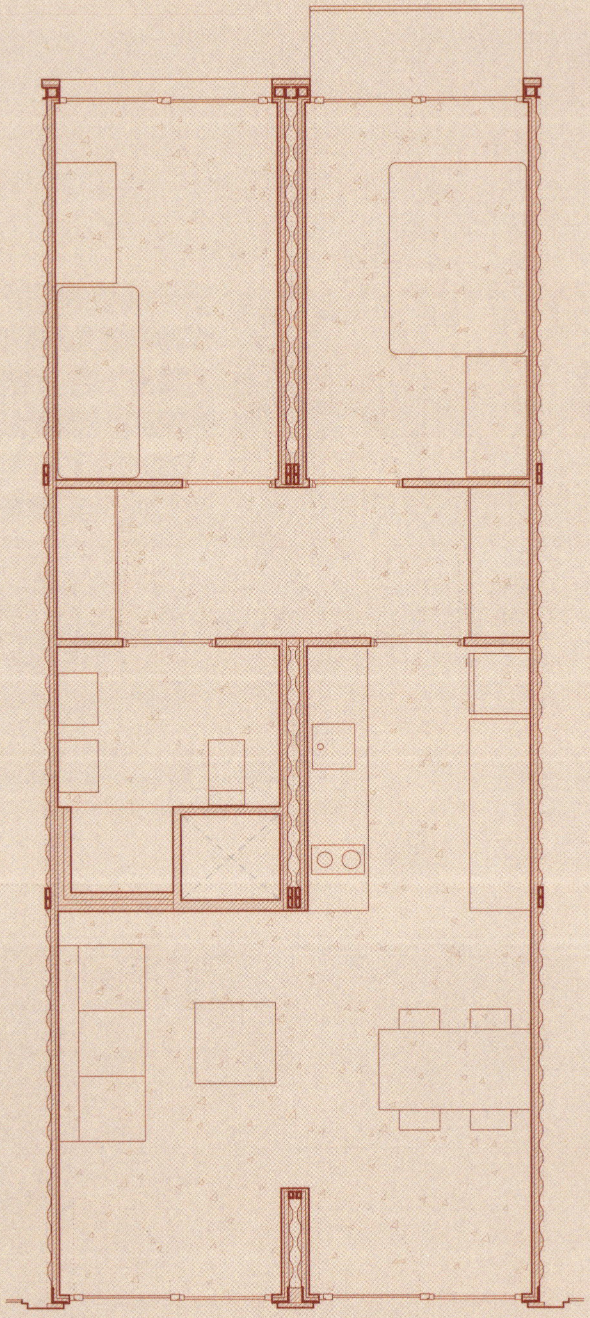

Floor plan of dwelling 1:75

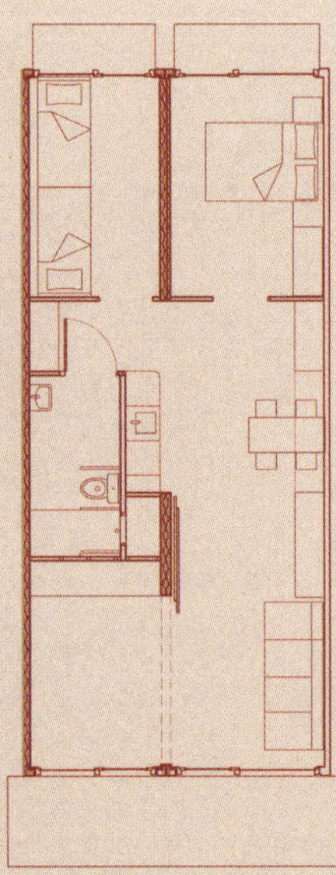

Floor plan of the dwelling version 1
Concept design

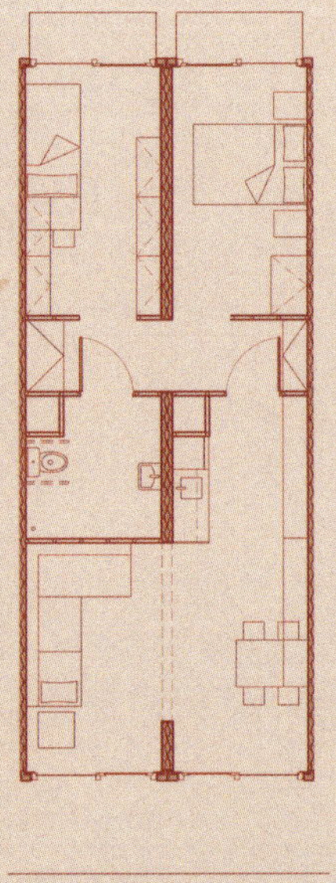

Floor plan of the dwelling version 2
Concept design

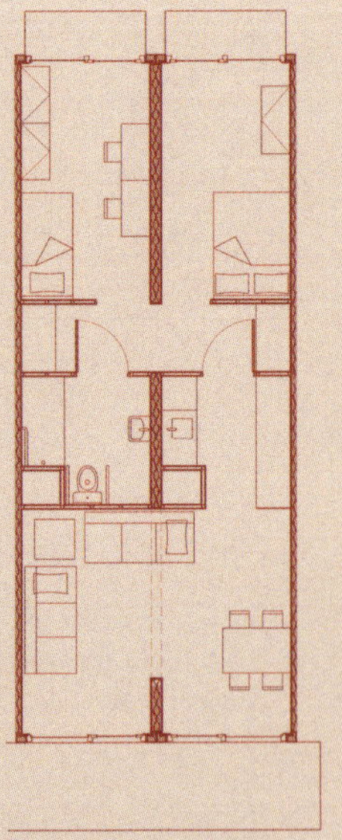

Floor plan of the dwelling versio
Concept design

Photographs - Maite Caramés © - 2022

Photograph of work

Photographs - Adrià Goula © - 2022

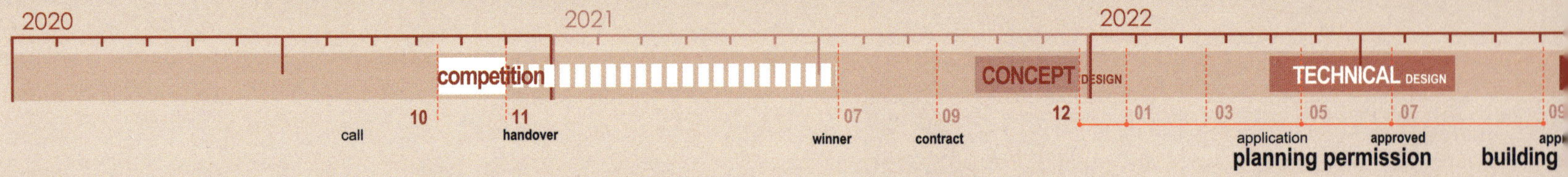

40 housing units / Arriassa LOTE 4

Guallart Architects

The building, situated on a rectangular plot of land (423 m^2) with three façades, is laid out according to a precise, economical floor plan, with five units of two double rooms per floor, all with similar dimensions to guarantee flexibility of space. Each home has a spacious 1.80-m-deep terrace that occupies at least two structural modules with lengths of between 7 and 14 metres.

The building is designed using prefabricated CLT panels, making for a much faster industrial construction process that is acoustically, thermally and environmentally more efficient than the usual methods. Wooden buildings are, in fact, CO_2 sinks, because they store the carbon dioxide absorbed throughout the trees' growth, thereby helping to combat climate change.

In the context of the fight against energy and food poverty, and the search for net-zero architecture, the concept of the rooftop solar conservatory is a new element that can be installed on any city terrace. Previous research was taken as the basis to study how to apply the concept in this building with the aim of potentially defining a new standard that can be implemented on many rooftops in the city of Barcelona and around the world.

A prototype solar greenhouse is proposed in the plot 4 building, marking the start of a new way of understanding sustainable urban architecture that can be set up on the roofs of existing and new buildings.

Greenhouse render

Façade render

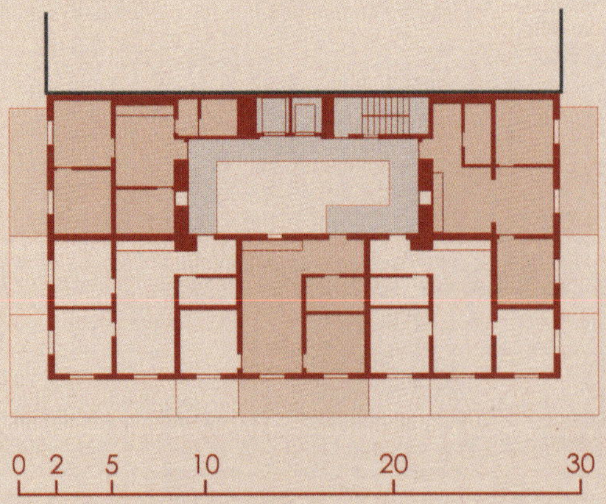

Typical floor plan 1:500

Location: c/Lola Iturbe Arizcuren, 13. Barcelona. **Programme:** 40 homes + Athenaeum on GF. **Surface area:** 3,803.49 m^2. **Cost:** 5,800,867.19 € **Architects:** Vicente Guallart, Daniel Ibáñez. **Collaborations:** Elisabet Fàbrega, Ramiro d'Elia, Firàs Safieddine, Irene Rodríguez, Andrea Puebla, Pieràngela Humet, Clara Sackman, Jesús Mora. **Contractor:** ACSA. **Consultancy:** JSS (installations), Enginyeria L3J (sustainability), ENMADERA, TALLFUSTA (structures), Sorigué (budget), Arquitectura Técnica Sequoia (site management).

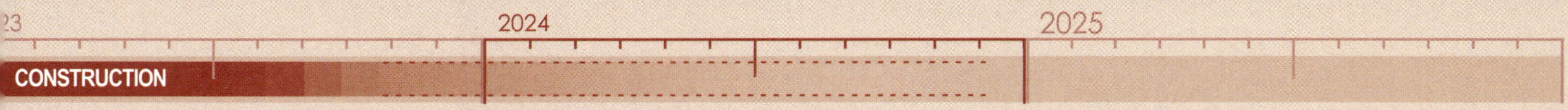

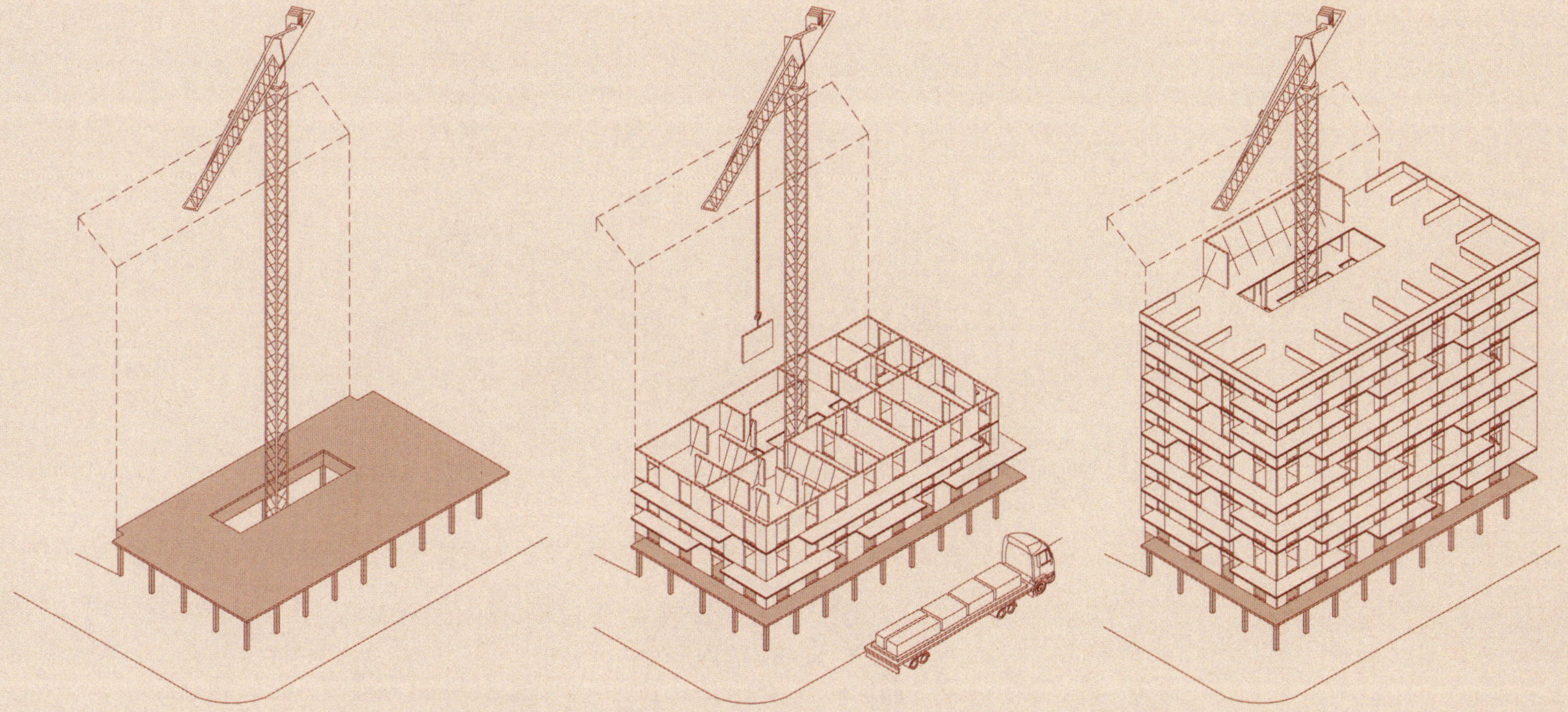

On-site assembly process

Project renders

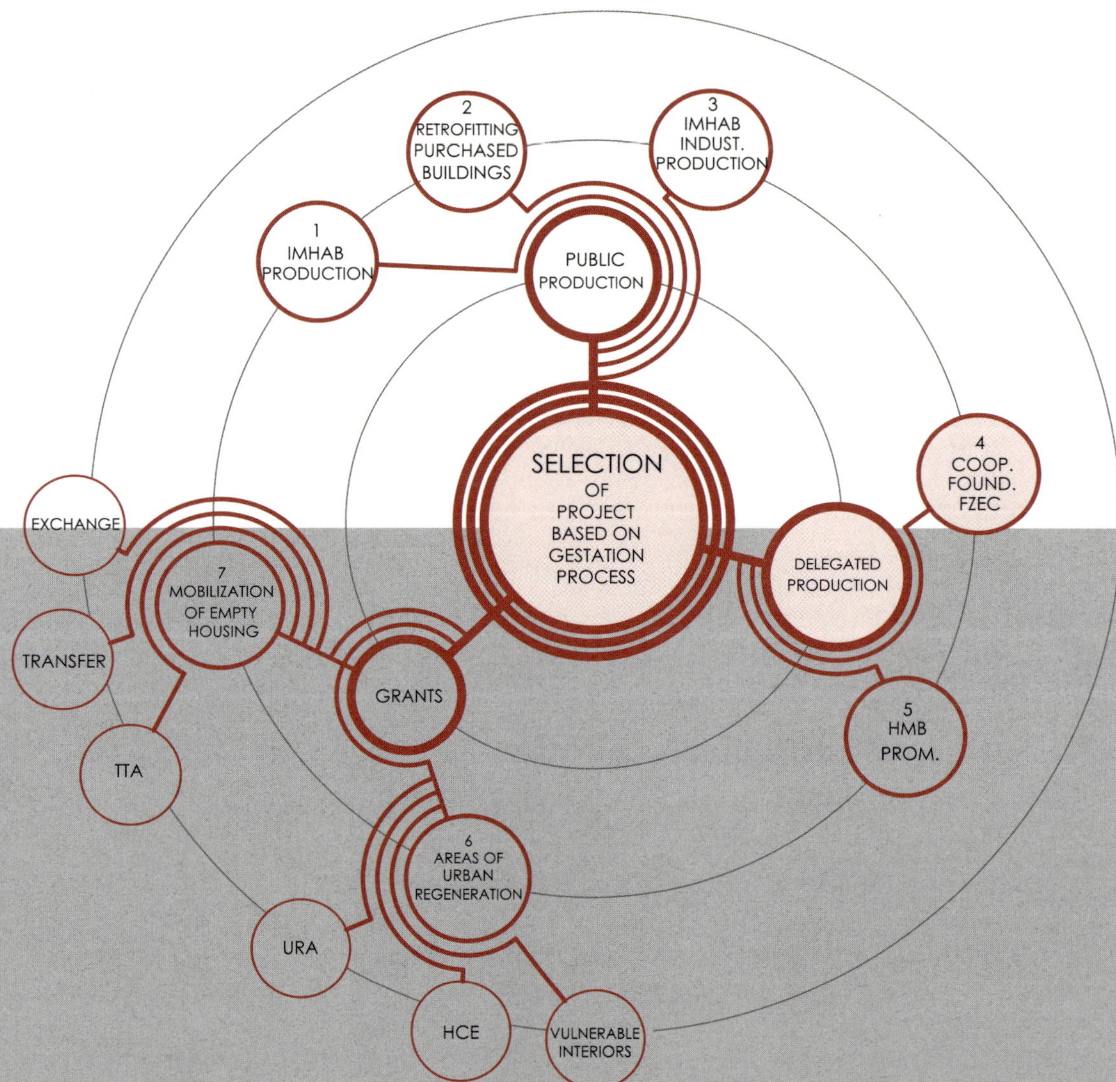
SELECTION OF PROJECT BASED ON GESTATION PROCESS
PUBLIC PRODUCTION
1 IMHAB PRODUCTION
2 RETROFITTING PURCHASED BUILDINGS
3 IMHAB INDUST. PRODUCTION
DELEGATED PRODUCTION
4 COOP. FOUND. FZEC
5 HMB PROM.
GRANTS
6 AREAS OF URBAN REGENERATION
URA
HCE
VULNERABLE INTERIORS
7 MOBILIZATION OF EMPTY HOUSING
EXCHANGE
TRANSFER
TTA

Foundations and Zero Equity Cooperatives. FZEC Agreement

01 20 housing units / La Balma Cooperativa **Lacol + LaBoqueria Taller**

02 32 housing units / Cirerers Cooperativa **Celobert**

03 44 housing units / Fundació Salas and Fundació Nou Lloc **011h Sustainable Construction**

Cohabitac, XES, Habicoop

The housing emergency that the city of Barcelona is experiencing is one of the most worrying indicators of inattention to basic rights. Added to energy poverty, evictions and the speculative pressure that is driving more and more people out of the city, it makes the right to housing a vital social priority.

These situations are not, however, a natural fact; they are the result of decades of public policies at all administrative levels to promote private property and speculative housing dynamics. This demonstrates the importance of administrations, organized civil society and associations taking action to ensure that decent, affordable housing is available.

Following the model of cities such as Vienna, Amsterdam or Berlin, the Foundations and Zero Equity Cooperatives (FZEC) has established a framework for public-social-community collaboration to help to respond to the housing needs of the population of Barcelona, with the firm commitment to speed up the expansion of social housing stock in the city, guaranteeing continued public ownership of the land and its development by non-profit social entities.

The agreement sets the goal of building or rehabilitating 1,000 homes in the coming years, with access to patrimonial assets of Barcelona Council. These plots and buildings, in accordance with legislation, can be transferred directly to non-profit organizations to promote social housing.

The signatories of this agreement are, on one side, the Federation of Housing Cooperatives of Catalonia (Habicoop), the Coordinator of Social Housing Foundations (Cohabitac) and the Solidarity Economy Network (XES), and on the other, Barcelona City Council, Barcelona Housing Authority (IMHAB) and the Association of Social Housing Policy Managers of Catalonia (GHS).

The signatory bodies must ensure that the proposals respond to the general interest, taking into account criteria such as speed of production, technical and economic capacity, and rental prices or transfer fees in keeping with protected prices. The aim is to avoid the concentration of projects among limited producers, provide measures to combat climate emergency, improve energy and limit polluting elements, discourage the use of private vehicles, and encourage community ties.

To guarantee the affordability of homes, the agreement establishes a fee of zero euros during the amortization of the financing, refundable subsidies of 7% to 16%, a municipal guarantee of non-payment of the loan in the event of more than five maturities, and specific financing from the Official Credit Institute-ICO, the Catalan Finance Institute-ICF (soft loan of 140 million euros guaranteed by the City Council), and other public and private financial entities.

Of the total number of homes, 40% will be assigned for use and 60% will be for rent promoted by foundations or cooperatives, with homes intended for specific groups such as young people, people with mental and physical diversity, and the elderly.

As well as speeding up the production of sheltered housing, the agreement also sets out to promote the social and solidarity economy. This is a diverse economic fabric that is very resilient in maintaining occupancy in times of crisis, which contributes particularly to building a more sustainable, equitable economic model.

The agreement is the first step towards a future social operator similar to the community land trusts that originated in Afro-descendant communities in the United States and northern European countries, in which the Administration, social producers and resident communities are jointly constituted as producers and managers of social housing stock. With this aim in mind, the agreement includes the decision to study the constitution of a social housing operator, and foresees that, once the credits have been repaid, the social organizations will allocate 50% of their results to it.

Shared domestic lives

Raül Avilla-Royo
Doctor of Architecture
Lecturer in Architecture Projects, UPC. ETSAB

Sharing domesticity. Our daily routine of being at home. Understanding that living and managing part of our home as a community multiplies its possibilities and improves the quality of our habitat at all levels. It might seem obvious, but perhaps it isn't, in an urban context based on individual horizontal ownership that also individualizes the way we think and what we value about home.

In this context, public-social agreement is committed to putting the focus on community. On the one hand, the Administration recognizes the shared responsibility of external agents in the production of affordable housing and their capacity to produce and manage it successfully. On the other, a degree of autonomy in the process allows the producer to refine existing processes or propose new strategies, and to address the needs of specific groups.

This framework offers the possibility of including users as active agents, allowing us proactively to question the values and cultural constructs of our collective lives. The resulting potential impact goes far beyond the urgent response to the lack of affordable housing, and addresses the social, political and regulatory levels. Examples are typological research into private and collective space, emphasis on sustainable construction, the ecological footprint of a building, gender perspective, caring and the strengthening of community bonds of mutual support, among others.

As a result, the building is lived and activated by the appropriation of space by the users, who give meaning to every corner of it. The limits of the home are not marked by private space, nor do they respond to the administrative definition of property (the flat, in conventional terms, adapted to the specifics of cohabitation units), being seen rather as soft limits that are constantly redefined.

The spaces in front of the home become a projection of it towards the community. The corridors, now more than passing places, become spaces for interrelation and meeting that acquire a life of their own, filled with their own objects, and demonstrate trust in the community and a desire to contribute to the improvement of shared space. These two attitudes of trust in your neighbours and caring for shared spaces, characteristic of small-scale rural areas and missed in big cities, are an intrinsic part of the everyday life of these buildings, now seen as social and spatial units.

In this way, living does not happen strictly in private space but in an ambiguous, intermediate space between the home and the street; a threshold of the scale of the building that allows simultaneous forms of living and collective activities in multiple spaces: rooms such as kitchens, laundry rooms and care spaces to collectively carry out domestic tasks; community energy management systems; communal spaces to leave bikes and other objects; rooftops that become the chosen place for recreation and interrelation (recovering the role they traditionally had); reading rooms and multipurpose spaces that allow new uses; shared guest rooms; ground floor spaces open to the neighbourhood... It is a long list that grows and adapts with each new initiative.

All this is accompanied by community management of the space, in which it is the users who agree the use to be made of it –conversations that begin not with the occupation of the building, but in its gestation phase– and keep up an open dialogue that adapts over time.

It is important to highlight that this process is only possible thanks to the active involvement of new agents who take on the risk and the leadership, and the complicity of the parties involved, giving rise to a certain type of shared space and community life. The resulting gestation, built form and cohabitation are three inseparable dimensions that cannot be understood independently.

No less important, and arising from the experimental nature of the project: the gestation, the materialization of the proposal and community cohabitation have a pedagogical effect on the agents involved. This learning process includes the technical teams and the Administration, the production agent, the users and even those who visit the building when it is inhabited and discover another way of living collectively with non-conventional answers –spatial and social– to everyday challenges that are both urgent and long-term.

We know how we live today, but not how we will live in the future. The constant redefinition of ways of living, of the structures of cohabitation units, and challenges such as the ageing of the population and the lack of affordable housing call for a pluralistic approach to research that allows different groups to find their own mechanisms to address these and other situations. If the city is, by definition, a meeting place for diverse people, then the response to the needs arising from it is also necessarily based on collective intelligence and multiple processes.

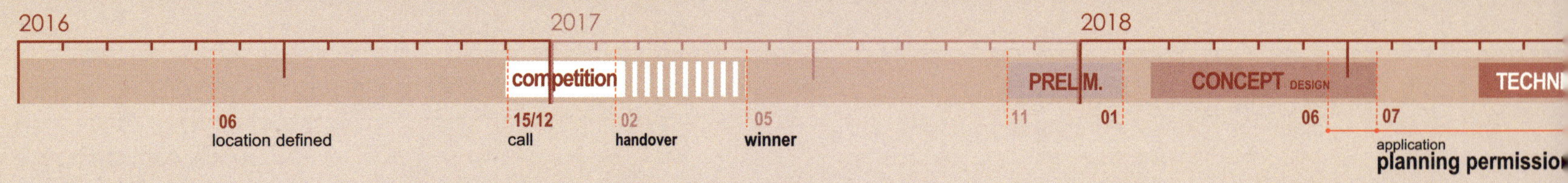

20 housing units La Balma Cooperative / Poblenou

Lacol + LaBoqueria Taller

La Balma focuses on the initial cost of construction and the use of the building during its useful life, thinking about the final economic impact for occupants. The aim of the building is to combat energy poverty and be an infrastructure that enhances the evolution of the three social levels: neighbourhood, community and home.

The cooperative is an apartment building, but it also aims to be a neighbourhood facility, which is why it opens onto the public space (strip of facilities on c/Antic de València) and is designed for this twofold function.

The homes are complemented by community spaces on all the building's floors. On the ground floor is the communal kitchen-dining room and two commercial premises that give onto c/Espronceda. The small format parts are laid out on the rest of the floors, which improves internal circulation. Finally, the fully accessible 300 m^2 roof is the cooperative's outdoor space.

The building's environmental strategy aims to reduce all the building's energy demands and generate the minimum environmental impact in its construction:

- Compaction of the heated/cooled areas.
- Work on a changing building section, equitable passive functioning.
- Centralization of installations.
- Perfectible installations.
- Heating and cooling, and DHW generation using geothermal energy.
- Low environmental impact construction. Wooden structure and dry construction.

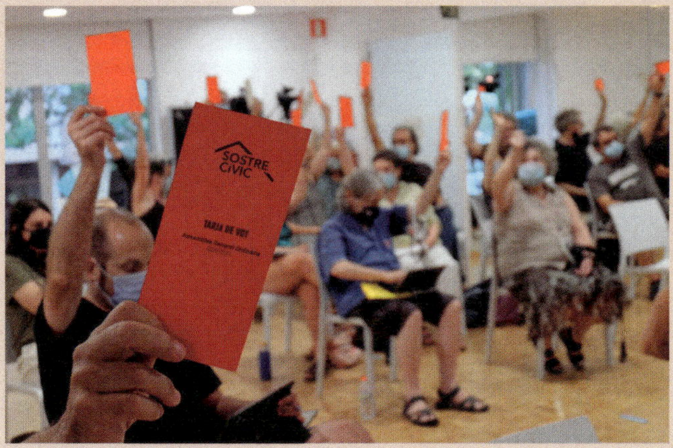

Sostre Cívic assembly

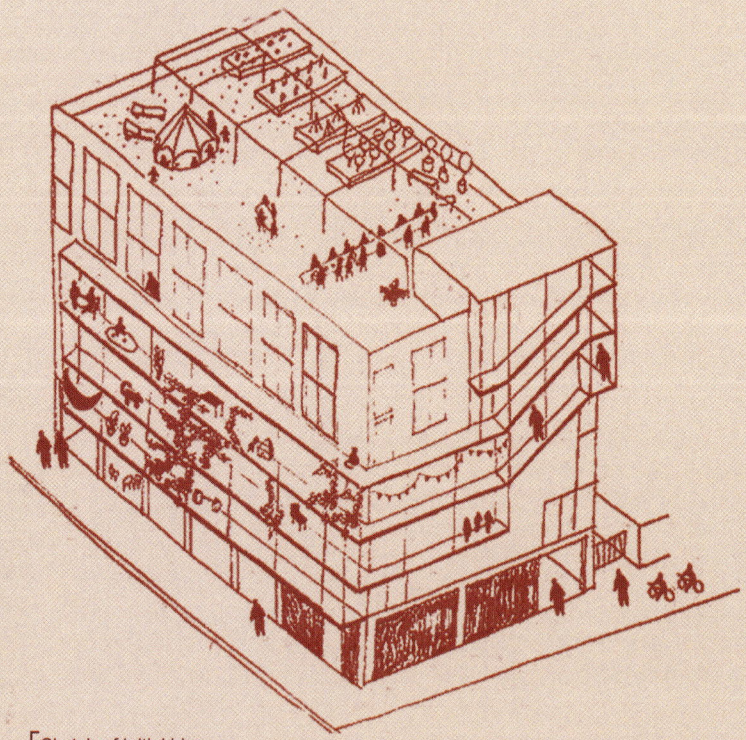

Sketch of initial idea

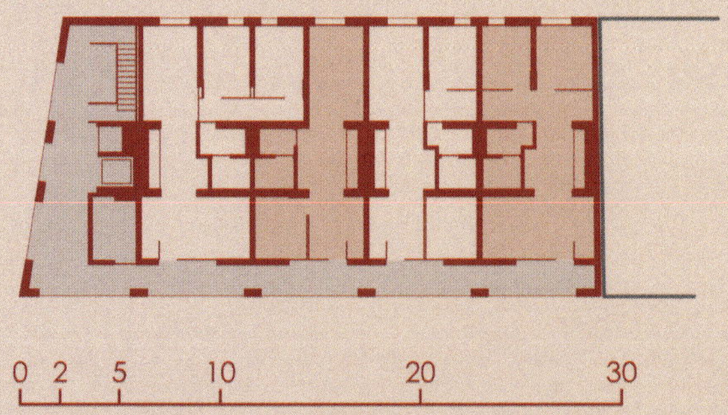

Typical floor plan 1:500

Production prior to Foundations and Zero Equity Cooperatives Agreement

Location: c/Espronceda, 131-135. Barcelona. **Programme:** 20 homes (19 + 1 social housing unit). **Surface area:** 2,347 m^2. **Cost:** 2,725,622.14 € (CEB VAT incl.). **Architects:** Lacol and LaBoqueria. **Contractor:** La Constructiva SCCL. **Consultancy:** Arkenova (installations), Societat Orgànica and PAuS (sustainability), Miguel Nevado (structures), Arrevol (building engineer), Sostre Cívic (developer).

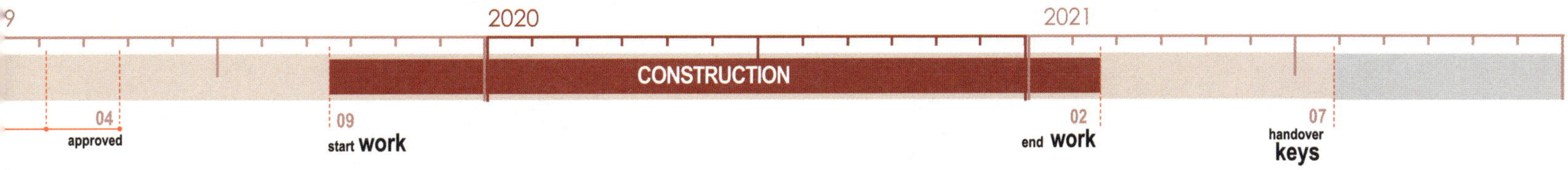

Photographs - Adrià Goula © - 2022

Render of walkway – Competition phase

Render of walkway – Project phase

Render – Competition phase

Render - Project phase

Photographs - Milena Villalba © - 2022

Photograph of work

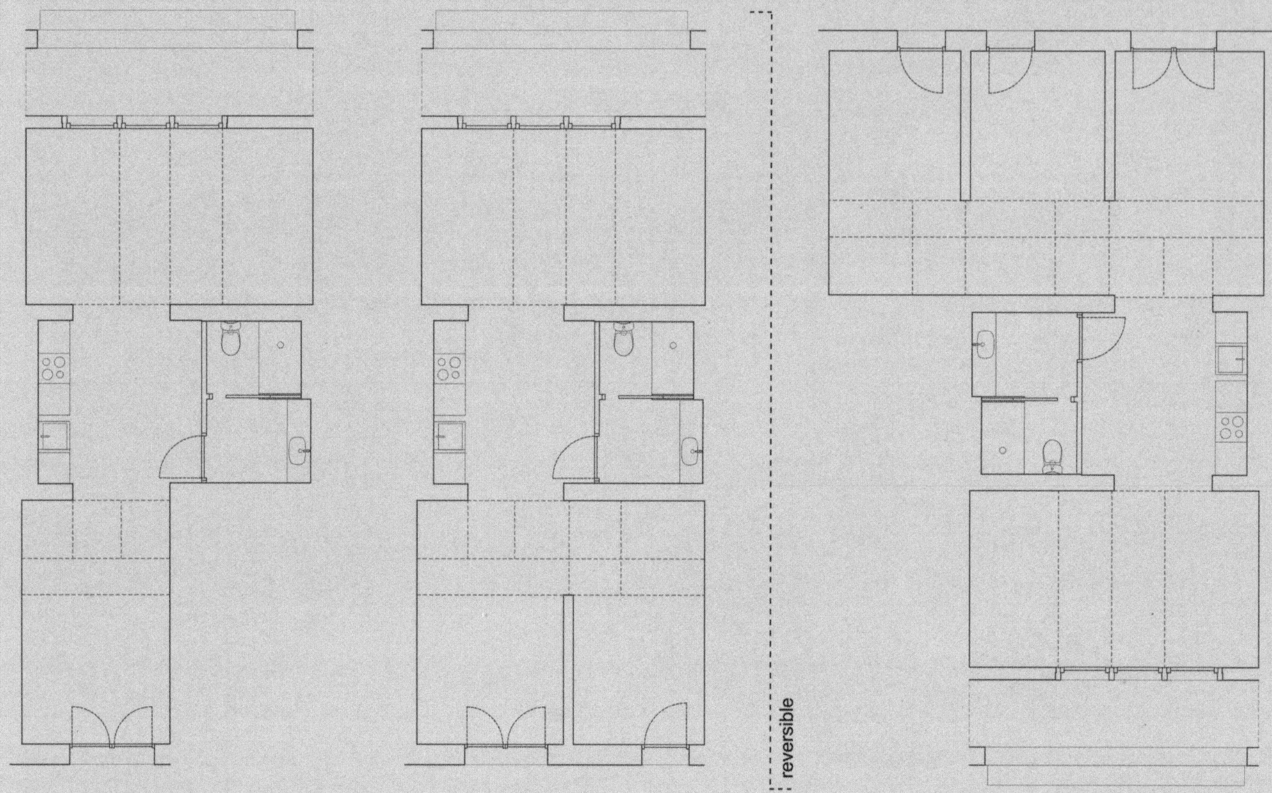

S version apartment

M version apartment

L version apartment

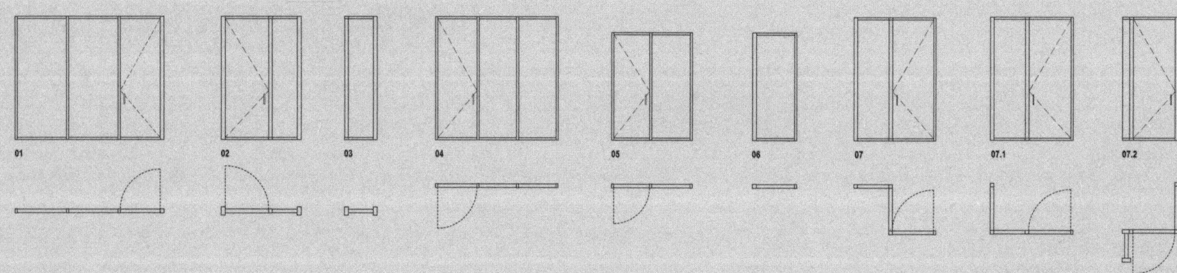

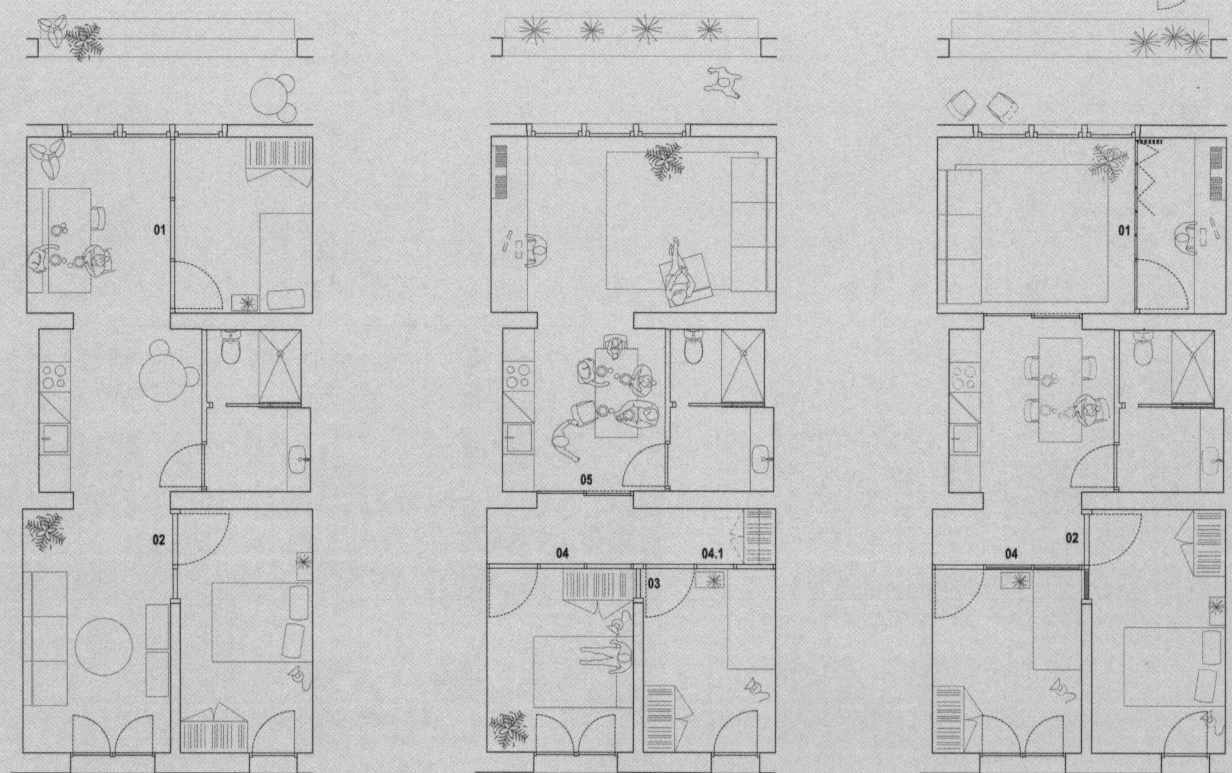

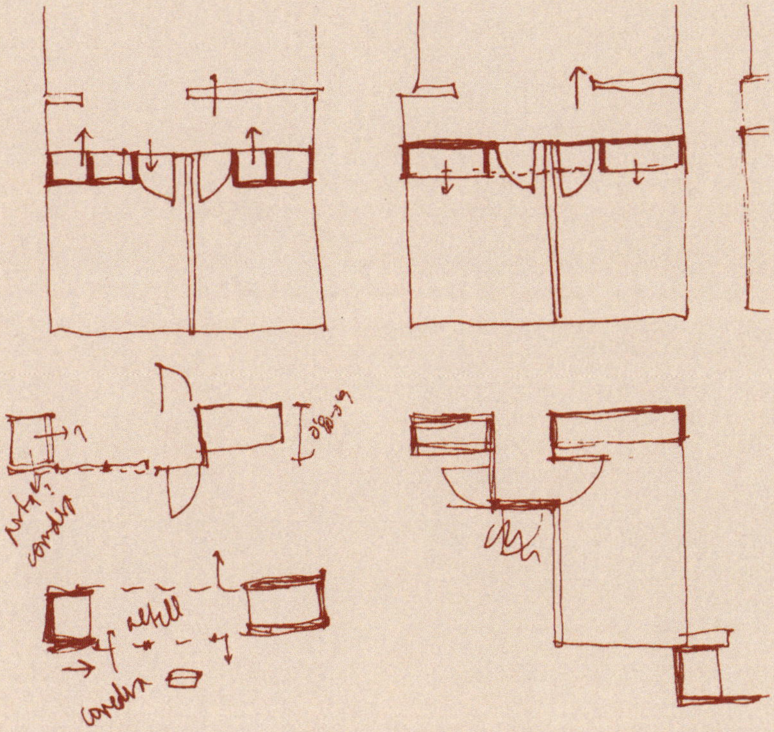

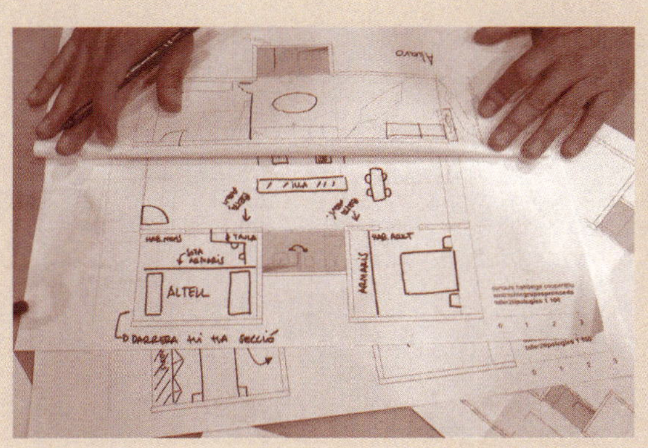

Drawings and photographs of cooperative work with the occupants

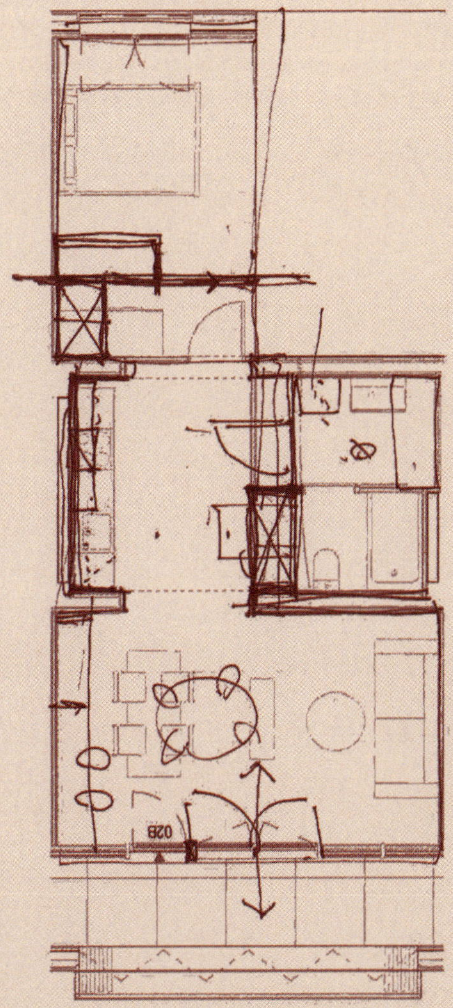

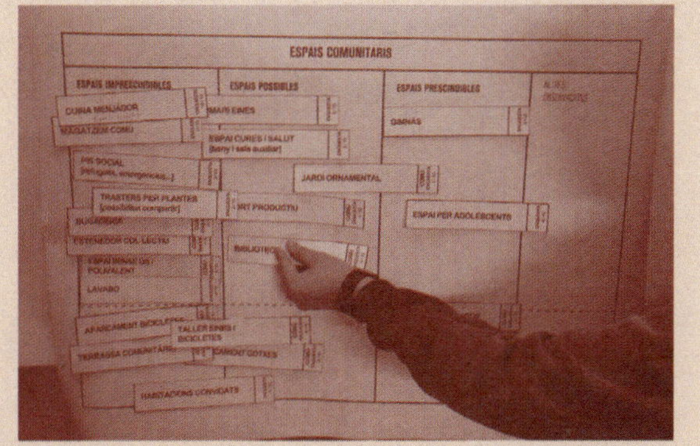

The proposal consists of 20 housing units. They all start from a grid of 16-m² pieces that allow the inhabitant to decide the interior layout. Each apartment has a fully equipped 50 m² basic unit that can be complemented with one or two pieces. The spaces resulting from this extension are managed by the cooperative. This management makes possible a real flexibility of the system.

The final distribution of each of the apartments has been worked on collaboratively with its inhabitant.

⌈Render of housing interior – Concept project phase

⌈Photograph of housing interior - Milena Villalba © - 2022

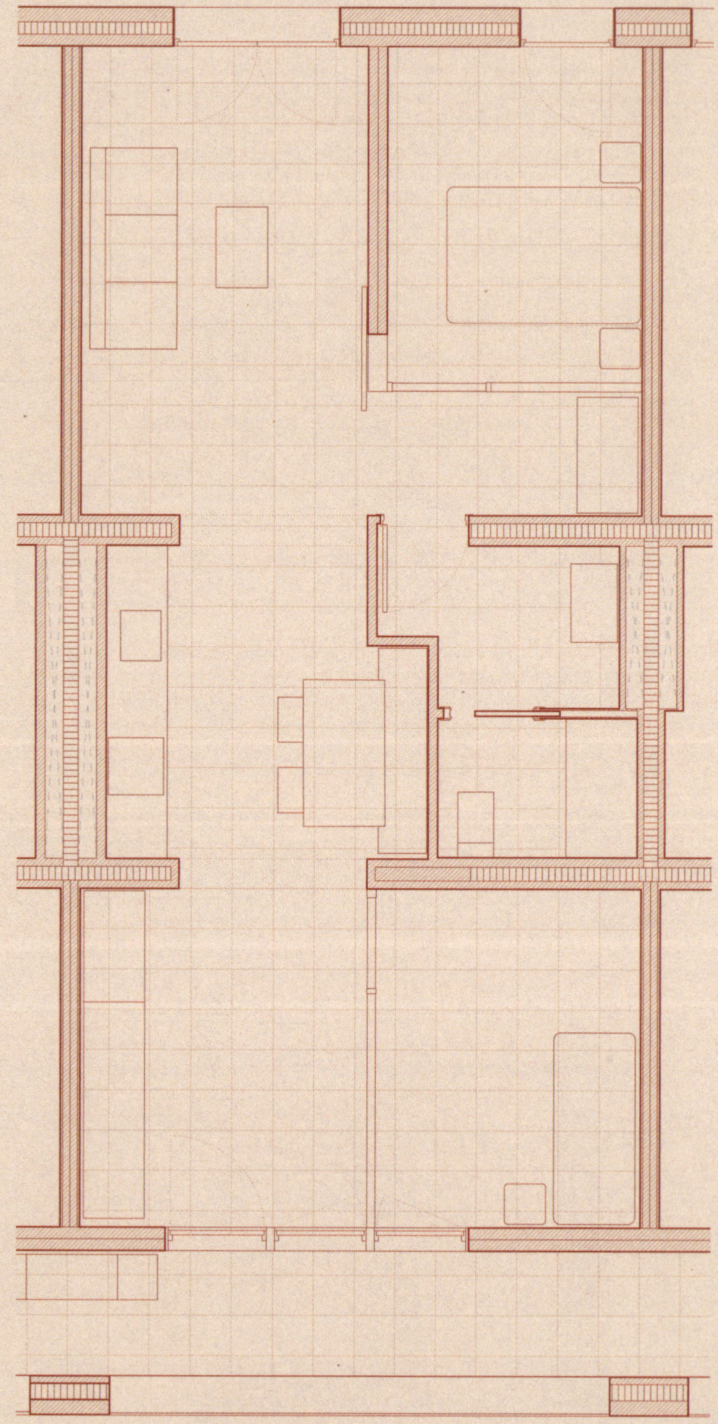

⌈Floor plan of apartment 1:75 – M version

Interview – 2022

“Well, it’s a building made by and for the people who live in it. There are lots of communal spaces and that, together with the architecture itself, with the open walkways where we have to go past the other flats to get to ours, makes them very important meeting places, for unorganized meetings. Then we have shared spaces where we organize things, like the ground-floor space, which is brilliant, we’ve got a communal kitchen...”

Lived-in floor plan 1:75 – S version

Render of concept design

Typical section

Render of concept design

Photographs - Milena Villalba © - 2022

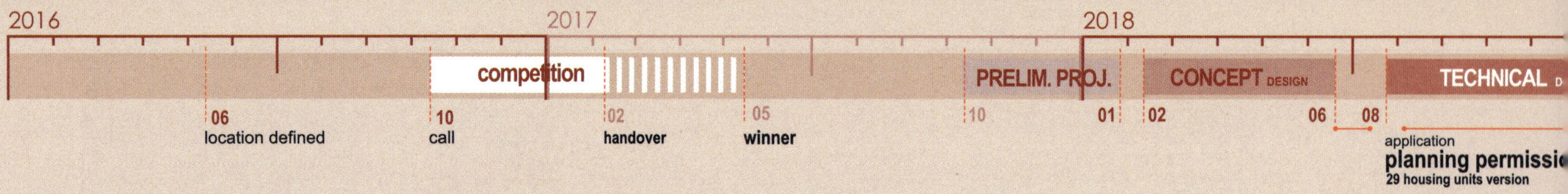

32 housing units Cirerers Cooperative / Roquetes

Celobert

At the centre of the triangle formed by Roquetes metro station, the Ateneu Popular 9 Barris and Montserrat Market, Cirerers co-operative co-housing stands on the corner of c/Pla dels Cirerers and pl/Dones de Nou Barris.

Produced by Sostre Cívic cooperative on a municipal site transferred from Barcelona City Council, designed by Celobert architecture cooperative and promoted by other social and solidarity economy associations, this project is based on a community logic that aims to do more than satisfy the individual needs of its inhabitants. Its cooperative model, shared spaces and bioclimatic design make it an exercise in community ecology with three objectives:

TO CREATE CITY by integration into a consolidated urban site in a working-class neighbourhood of Barcelona. Its geometry adapts to the existing fabric, and the transfer of surface rights to the cooperative model, promoted by public-private collaboration, offers collectively-owned housing at a more affordable price.

TO BE A COMMUNITY in the form of a cooperative model that represents an alternative to buying and renting, and encourages the participation and empowerment of citizens. It is a cohabitation project that sees the act of dwelling as a collective act, in which the whole building is home, and the spaces are co-designed with its future inhabitants.

TO HAVE A POSITIVE ENERGY BALANCE thanks to its low demand and minimal environmental impact, during construction and after. The building is committed to self-sufficiency with the use of renewable centralized community energy and ecological materials such as timber.

Production prior to Foundations and Zero Equity Cooperatives Agreement

Location: c/Pla dels Cirerers, 2-4. Barcelona. **Programme:** 32 homes. **Surface area:** 2,745 m². **Cost:** 3,741,200 € (CEB VAT incl.). **Architects:** Celobert Cooperativa (Jordi Carbó Boix, Diego Carrillo Messa, Ana Taratiel González, David Fernández Gutiérrez). **Collaborations:** Julieta Duran, COLANA Arquitectura, Andreu Ambrose. **Contractor:** La Constructiva SCCL (Yon Sánchez, Eugènia Ruiz, Borja Fernández, Marta Jené). **Consultancy:** Grup Nou (Xavier Humet, Jan Dinarès, Maria Verdaguer), Estudi M103, Jorge Blasco, Ferran Peralba (structures), Àurea Acústica, Sergi Soler, Grisel·la Iglesias (acoustics), Sostre Cívic, Núria Petit, Arantxa Garcia, Eva Ortigosa, David Guàrdia (developer).

Photograph of the participatory process

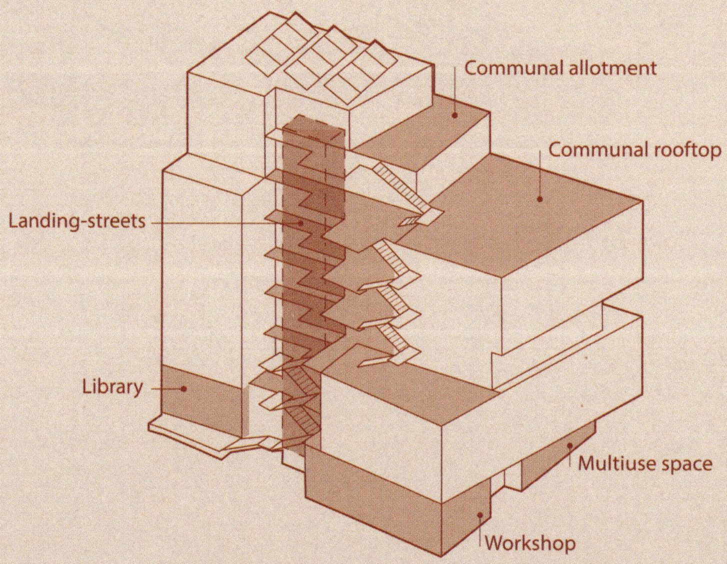

Study of the building's volumes - Communal spaces

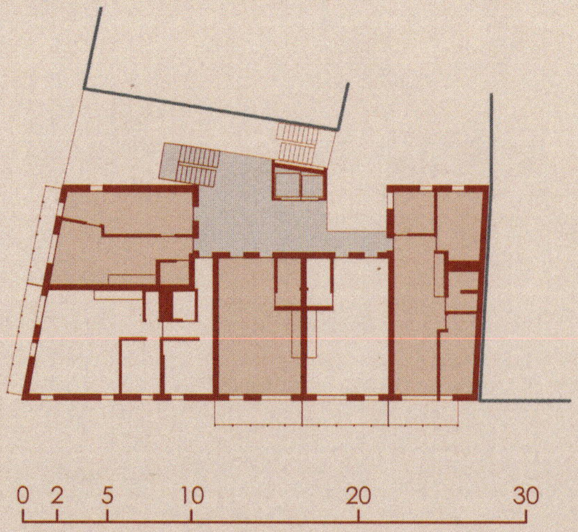

Typical floor plan 1:500

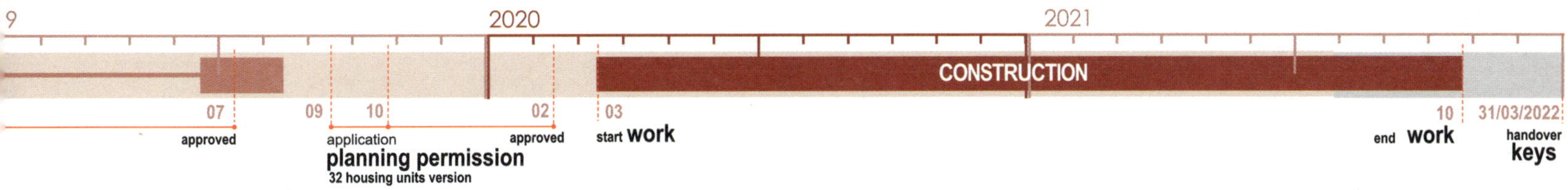

Photographs - Adrià Goula © - 2022

Floor plan of apartment 1:75

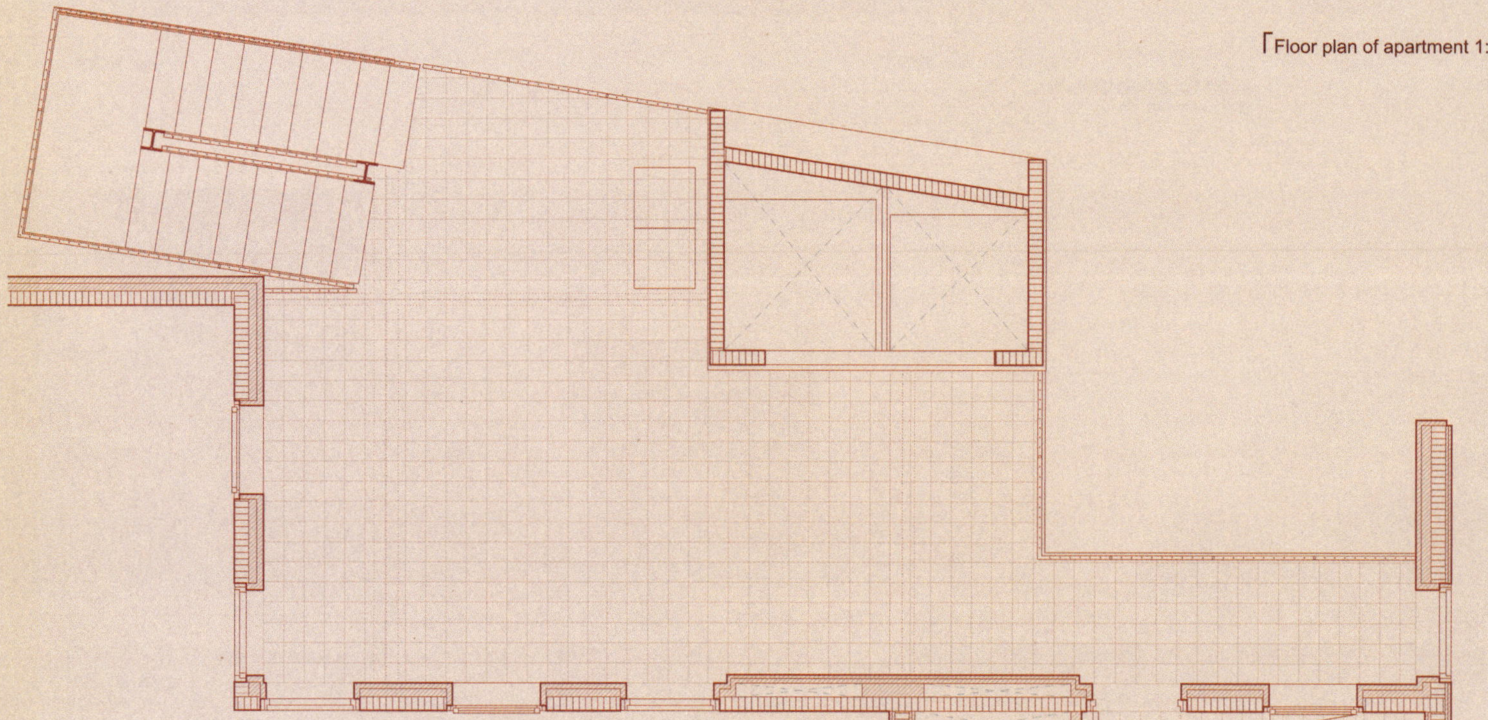

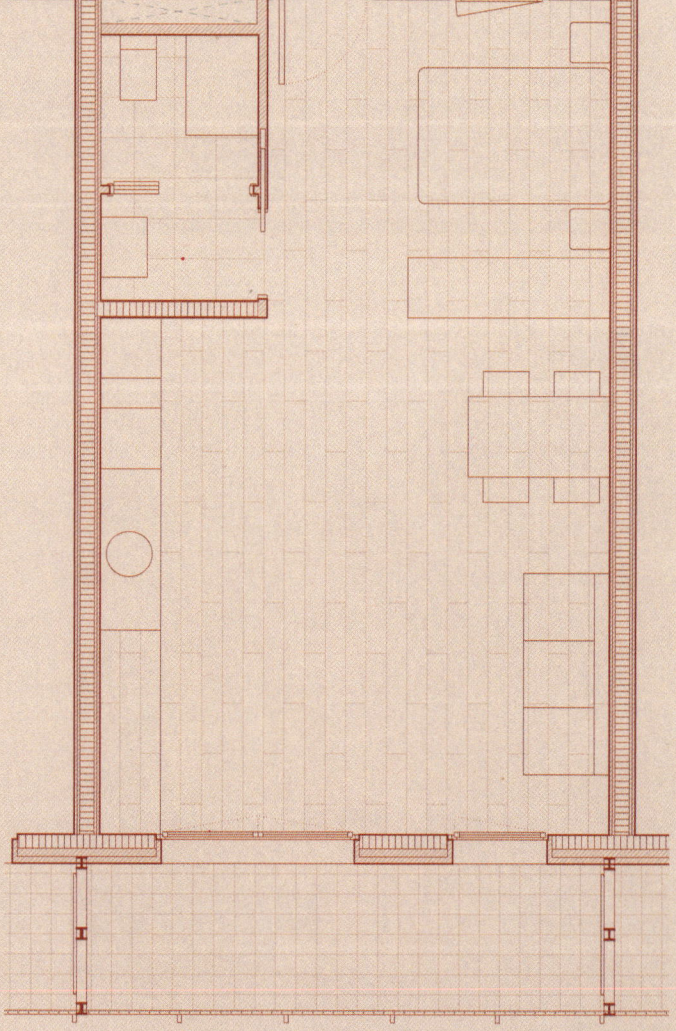

Site photograph - Guifré de Peray

Photograph of finished work – Joan Guillamat

Lived-in floor plan 1:75

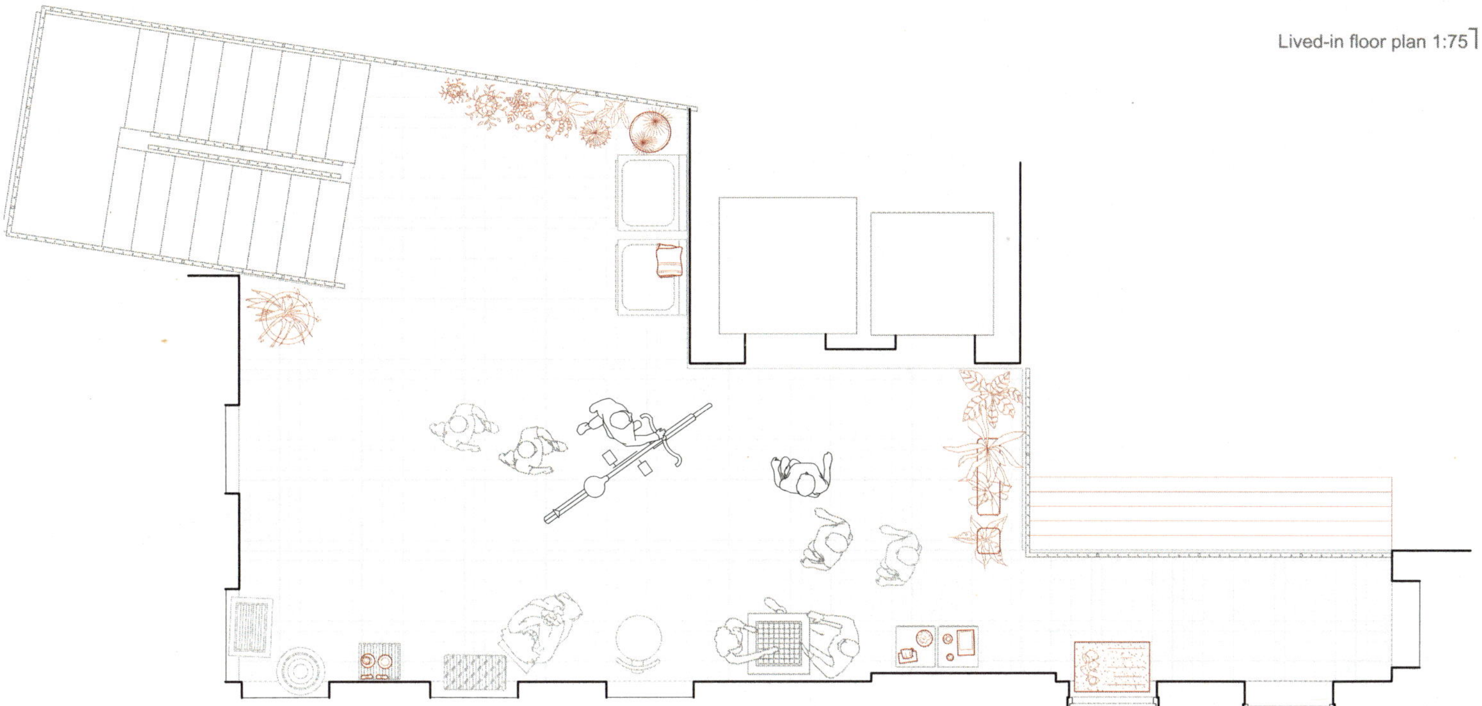

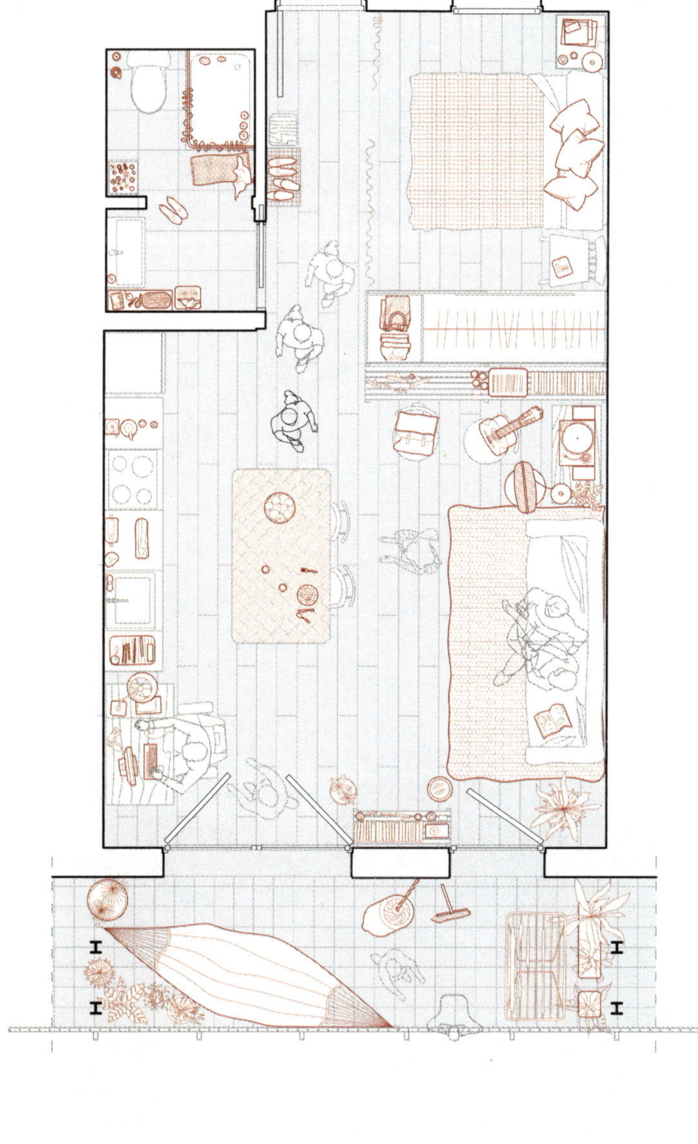

Interview – 2022

"The building's designed not just to live in, but for community life. Even though we've got our own private space, there are these communal spaces for community life, and not just community life for those of us who live in the building, but open to the neighbourhood."

LJUSKRAFTIG
LJUSKRA

Site photograph - Guifré de Peray

Photograph of finished work - Celobert

Cirerers Instagram © - 2022

Photographs - Maite Caramés © - 2022

Photographs - Maite Caramés © - 2022

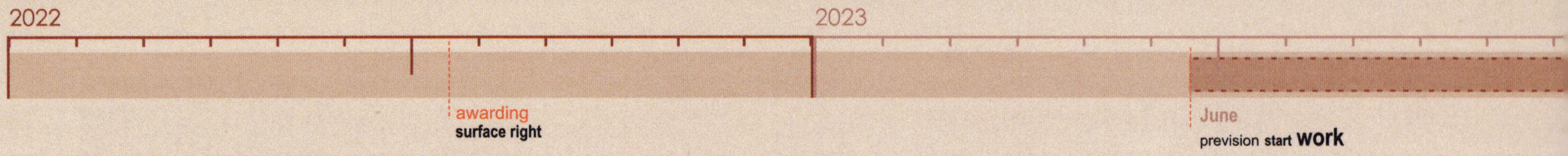

44 housing units / Fundació Salas + Fundació Nou Lloc

011h

The temporary union of Fundació Salas and Fundació Nou Lloc is jointly producing 44 social housing units, in public-private collaboration with Barcelona City Council, in the framework of the FZEC Agreement, which regulates and establishes the mechanisms for allocating public plots to organizations, transferring land and public grants.

The development is possible thanks to the professional management of these two non-profit bodies, with a strong track record in the sector, whose mission is to promote affordable housing that responds to social needs.

The principal values of these two foundations are:

- Commitment
- Social vocation
- Accessibility
- Awareness-raising
- Cooperation
- Innovation
- Environmental respect

In this case, the foundations propose a building to be produced using an industrialized system of wood, which is a natural, sustainable material with excellent mechanical properties that offers freedom of design and precision in construction. The high level of prefabrication makes construction more efficient from a technical point of view, producing buildings that are robust, lightweight, watertight and sustainable, as well as acoustically and thermally insulated. Wood makes for faster construction than traditional methods using concrete or steel.

Wood is a fully recyclable material that continues its life cycle once the building has been dismantled and can be reused to manufacture numerous products. This represents a very significant reduction in greenhouse gases.

Prefabrication of part of the process off site considerably reduces the level of waste. In addition, the number of trucks needed during onsite work is reduced by between six and eight. The use of local materials and the associated construction techniques reduces wood's carbon footprint because it does not have to be transported long distances and has a positive impact on the local economy.

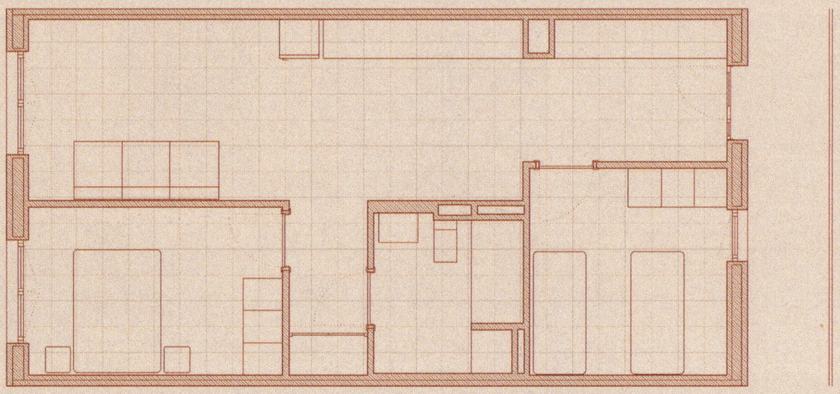

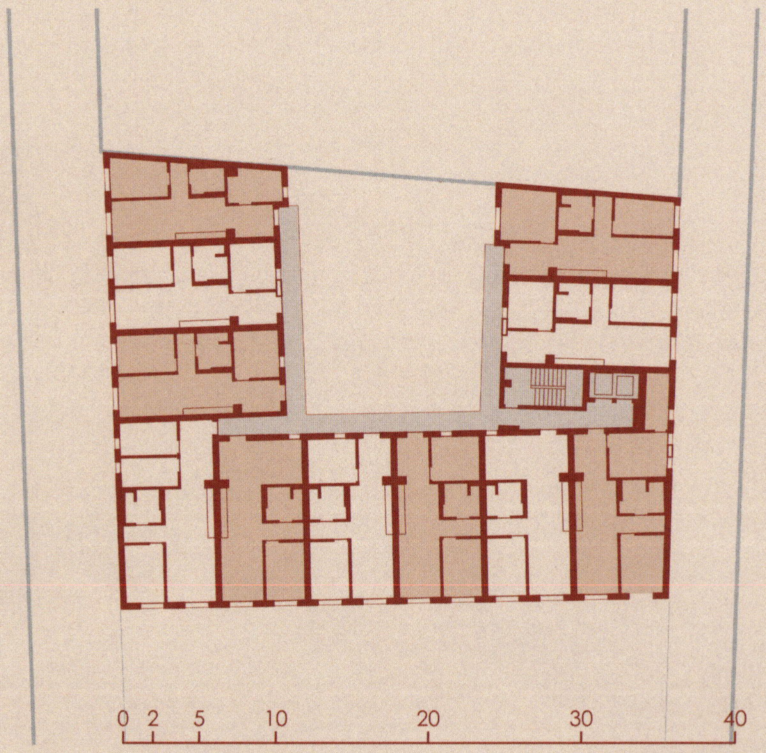

Typical floor plan 1:500

Location: c/Sant Martí, 12-16. Barcelona.
Programme: 44 homes. **Surface area:** 4,436.46 m².
Architects: 011h

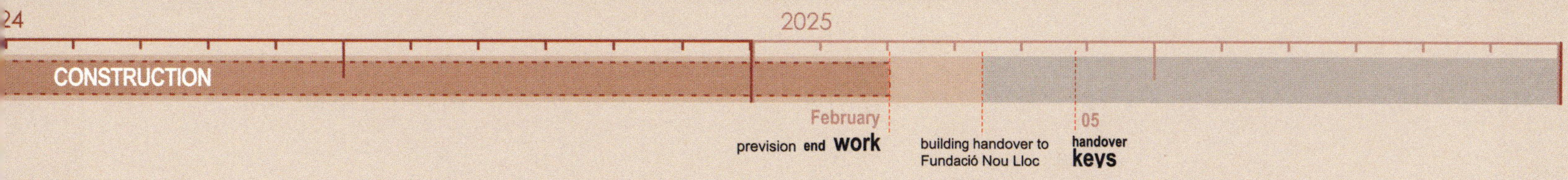

Photograph of prefabrication process

Photograph of assembly

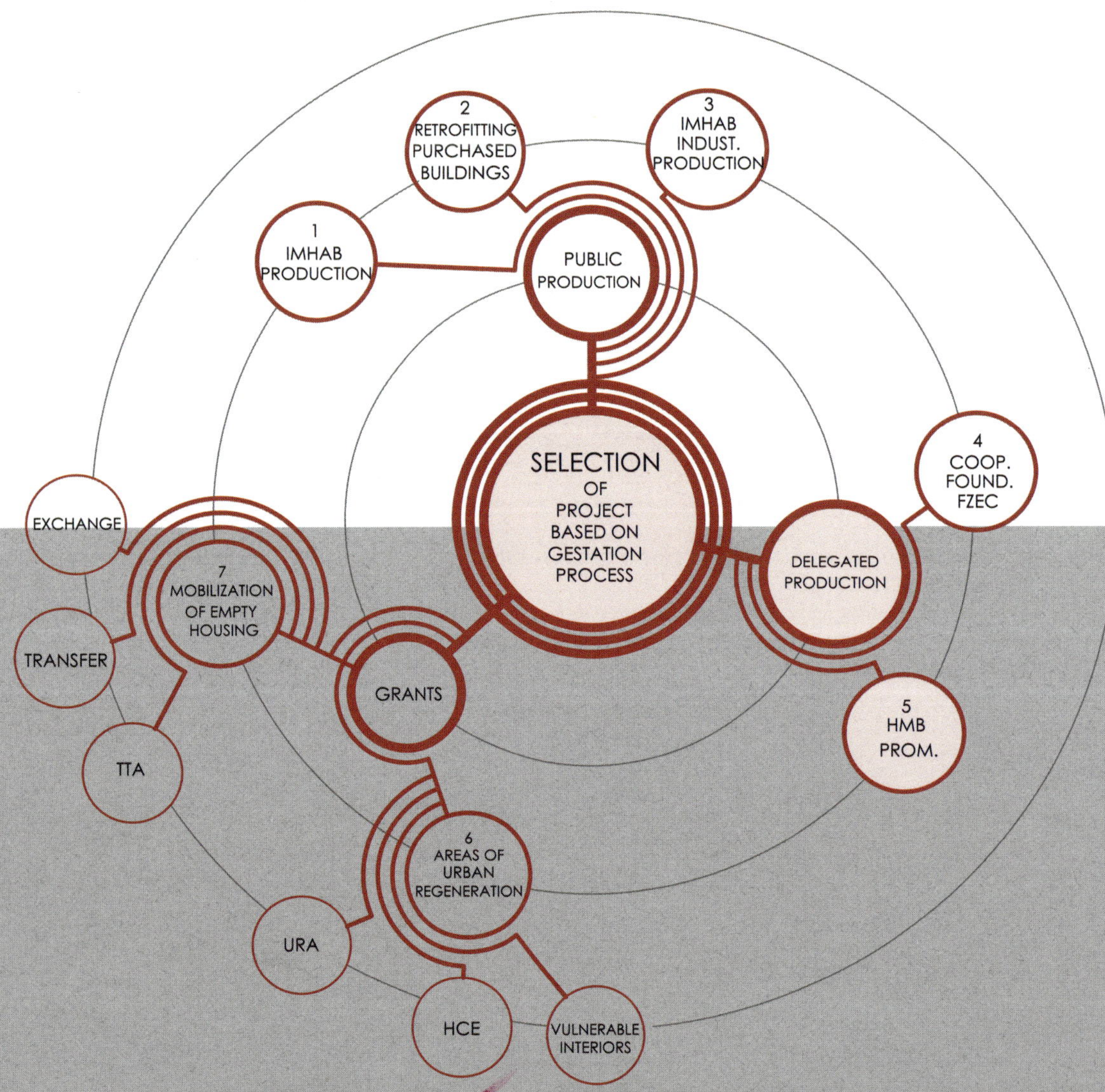
SELECTION OF PROJECT BASED ON GESTATION PROCESS
PUBLIC PRODUCTION
1 IMHAB PRODUCTION
2 RETROFITTING PURCHASED BUILDINGS
3 IMHAB INDUST. PRODUCTION
DELEGATED PRODUCTION
4 COOP. FOUND. FZEC
5 HMB PROM.
GRANTS
6 AREAS OF URBAN REGENERATION
7 MOBILIZATION OF EMPTY HOUSING
EXCHANGE
TRANSFER
TTA
URA
HCE
VULNERABLE INTERIORS

Habitatge Metròpolis Barcelona's affordable housing production

01 63 housing units / Ulldecona **Musquera Arquitectura**

Habitatge Metròpolis Barcelona: a public-private rental housing company with purpose

Javier Burón / Eduardo González de Molina

Housing Manager, Barcelona City Council / Housing Management Consultant, Barcelona City Council

Since 2015, Barcelona City Council has brought about a deep-seated paradigm shift in its housing policies. Instead of a model focused on producing subsidized housing for sale and subsequent recategorization, it aims to generate a real public service of permanent rental housing. To this end, it promotes policies to generate affordable social housing stock according to the European model. Starting with a stock of 2.5% subsidized rental housing, Barcelona has a deficit of up to 90,000 subsidized homes to reach 15% of affordable social housing stock, as established by the urban solidarity objectives of the Right to Housing Act 18/2007 of Catalonia. Faced with a challenge of this magnitude, in the field of new construction Barcelona has not only opted for public housing production with the Barcelona Housing Authority (IMHAB), it has also strategically chosen delegated production, collaborating both with non-profit organizations (FZEC Agreement) and for-profit bodies (HMB).

For the public-private partnership to work, however, it is essential to design collaboration mechanisms that are symbiotic rather than parasitic. Collaboration cannot be used to privatize profits and socialize losses, transferring the risk to the public sector without sharing the benefits. Like in other European countries, public-private collaboration has to involve creating new organizational structures and taking advantage of the synergies of both sectors to build capacities: pooling knowledge and resources; sharing risks, costs and benefits, and working together in the search for innovative solutions to public problems like the housing crisis. And for this to happen, it is essential that there be private actors in the market, proactively seeking investments with limited, patient and safe profitability in projects with a high social impact.

With these coordinates, Barcelona City Council and Greater Barcelona created a business organization, Habitatge Metròpolis Barcelona (HMB), to produce 4,500 affordable rental homes in six years in the city of Barcelona (50%) and its metropolitan area (50%). After the public constitution of the company, a private partner was found by means market consultation, an open tender and, finally, a publicized negotiated procedure. The result of this process was the selection of the company NiCRent, made up of Neinor and Cevasa. Governance presents a balance of 50% public capital (half owned by Barcelona City Council and the other half by the AMB) and 50% private capital (in equal parts between the two companies), with a maximum capital contribution of 58 million euros per sector, producing a board of directors made up of nine persons: four elected by the public partners, four by the private partners, and one independent member chosen by mutual agreement. No one has the casting vote. In this way, risks and benefits are shared.

The total investment in producing these homes amounts to some 650 million euros. The project will be carried out in four phases, and it is estimated that the first homes will be delivered in 2025 and the last in 2028. The first phase foresees the development of approximately 640 homes in Barcelona (La Marina del Prat Vermell, La Sagrera and Les Casernes de Sant Andreu), Sant Boi de Llobregat, Montgat and Sant Adrià de Besòs. As well as being affordable, all the homes will be sustainable and healthy, built according to criteria of environmental design and energy efficiency. The land will be provided by public institutions, almost entirely with very long-term surface right contracts (99 years). The prices will be those of general subsidized housing: around nine euros/m^2/month, whereas the average market rent in the city is over 15 euros. The tenants will be proposed by the administrations on the basis of the register of social housing applicants.

The Habitatge Metròpolis Barcelona project is a pioneering model of public-private collaboration with purpose. A partnership based on social impact investments that meet public objectives and fulfil the social function of property. Providing affordable rental housing and guaranteeing that land ownership remains public and housing is always protected. Aimed at producing flexible, innovative solutions to build housing in the fastest, most sustainable and efficient way possible. Public and private partners generate a long-term relationship of equality, commitment and mutual trust. Equitably sharing (everything is divided 50/50 between public and private partners) investment effort, risks, costs and profits. And taking advantage of the complementarity of resources, capacities and knowledge. Private partners accept limited returns in exchange for lower risk. And finally, the presence of the public on the board of directors guarantees a governance that looks not only to shareholders but to all stakeholders: tenants, workers, suppliers and society in general.

Habitatge Metròpolis Barcelona is, then, the biggest experience of institutional public-private collaboration for affordable rental housing in all of Spain, it is the first public-private housing partnership with a 50-50 balance, and is also the first experience of delegated production limited by guarantee in the city of Barcelona, aspiring to spearhead an innovative ecosystem of professionalized providers of affordable social housing.

gestating

Public-private collaboration in the production of affordable rental housing. Habitatge Metròpolis Barcelona

Donato Muñoz

Chief Executive Officer of Cevasa

As in any collaboration, there has to be a coincidence in business visions, and, when dealing with housing rather than business, we need to talk about the activity, where one of the keys to success is the existence of complementarity between public and private capacities, and a coincidence of objectives.

Affordable housing is one of the areas where there is the most evident need for collaboration to address the current deficit. Some studies suggest that around 2.5 million rental homes are needed in Spain, at prices below the market. If we calculate a minimum construction cost of 100,000 euros per home, the investment needed would be at least 250,000 million euros, over 25% of the country's GDP. An intervention of this scope necessarily requires collaboration between public and private initiatives, especially if the effort is to be effective in the long term, and both public and private initiatives contribute elements that improve performance in terms of public interest, with a lasting, higher level of satisfaction for citizens.

In the city of Barcelona, this deficit is estimated to be of the order of 80,000 homes, which requires not only a major municipal effort, but also a search for formulas that increase the capacity to achieve solidarity objectives in the shortest possible time, guaranteeing quality, sustainability and stability. This necessarily implies collaboration with the private sector.

One of these collaboration formulas is represented by HMB (Habitatge Metròpolis Barcelona, SA), a mixed company created as a public initiative: Greater Barcelona and Barcelona City Council, with the addition as a private partner, after a public bidding process, of the company NiCrent (Nicrent Residencial, SA), a company 50% owned by CEVASA and Neinor Homes. HMB's goal is to produce a total of some 4,500 homes for affordable rent over the next six years. This is the first 50-50 public-private partnership, covering the metropolitan area and devoted exclusively to the production of affordable rental housing.

The HMB project is developed in four phases: the first with a total of 650 homes, the second with 850, and the third and fourth each with a total of 1,500. Between each phase there is a period of one year, so after the initial two years of construction, from year three onwards the handovers will take place successively for the remaining four.

HMB will represent a total investment of approximately 600 million euros, which will be financed by the capital contributed by its partners: 25% by Greater Barcelona, 25% by Barcelona City Council and 50% by NiCrent, plus the additional bank financing needed to complete financial requirements. All partners will participate not only in the capital, but also in strategic decisions, risks and benefits, shared 50% between the public and private partners.

The land will be provided entirely by public administrations, mostly by means of surface right contracts for 75 years, and management of production and subsequent rental activity will be carried out by the private partner.

This is a very long-term project for which efficient management is essential in all areas, from the design and production, economically and in terms of quality, comfort and sustainability, to subsequent management. Economic efficiency in maintenance and services to tenants will also be essential.

The issue of long-term management has direct implications for the future quality of the homes, which must be kept in optimum conditions for use at all times. This includes routine maintenance and regular rehabilitation and improvement over the years. For all these reasons, when the time comes, the appropriate formulas must be found to make these investments and ensure the permanent classification of these homes as affordable housing for citizens.

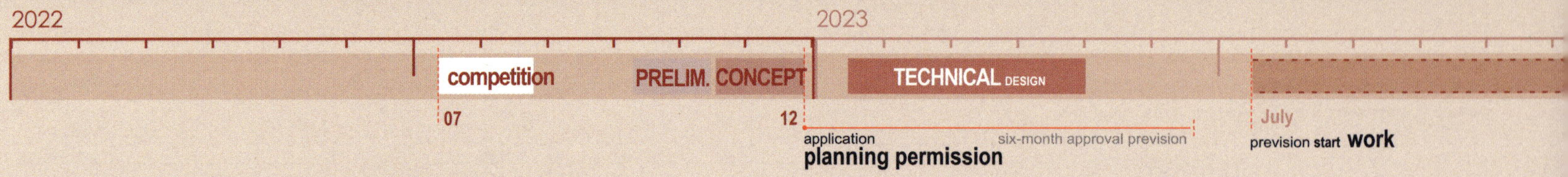

63 housing units / Ulldecona

Musquera Arquitectura

This 63-apartment building in the Marina del Prat Vermell district of Zona Franca offers affordable housing thanks to the occupation of land by surface right granted by Barcelona City Council for 75 years. With a view to increasing social housing in the city, this is the first public-private collaboration agreement made.

The proposal is based on three pivotal strategies: urban consolidation and adaptation to the surrounding fabric; creation of 100% exterior modular homes with interchangeable uses, and healthy design criteria to promote the energy efficiency of the building.

The project proposes a volume that adapts to the adjacent buildings in height and connects the green space on the ground floor. The building, which stands six floors high throughout, reduces its height to four to adapt to the neighbouring volumes. At this same point, the building frees up the ground floor, generating a new passage for the city that reconnects the surrounding green spaces that were previously fragmented.

The 63 homes are laid out around four atriums that lead to each of the units, guaranteeing cross-ventilation and giving the apartment added interior quality, as there are no rooms in this space. In this way, all the homes have rooms of equal dimensions with no hierarchy, in contact with the outside. The project also promotes the creation of terraces for community use to encourage interaction between its occupants.

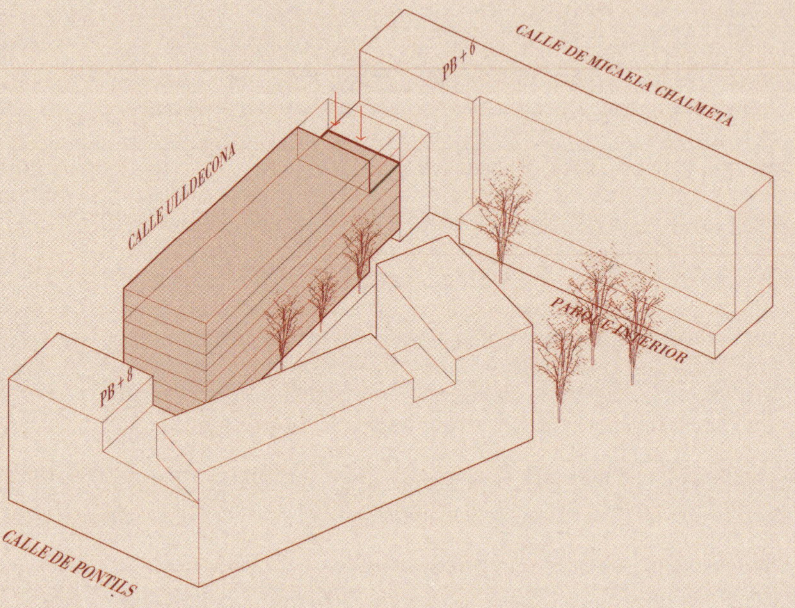

Fit of building volumes

Render – Competition phase

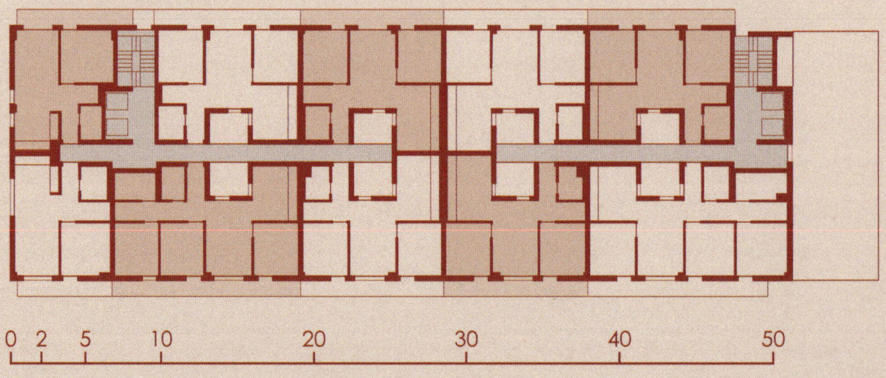

Typical floor plan 1:500

Location: c/ d'Ulldecona, 16-24. Barcelona. Programme: 63 homes. Surface area: 8,748 m². Cost: €7,122,182.36 (Ceb Vat incl.). Architects: Noemí Musquera Ferrer and Sergi Viñals Musquera (Musquera Arquitectura). Collaborations: Gemma Haase and Daniel Martínez. Consultancy: Paci Global (installations), Static Ingeniería slp (structures), Ferran Pelegrina Associats (budget).

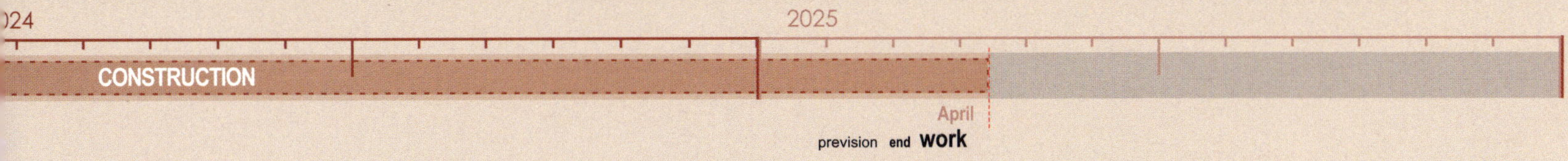

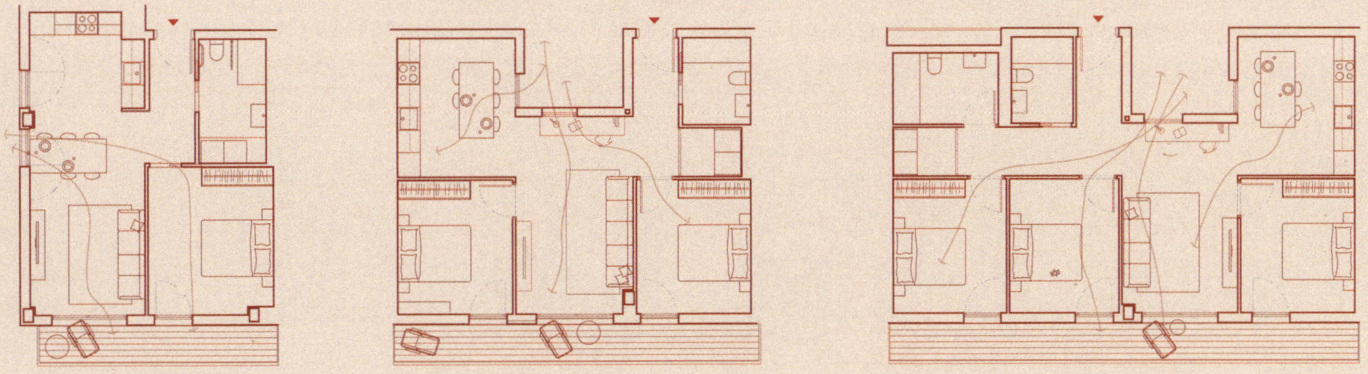

MODULE - 1D

MODULE - 2D

MODULE - 3D

Housing typologies – Concept design - 1:200

Render - Concept design phase

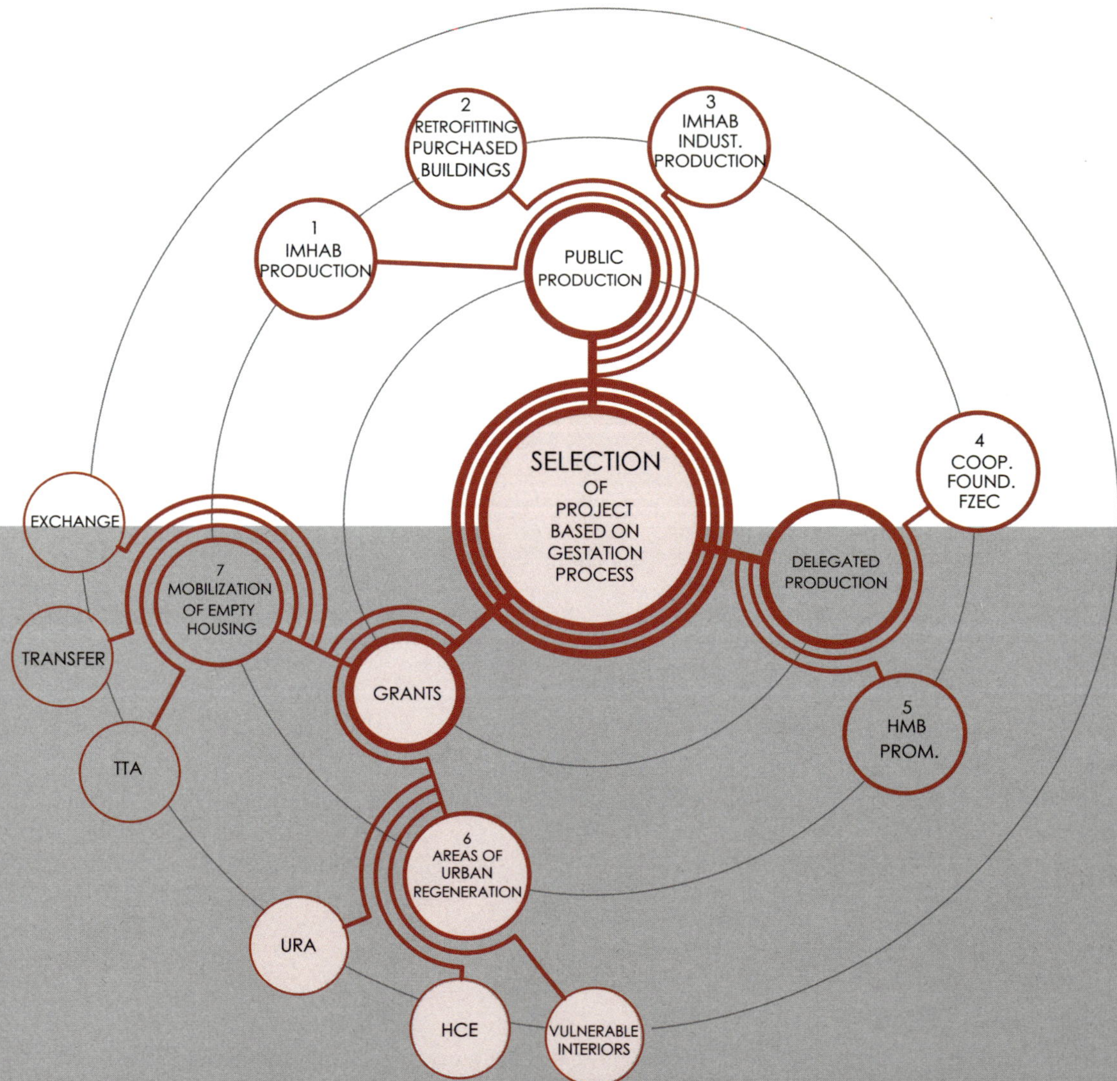
SELECTION
OF
PROJECT
BASED ON
GESTATION
PROCESS
PUBLIC
PRODUCTION
1
IMHAB
PRODUCTION
2
RETROFITTING
PURCHASED
BUILDINGS
3
IMHAB
INDUST.
PRODUCTION
DELEGATED
PRODUCTION
4
COOP.
FOUND.
FZEC
5
HMB
PROM.
GRANTS
6
AREAS OF
URBAN
REGENERATION
URA
HCE
VULNERABLE
INTERIORS
7
MOBILIZATION
OF EMPTY
HOUSING
EXCHANGE
TRANSFER
TTA

Areas of urban regeneration

Urban regeneration areas and high complexity estates retrofit management

David Martínez - Anna Terra

Director of the Municipal Urban Planning Institute - Director General of Foment de Ciutat

In recent years, Barcelona City Council has launched a series of programmes with the aim of intensifying intervention in the city's most vulnerable properties and environments. The rehabilitation of high-complexity properties, the management of urban regeneration areas and the improvement of home interiors are the main examples. In all cases, just as important as the ultimate aim of the policy are the way the programmes are implemented and a management model based on ongoing support for residents.

High-complexity properties

It became clear that the usual way of operating, publishing calls for grants and expecting communities to apply, excluded the city's most complex properties, which are those that need it most. Rehabilitating with the support of public competition subsidy mechanisms is a complex administrative process, which is why only the best organized properties applied for and obtained the grants.

As the most vulnerable communities were excluded from the system, their situation became worse. A proactive approach was needed to locate them and accompany them throughout the process, working together on a basis of recognition and empowerment, since in the high-complexity properties programme (unlike the URA), it is the communities that end up being the producers.

The complexity of the properties, due to the state of the buildings and their rehabilitation needs, but also to their social makeup, called for a comprehensive approach and support, with architects, lawyers, administrators and professionals who could offer social intervention.

The Neighbourhoods Plan is a comprehensive intervention project that acts in all areas of local development with a marked community approach, seeking always to generate connections and networking. Working under the umbrella of this plan is an opportunity for the high-complexity estates programme to go beyond supporting the community in the rehabilitation process, to get the people who live there to link up with other Neighbourhoods Plan programmes and create links with their surroundings.

Urban regeneration areas

In the case of urban regeneration areas, intensive interventions are programmed in very specific areas of the city, addressing both the retrofitting of residential buildings and the redevelopment of public space. These areas are characterized by the homogeneity of their urban fabric, with similar material and functional problems in housing, and also in their social fabric, with medium or low income levels and other characteristics that make interventions unfeasible unless they are in a turnkey format. In other words, the public manager carries out all the interventions on behalf of the community (inspections, drafting the project, tender and construction), and delivers the property completely rehabilitated with good levels of services that will allow good functionality in the future.

The management of these areas comprises several phases. First, an information session communicates the objectives of the urban regeneration programme. In this phase, the involvement of neighbourhood fabric is key, both formally (local associations and bodies) and informally (leading figures in the community). Proximity is vital to the success of these programmes, and in these territories certain social structures can act as sounding boards and natural facilitators of information.

The second phase is diagnosis, documentation and home inspections, as necessary. Visiting the homes of residents represents an initial contact with the particular physical and human reality of each.

The architectural project is then drafted, subject to agreement with the community. Once validated, construction work is tendered and carried out, by the MUPI itself. These are widely subsidized interventions that include actions to guarantee the building's structural safety and retrofit the envelope (façades, roofs and party walls) according to energy efficiency criteria, and install lifts, if applicable. Depending on the extent of the interventions, on some occasions it may be necessary to temporarily relocate families, empty homes of furniture and take other actions.

Improvements to the homes of persons in a situation of vulnerability

The call for improvements to homes of vulnerable people, published for the first time in 2017, complements and strengthens interventions in high-complexity estates. Unlike the other programmes, which have a pre-established territorial boundary, this line is aimed at the entire city and concentrates on the individual vulnerability of the person, though the highest percentage of applicants and beneficiaries is still located in the city's most vulnerable areas. Support throughout the application and retrofitting process continues to be a central element in promoting the programme.

This programme centres on retrofitting in the usual permanent homes of the most vulnerable population and aims to guarantee basic conditions of habitability, safety, accessibility, hygiene and energy efficiency, and to promote actions to facilitate the everyday lives of people with functional diversity by installing home automation systems, accessibility technology and elements to ensure accessible communication in the home.

Who is the downtown for?

David Bravo
Architect. Member of the Atri team

“Who is that madwoman?” cried the editor of *Fortune* magazine when a woman, with no public office or technical credentials, popularized the slogan “Downtown is for people!”. With her cry, that New York activist managed to paralyse the entire Lower Manhattan “regeneration” plan devised by Robert Moses in the early sixties. What the prestigious urban planner pretended was none other than running a new eight-lane elevated expressway through the city-centre neighbourhood, an urbicide with collateral effects as not inconsiderable as the demolition of many housing blocks and the expulsion of thousands of families and businesses. Over six decades have passed, the manwoman was Jane Jacobs, and it is worth asking whether time has proved her right. Is the centre for “people”?

The truth is that, before the industrial age, it wasn’t. When cities were markets rather than factories, dominance inside their walls was reserved for powerful and wealthy minorities, while the vast majority of the population spread out across the agricultural territory. This is reflected in the etymology of the Catalan *barri*, or neighbourhood, which, although today it refers to the urban landscape, comes from the Arabic *barrî* (exterior, country, wood), formerly used to designate settlements outside the walls. In fact, the entire 20th century had to pass before the percentage of the Spanish population living in cities went from 10 to 90%. It was industrialization that suddenly, between the 19th and 20th centuries, brought the social majorities together for the first time in urban centres. As the working class emerged, as large as it was necessary, the seams of what had, until then, been understood as “city” were torn open.

From that industrial background comes the idea of neighbourhood as we understand it –or miss it– today. A densely populated, intensely crowded anthill where “people” can make a living and even carve out a place to live. An ecosystem where “hands” crowd factories, workshops, shops and markets, while balconies and windows emit the daily symphony of people singing to a crying child or beating eggs to make an omelette. This vibrant landscape lives on in old towns like Naples, where washing hung out to dry desecrates Corinthian capitals, but it has met its death in Venice, a stuffed prize with glass eyes. In fact, living neighbourhoods not only allow “people” to have a roof and a job in the urban centre; they make them dominate. They make, as Jacobs claimed, the centre belong to “people”.

It’s hard to believe today, but this is what happened in pre-Olympic Barcelona, when not everyone dared to venture into the Born or the Barri Xino districts, and, amid dripping soot, a bingo poster desecrated the façade of La Pedrera. The bourgeoisie, meanwhile, retreated to the outskirts or to higher-lying ghettos, always above Diagonal.

It is precisely this physical congregation of residents and workers in urban centres that has given social and trade union movements the necessary strength to conquer the rights and services of the welfare state. Public schools, health facilities, basic infrastructure, collective transport, green areas and heritage saved from the pillory are the work not of councils and ministries, but of neighbourhood struggles in the street.

But does post-industrial Barcelona need populous, congested neighbourhoods? Is calling for them a nostalgic stance, or are they still a valid solution? It is just over 30 years since the 1992 Games, and there is no doubt that the Catalan capital has changed a lot. Offshoring took much of its industrial production to far-flung parts of the globe, where it was easier to exploit workers and the environment. Barcelona’s factories became as inactive as their workforce. Uncertain times were coming, and it was necessary to think about what it was going to live on. It was clear to the local authorities: they would make Barcelona a global city. Instead of advising it to find a nice flat –good public housing stock, for example– and stop smoking –it was addicted to fossil fuels– they demanded that it “prettify” itself and go out to attract the money of investors, tourists and big events.

Since then, the city has ceased to be a factory and become a circus. In this urban model, “people” have no place in the centre. Housing is increasingly expensive, and jobs are increasingly precarious. Beyond serving tapas and drinks to Port Vell cruise passengers, Mobile World Congress attendees and Primavera Sound fans, “people” are increasingly expendable in the centre. The global city casts out the local population because it does not need it. That is why it reserves the most central public space for the Hotel Vela, the Macba extension and the revamped Montjuïc Trade Fair. But what if this model is madness? And what if global warming and the energy crisis make it completely unviable? And what if it was necessary to reserve central space for public housing, local facilities and productive places of an economy rooted in the territory? What if Jane Jacobs wasn’t a madwoman?

Urban regeneration areas

Trinitat Vella + Besòs and Maresme

The Urban Regeneration Programme is currently active in six neighbourhoods: Besòs, Canyelles, Trinitat Vella, Can Peguera, La Pau and Congrés-Indians. The interventions planned in these areas are designed to achieve three main objectives:

- To retrofit residential buildings so that they offer the best possible services, comfort and living conditions. Interventions mainly involve improving the energy efficiency of the envelope, repairing the waterproofing of roofs and addressing structural pathologies caused by the presence of cement.
- To promote the generation of green energy, both in the buildings themselves and in public space.
- To redevelop public space, bringing the streets up to date and providing local people with a new, quality urban environment that invites them to use it.

Two of the areas where most progress has been made in pilot projects are the Besòs and Trinitat Vella neighbourhoods.

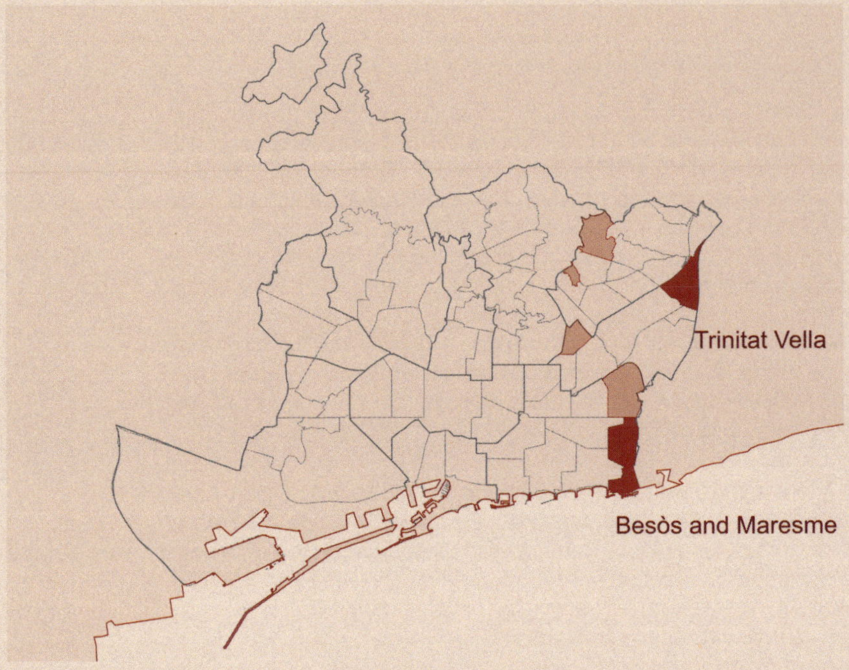

Neighbourhoods in the Urban Regeneration Programme

G + 1 (low density)

A. Single-family row housing
B. Multifamily buildings
C. Mixed blocks

G + 5 (medium density)

Residential blocks
of multifamily homes

D. E. F. G. H. I.

G + 11 (high density)

Mixed blocks of multifamily homes
with ground-floor commercial premises

J. K. L. M. N.

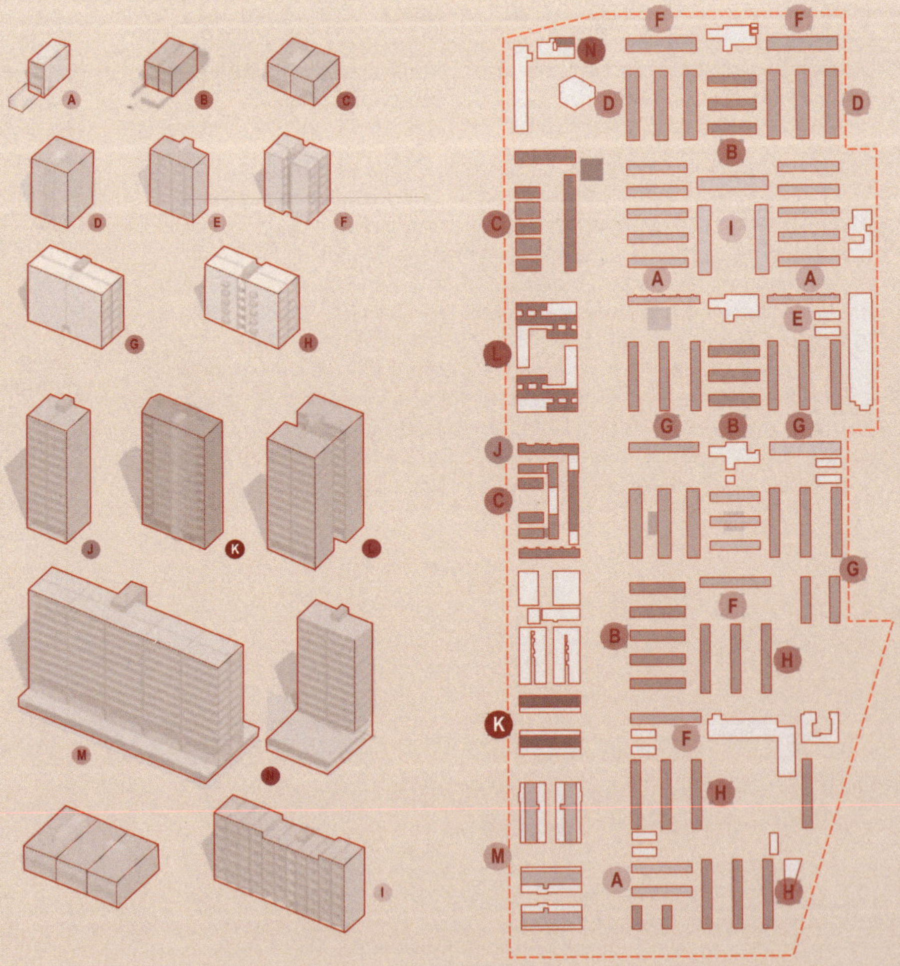

Typological analysis of housing blocks
Besòs and Maresme
Municipal Urban Planning Institute

Trinitat Vella

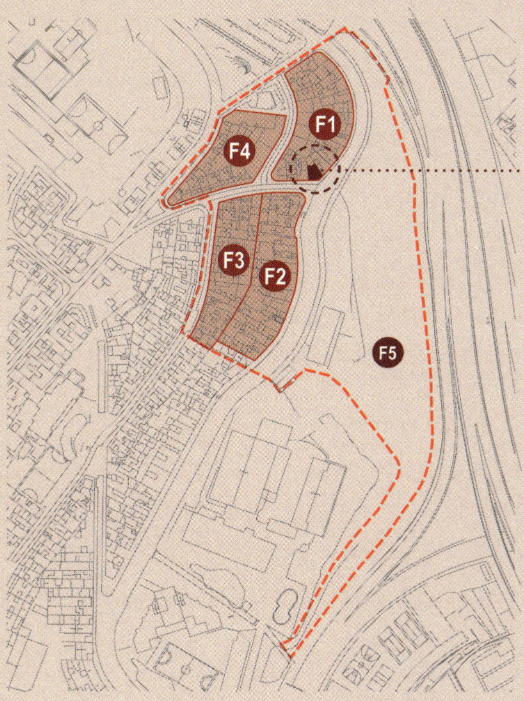

5 housing units - c/ Foradada

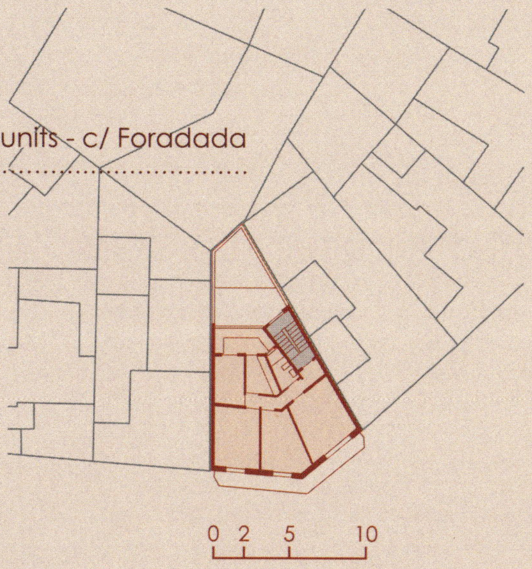

Typical floor plan 1:500

Area of the Urban Regeneration Programme in the Trinitat Vella neighbourhood

Five phases of intervention:

F1 F2 F3 F4

F5 Parc de la Trinitat Vella

Map based on information provided by the Municipal Urban Planning Institute (MUPI)

Besòs and Maresme

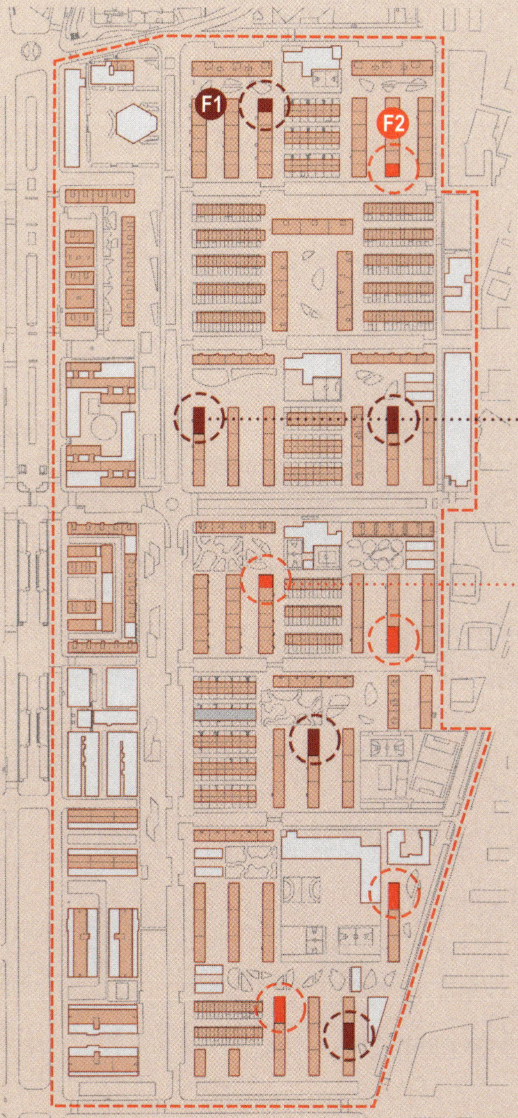

Area of the Urban Regeneration Programme in the Besòs neighbourhood and Maresme

Phases of intervention:

Pilot tests:

F1 Phase 1: 96 housing units

F2 Phase 2: 108 housing units
Total: 204 housing units

24 housing units - c/ Alfons el Magnànim

12 housing units - c/ Messina

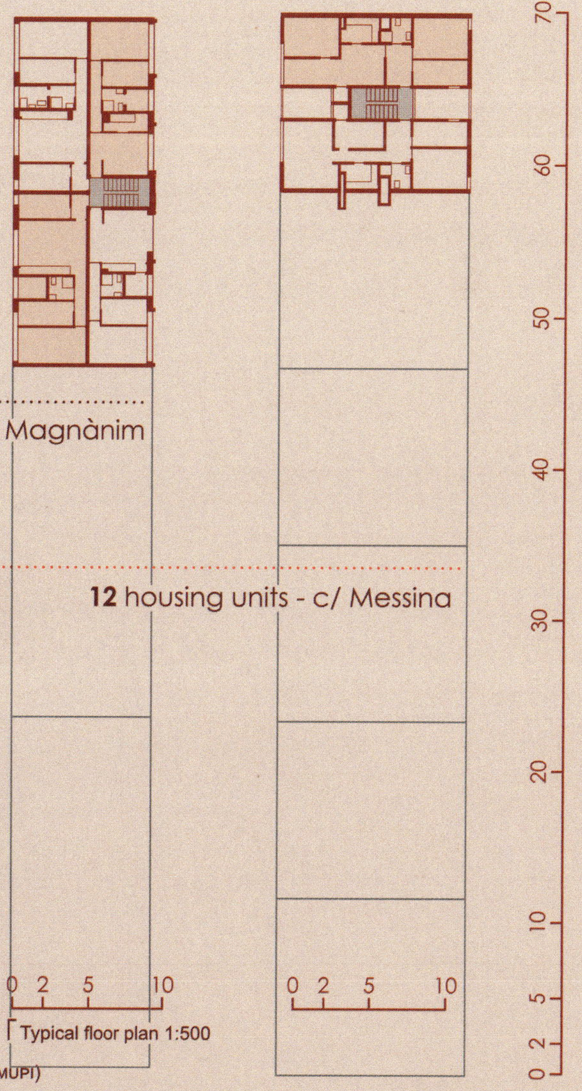

Typical floor plan 1:500

Map based on information provided by the Municipal Urban Planning Institute (MUPI)

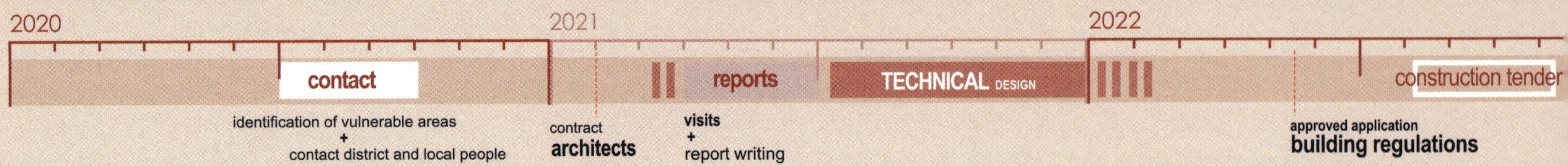

24 housing units - Alfons el Magnànim

Estudi d'Arquitectura CODI

The main aim of the project is to improve the overall energy efficiency compared to the current state, intervening in the envelope and carrying out structural consolidation, as the building presents concrete pathologies. The building will be also equipped with a lift tower and a new stairway to improve accessibility, balconies will be built and the bathrooms in all the homes will be renovated.

Interventions to improve energy efficiency will consist of replacing all outside frames for better energy performance, changing the roof solution by adding 8 cm of XPS insulation and supplementing the façades that form the building's envelope with thermal insulation using the ETICS system.

These interventions will decrease the consumption of non-renewable primary energy by more than 45%, with a reduction in heating and cooling demands of over 60% compared to the initial situation.

Location: c/Alfons el Magnànim, 44. Barcelona. **Programme:** building energy rehabilitation (24 homes). **Surface area:** 1,326 m^2. **Cost:** 1,685,315.83 € (CEB VAT incl.). **Architects:** CODI Estudi d'Arquitectura, Oscar Frago. **Collaborations:** Kenneth McGuire and Jaime García Martín. **Contractor:** GUINOVART & OHL. **Consultancy:** E3G Enginyeria i Energia (installations), Brufau-Cusó Estudi d'Arquitectura (cost study), Sulmag (photovoltaics).

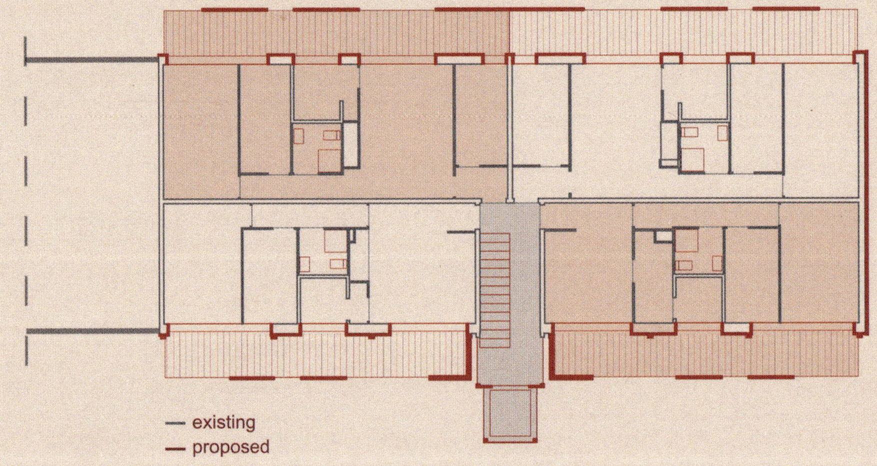

Typical floor plan

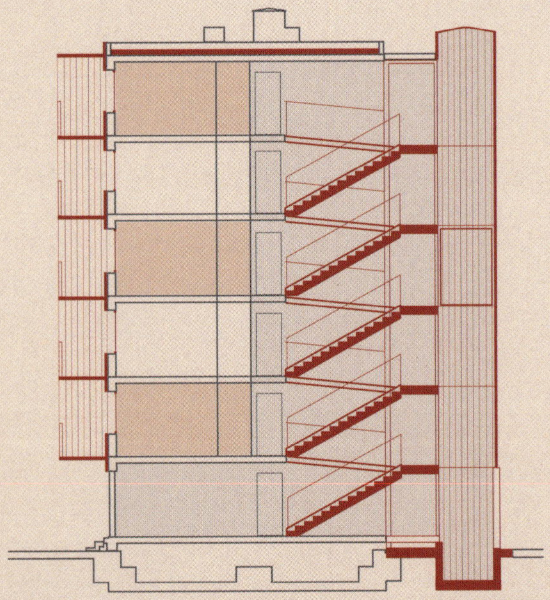
Typical section 1:250

Render of the first version of the façade

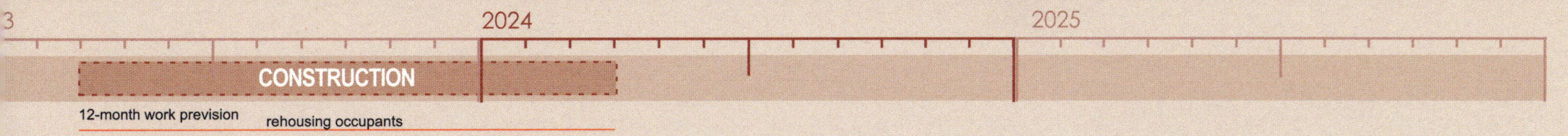

Photograph of current state

Photograph of current state

Render of second version of façade project

High complexity estates

The maintenance problems of residential housing especially affect cohabitation units that have fewer resources to deal with home improvements. The increase in socio-economic inequalities accordingly represents an increase in differences between the living conditions of the city's population. A study commissioned to the Polytechnic University of Catalonia in 2017 detected the city's most vulnerable buildings.

Taking this study as its basis, Barcelona City Council defined the areas of the Neighbourhoods Plan where the High Complexity Estates programme is applied. This programme proactively targets properties that, due to their socio-economic complexity, tend to get left out of general calls for grants and require specific support to carry out improvements. This measure is a clear example of the City Council's new approach to retrofitting, as it targets the areas in the city that have the most deficiencies, with populations that are least able to afford housing maintenance.

This measure serves to promote rehabilitation agreements to improve buildings in areas included in the Neighbourhoods Plan by means of support and advice from the Council. This produces benefits for the cohesion and organization of the community, agreement between private individuals, communities and contractors, and subsequently, the physical state of the building.

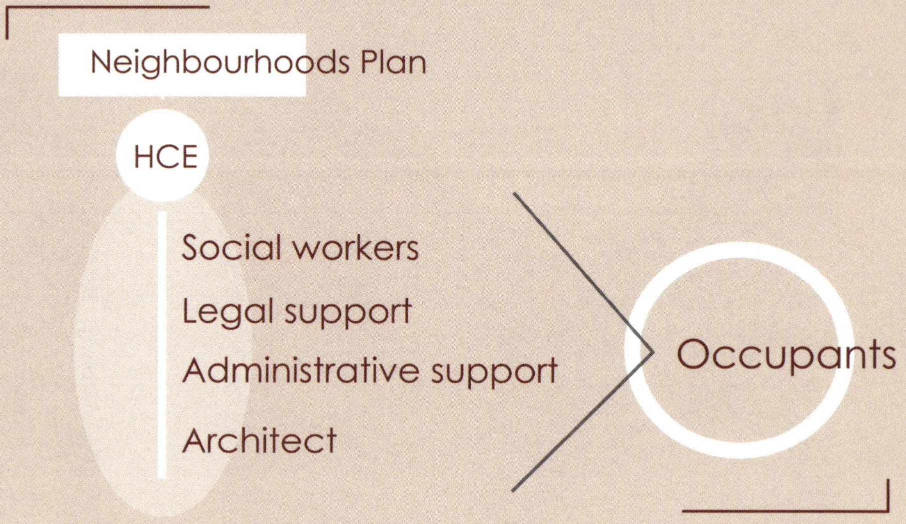

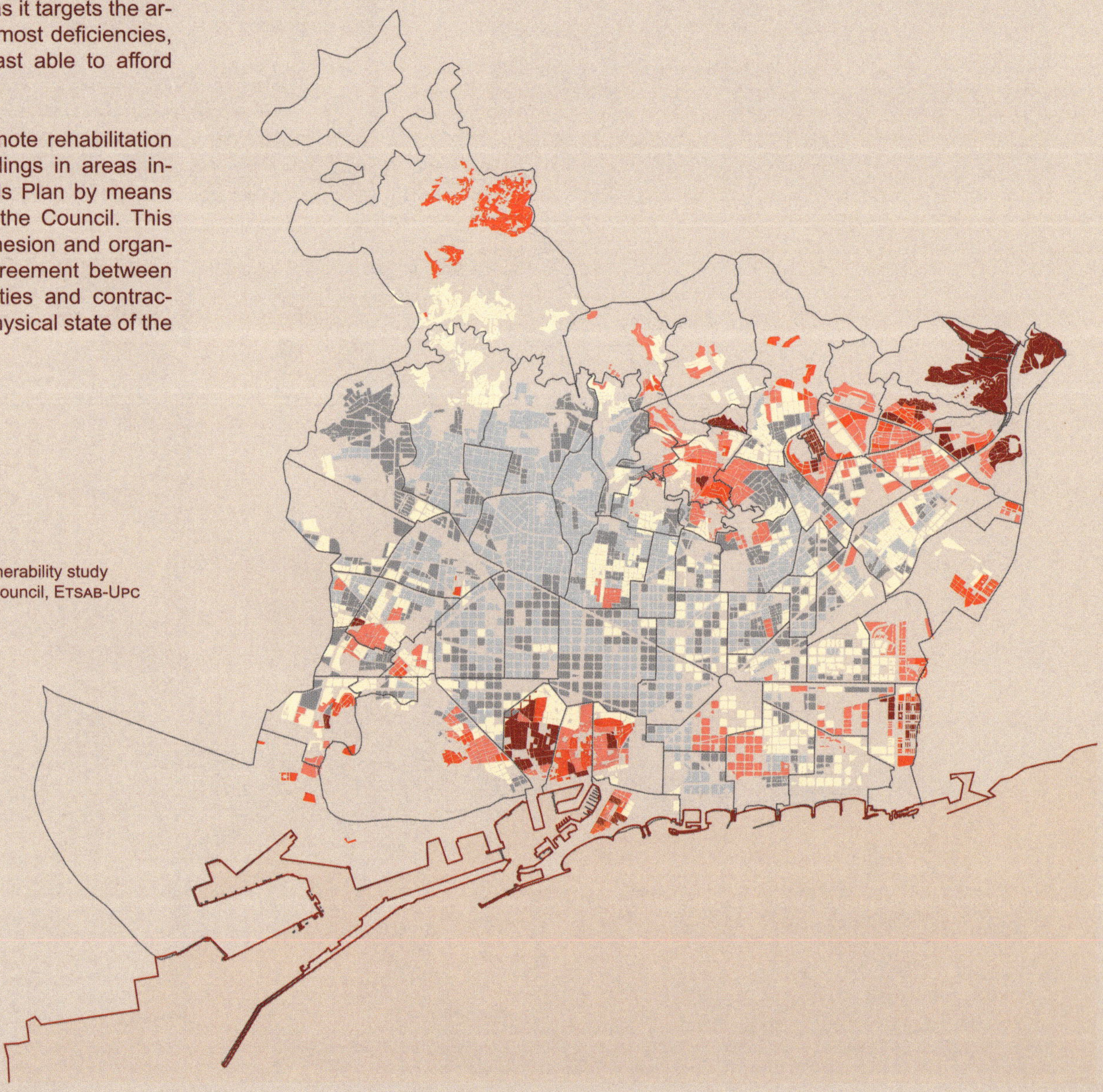

Barcelona residential vulnerability study
Source: Barcelona City Council, Etsab-Upc

- Imperceptible
- Low
- Moderate
- High
- Very high
- Extreme

A. Reduction in energy demand

A.1 Façades
A.2 Rooftops
A.3 Party walls
A.4 Lightwells and courtyards
A.5 Green roofs

B. Work to be carried out to the general communal installations

B.1 Water, gas, electricity and drainage
B.2 Direct water
B.3 Elimination of obsolete asbestos elements
B.4 Installation of alternative energies: solar, thermal energy or photovoltaic panels

C. Work to improve accessibility

C.1 Lift
C.2 Removal of architectural barriers
C.3 Stairways
C.4 Foyers

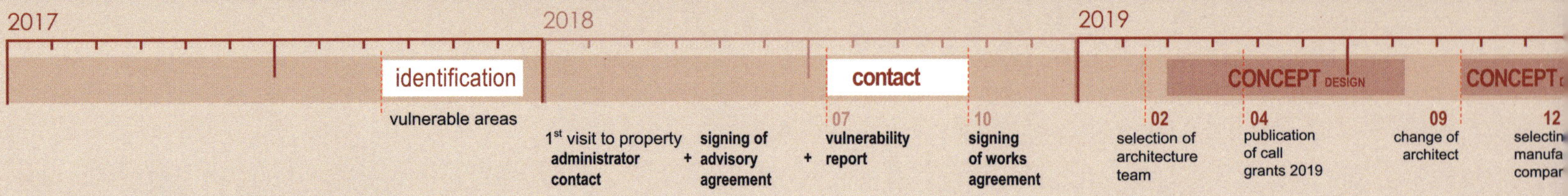

5 housing units / Gòtic

Heres Arquitectura

The building dates from 1850, with the typical structure of the time of bearing walls and a floor slab of metal joists with flat bricks. The Catalan-style roof incorporates a crawl space, with ventilation integrated in the flashing.

The project involves rehabilitation of the façade, cleaning the lime mortar surface and painting with a layer of glaze, removing obsolete elements, replacing window frames in the façade to unify its aesthetics and retrofitting the entrance door of the building.

Rehabilitation of the two courtyards, elimination of obsolete elements and painting claddings and drainpipes.

Rehabilitation of the lobby, replacement of paving and cladding of the stairway, replacement of the electrical installation and lighting. Replacement of the skylight that gives onto the stairway.

On the roof: replacement of the skylight in the stairwell and rehabilitation of the walls of the stairwell and the railings that were not addressed when the roofs were repaired. Inside the homes, repair of localized cracks and reinforcement of beam heads on the ground floor.

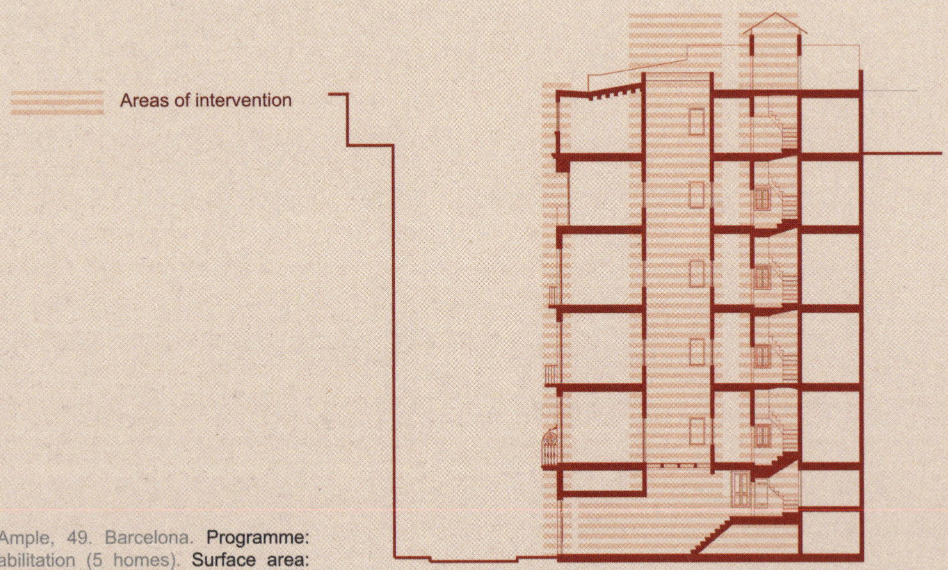

Location: c/Ample, 49. Barcelona. **Programme:** building rehabilitation (5 homes). **Surface area:** 283.5 m² (rehabilitated surface area). **Cost:** 224,812.19 € (CEB). **Architect:** Hector Restrepo Calvo / Heres Arquitectura.

Typical section / Not to scale

Proposed elevation

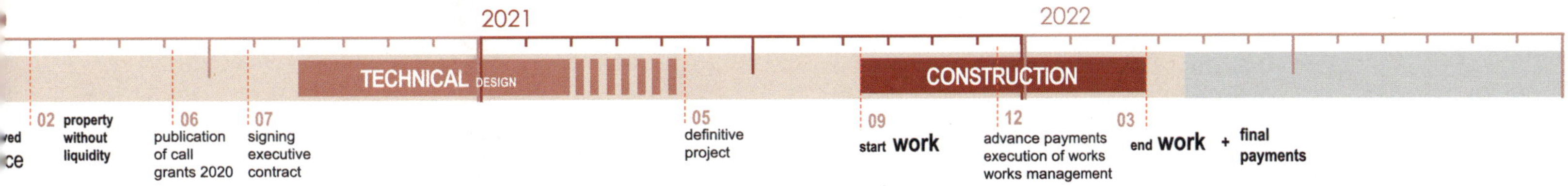

[Photographs - Adrià Goula © - 2022

Photographs - Maite Caramés © -]

Interiors of vulnerable housing units

Retrofitting is a means to guarantee basic conditions of habitability, safety, accessibility, hygiene and energy efficiency of the dwellings of vulnerable cohabitation units with limited economic resources. This strategy can be applied to both owner-occupied and rental properties. Grants for people in a vulnerable situation tend to be given in cases detected by social workers and based on consultations at energy advice centres (EAC) in each district.

There are two basic requirements for inclusion in the programme: a report detailing the deficiencies of the dwelling, and proof of the situation of vulnerability of the occupants.

This programme involved a great deal of technical coordination, as retrofitting is carried out directly by the City Council, based on a turnkey model, in order to avoid residents having to undertake the work.

A. General interventions

A.1 Improvement of finishes: painting, replacement and repair. Floors, false ceilings, tiling.

A.2 Improvement of electrical installation: repair distribution panel, plug circuit.

A.3 Waste management: elimination of old heating elements.

B. Interventions in bathrooms

B.1 Repair of false ceiling.

B.2 Replacement of damp fittings.

B.3 Repair of tiling.

B.4 Replacement of bath/shower.

C. Interventions in kitchens

C.1 Replacement of fittings.

C.2 Incorporation of vitroceramic hob.

C.3 Smoke extraction hood.

C.4 Replacement of electrical domestic appliances.

D. Complementary interventions

D.1 Window improvements: replacement, stop thermal bridges, insulate glass with air chamber.

D.2 Window improvements: roller blinds.

D.3 Intervention in façade to improve sealing and waterproofing. Thermal insulation.

E. Functional adaptation interventions

E.1 Incorporation of elements to improve accessibility

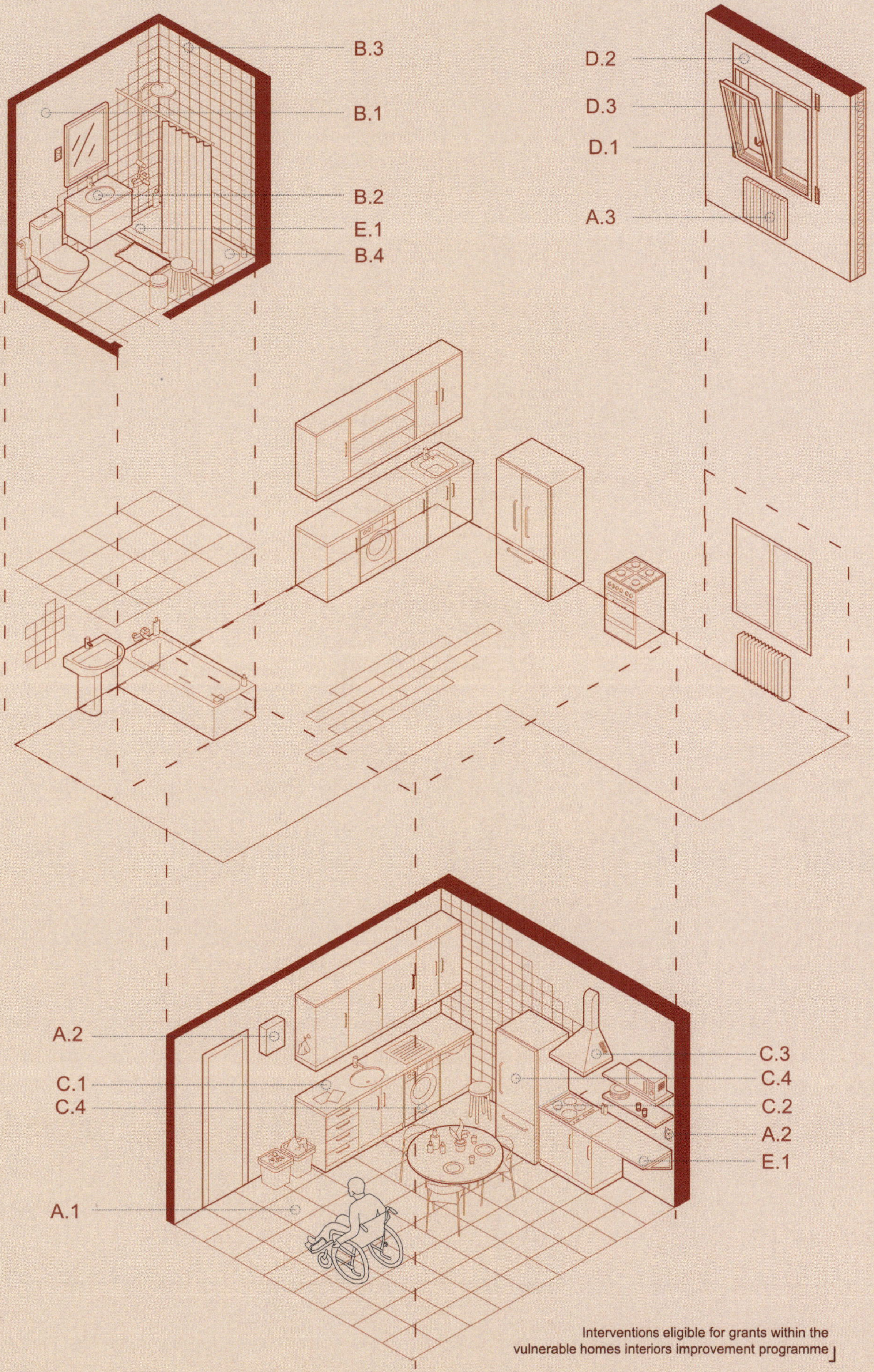

Interventions eligible for grants within the vulnerable homes interiors improvement programme

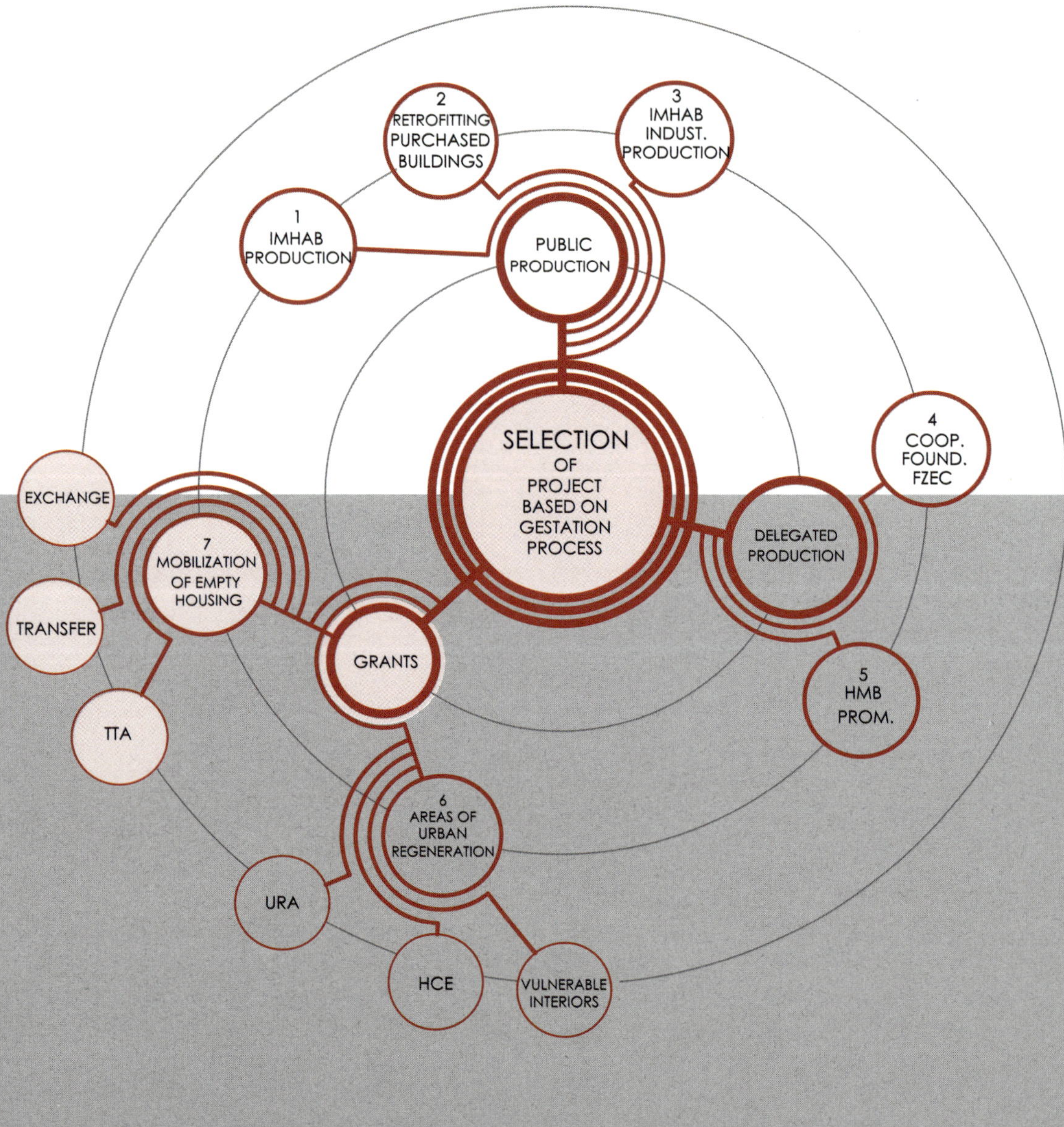
SELECTION OF PROJECT BASED ON GESTATION PROCESS
PUBLIC PRODUCTION
1 IMHAB PRODUCTION
2 RETROFITTING PURCHASED BUILDINGS
3 IMHAB INDUST. PRODUCTION
DELEGATED PRODUCTION
4 COOP. FOUND. FZEC
5 HMB PROM.
GRANTS
6 AREAS OF URBAN REGENERATION
URA
HCE
VULNERABLE INTERIORS
7 MOBILIZATION OF EMPTY HOUSING
EXCHANGE
TRANSFER
TTA

Mobilization of empty housing

01	18 housing units / Floridablanca	Exchange
02	2 housing units / Poble-sec **Fundación Hàbitat3**	Transfer
03	17 housing units / Casa Bloc residential home **Estudi fàbric**	Transfer
04	1 housing unit / Gran de Gràcia	Primer la Llar
05	10 housing units / Independència	TTA

Social housing programmes in collaboration with the private sector

Anna Soler - Cristina Valios
Head of the Adequate Use of Housing Department - Project manager of People Services, IMHAB

At the start of 2000, studies showed that the production of social housing had not worked since the latter half of the 1990s, and that the percentages of compliance with the objectives planned and agreed with the central government had repeatedly been low in the area of social housing production.

Decrees 454/2004 and 244/205 of the Right to Housing Plan were key regulations in establishing a series of measures to reinforce and promote the various forms of affordable housing in Catalonia (social and coordinated), prevent residential social exclusion, mediate in the social rental market, mobilize unoccupied stock and make existing rental stock profitable, with a view to increasing the number of properties for rent.

It was in this regulatory framework that social housing programmes were set up in 2005 to seek the collaboration of the private sector in mobilizing housing that was not available on the market, but that, with the support of the Administration, could be incentivized to extend housing supply and contain rental prices.

The current programmes of the Barcelona Rental Housing Exchange or the transfer of homes for social purposes are examples of the evolution of incipient collaboration with home owners and administrators, and are included in the 2016-2025 Right to Housing Plan of Barcelona City Council.

This plan has four strategic lines of intervention:

- o Preventing and responding to housing emergency
- o Guaranteeing the appropriate use of housing
- o Increasing the number of affordable housing units
- o Retrofitting existing housing stock

The four lines address the concept of gestating, generating or producing, or, ultimately, mobilizing empty housing.

All cities have private housing stock that is not on the market, principally because it does not meet the minimum standards of habitability and its owners do not have the financial capacity to carry out the necessary interventions. Facilitating the rehabilitation of homes with property grants for owners is therefore an incentive to incorporate them into the property market, increasing the supply of flats and containing rental prices, and making more affordable homes available.

Social housing programmes offer mediation services between the owners of empty homes and potential tenants. The Barcelona Rental Housing Exchange and the Programme for the transfer of homes for social purposes provide owners of empty housing with a technical evaluation of the homes to detect possible interventions needed to make them habitable, and advise and accompany them in the rehabilitation process until completion. These interventions can be subsidized provided the homes are included in the programmes and rented to the users proposed.

Homes included in social housing programmes are declared of municipal social interest, which may allow owners to access other housing incentives, financial guarantees and tax rebates. Throughout the contractual relationship, both the owner and the users of the homes enjoy social, legal and technical support to ensure compliance with the rights and obligations of all parties, and guarantee appropriate use of the home.

Over the years, social housing programmes have developed and evolved to adapt to users' circumstances and needs, providing residential solutions to different groups such as families and cohabitation units, young people, people at risk of losing their home, homeless people, etc.

In 2022, the private stock mobilized by Barcelona Council's social housing programmes represented over 1,700 homes with current rental or use contracts, and housed more than 5,000 people.

As the slogan says: “In Barcelona, we're convinced that housing is a basic right”; and this is how it should be to guarantee a decent life for everyone.

For this reason, the future means continuing to promote public-private collaboration, which should allow us to increase the supply of affordable homes and complement the council housing supply with the aim of accommodating more families and maintaining the habitability of private housing stock.

living

Living in everyday life

Caterina Figuerola
Architect. Co-founder of Llindarquitectura

"I was able to put my boxes on the bedside table." This is the experience of Living of a person for whom, until then, day-to-day life had consisted of passing through. Having a place where you can arrange the personal objects that accompany you in your life becomes, in this case, the daily expression of living, thanks to the space-time relationship that the subject has with their immediate environment.

The experience of Living means belonging to a specific place and the fact that everyday life becomes something habitual. Recognizing the spaces through which you move and where you carry out domestic tasks, being aware of the known, being able to name the spaces and position yourself in them is what the subject ends up doing when living. Creating the habits of Living is what allows them to recover the project of everyday life. The light, the colour, the smells, a whole sensory and dimensional world awakens when the passage from day to day becomes Living. Living as the construction of a new reality.

In a second connotation, Living also has to do with feeling relieved and cared for. If the subject does not have a place to live, they are unprotected; their body does not have sufficient defences to face the world in which they are immersed. The lived experience of Not Dwelling could be any situation of homelessness. The experience of Dwelling, on the other hand, could be sitting in a room next to a window, watching a ray of sunlight illuminate the space. Dwelling as a way of ensuring survival.

If Dwelling is this space-time dimension in which objects and subjects identify with a place, where they feel comforted, this feeling of identity and security is what makes it possible to create a new viewfinder. This viewfinder allows us to see from a distance the world from which we come and prompt the confidence needed to project where we are going. It allows us to conceive new imaginaries based on the perceptions, sensations, and physical and intellectual stimuli created in the act of Living. This viewfinder is the home, a refuge that guarantees shelter.

The transition from being a passer-by to dwelling means relearning habits and perceptions, knowing how to value this space-time dimension that has been forgotten due to the absence of a home. If guaranteeing the act of Dwelling involves recovering customs and habits, it is also necessary to recover the space dimension in things that exist. In the built-up, consolidated city, it seems logical to think about infiltration and urban surgery to recycle an urban fabric that is apparently full. Even if available land is practically exhausted, there are lots of empty cubic metres, private property in the form of homes that are unoccupied. Redistributing, reorganizing, recovering these empty homes generates a new process of building: re-building. In this process, an unsheltered space is turned into shelter by giving meaning to what already exists. Traces of the past that convey something are recovered, and space is examined in terms of different concepts. Finally, a shelter is re-built.

The prefix *re-* seems to be the most commended in the climate and energy emergency in which we are living. Rebuilding, recovering, rehabilitating, reorganizing are concepts that must be brought to the various social spaces of today's life –the city, the neighbourhood, the home– affected by the different growth dynamics driven by globalization. I wonder if, by slowing down this capitalist growth and incorporating the word degrowth into our everyday vocabulary, we could adapt the present-day scale to the local and close at hand. We could come to Inhabit our different social environments; starting by inhabiting the houses, we would end up inhabiting the neighbourhood, and then inhabiting the city, and in this way we would come to humanize wherever the act of Dwelling takes root.

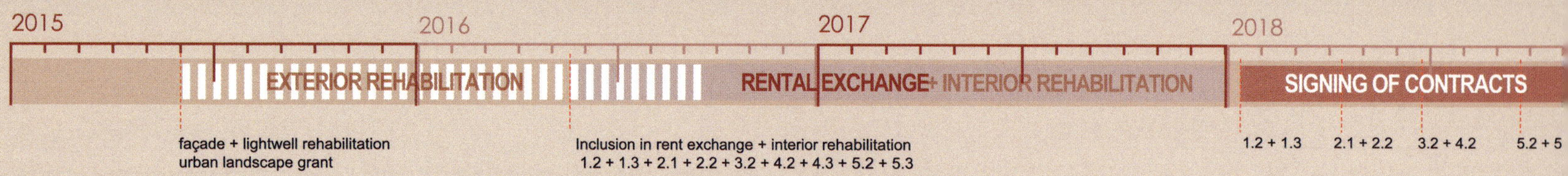

18 housing units / Floridablanca

Rental Exchange + Purchase

Creating interactions between the various housing programmes is one management objective. Calls for grants to retrofit buildings therefore allow for empty homes in a property to be included in the Housing Exchange and, if necessary, rehabilitated with municipal grants.

Homes included in the Rental Exchange after the rehabilitation of buildings have the same incentives for owners: grants for work carried out of up to €20,000; for inclusion, of €1,500, 95% of property tax, and guaranteed collection of rental income, among others.

Work at Floridablanca 106 started with the retrofitting of communal elements such as the façade, stairs and lifts, and the empty homes, which were then put up for rent on the Rental Exchange. In this way, the tenants, proposed by the Exchange, had access to a renovated home with a significantly lower rent than free-market prices.

The Rental Exchange accompanied the tenants and the owner in their contractual relationship, until the owner expressed the desire to sell the building. The sale did not represent a risk for the tenants, since the new owner has to respect the same conditions for the full term of the contract.

Given this circumstance, the City Council decided to exercise the right to first refusal and became the owner of the property, thereby increasing the city's council housing stock. The tenants then entered into a contractual agreement with the Barcelona Housing Authority

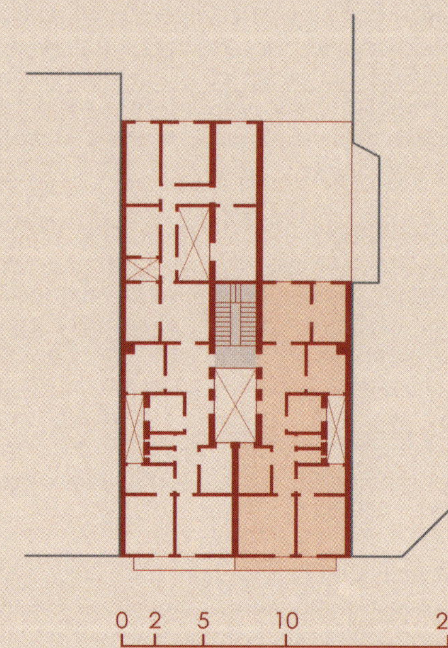

Typical floor plan 1:500

"Since they created this superblock, with the new market and everything that's been done with pedestrians in mind... the truth is, we're delighted with the neighbourhood. I suppose there're some people who aren't, but most are. Lots of elderly people live here, and it's been a real respite. Everything was so dirty, it was... and now we've got the new market and everything, fantastic."

Interview – 2022

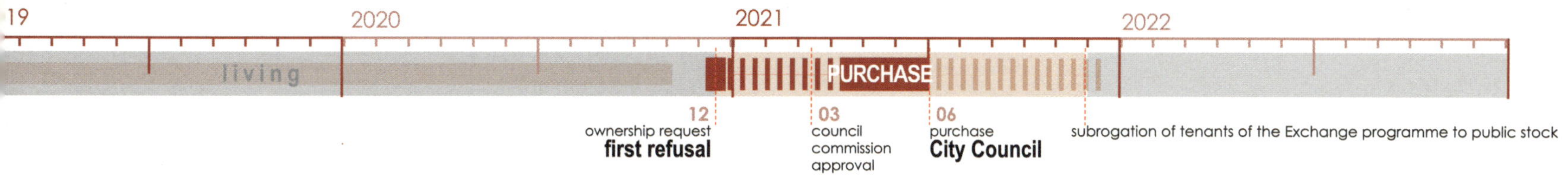

Photographs - Adrià Goula © - 2022

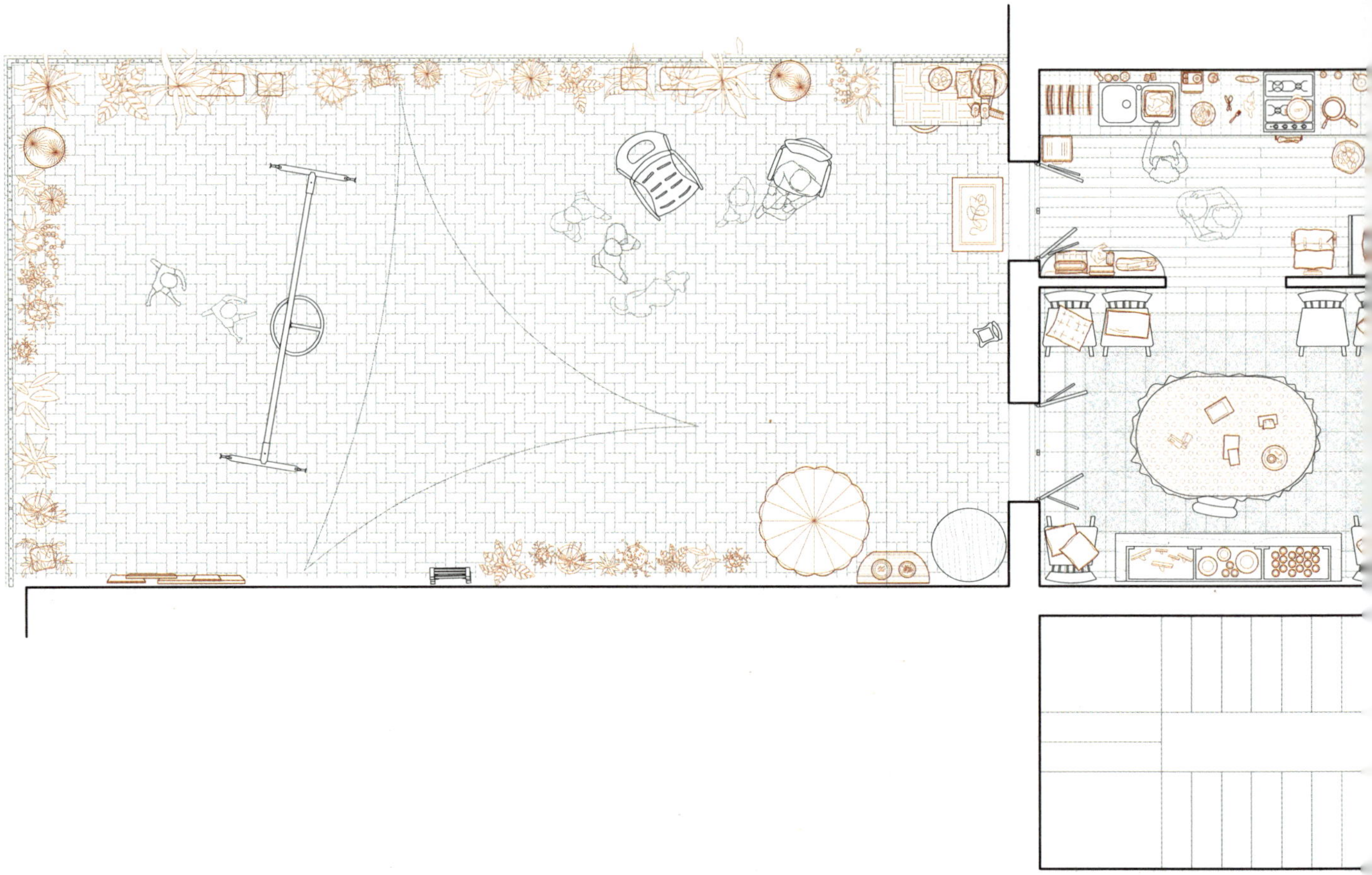

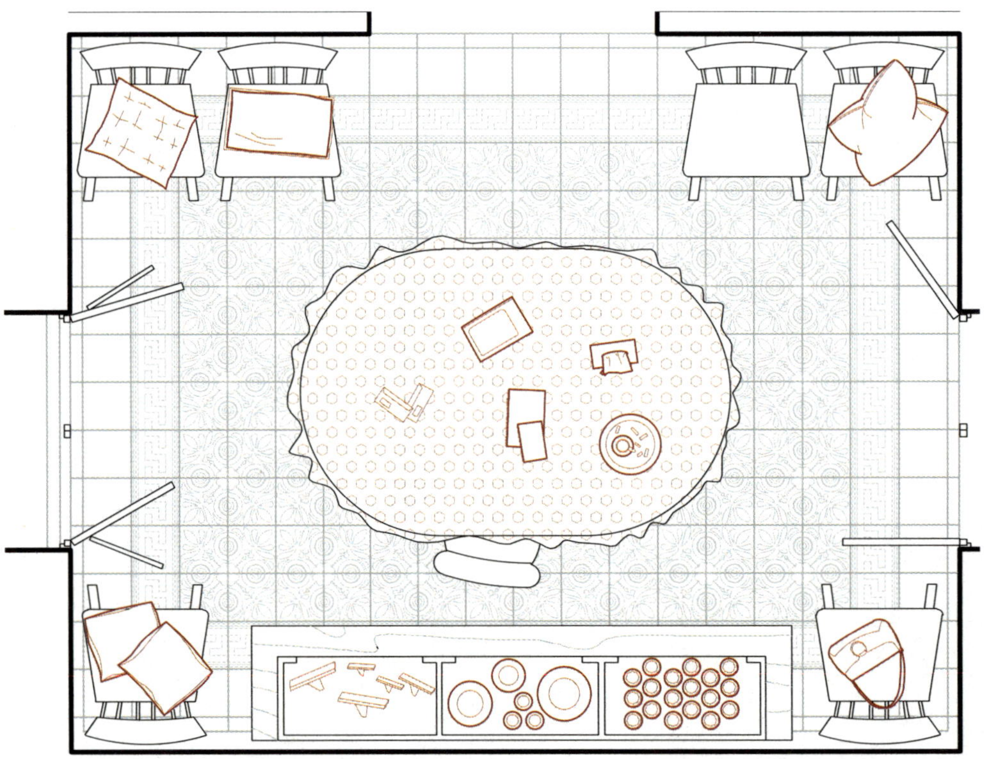

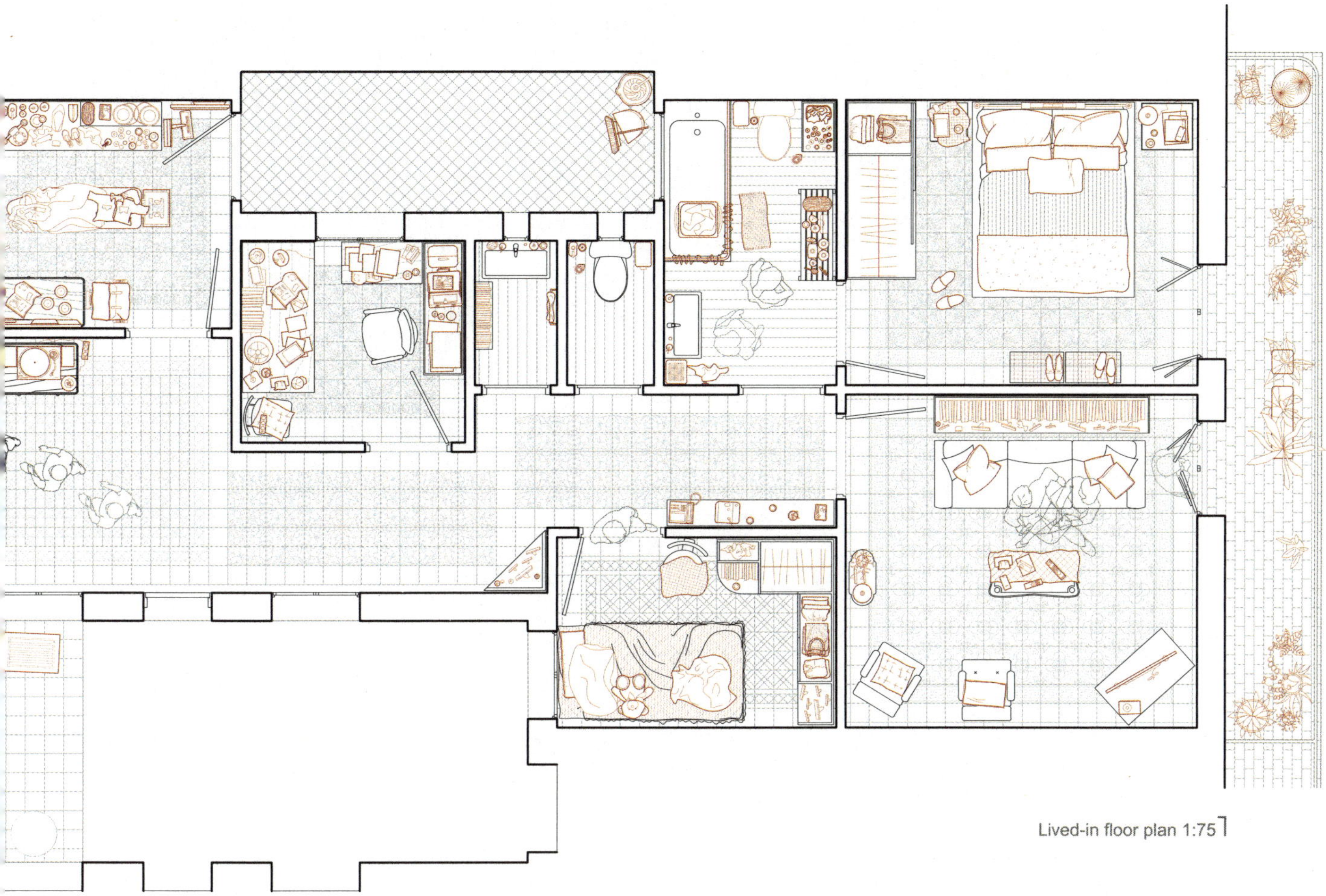

Lived-in floor plan 1:75

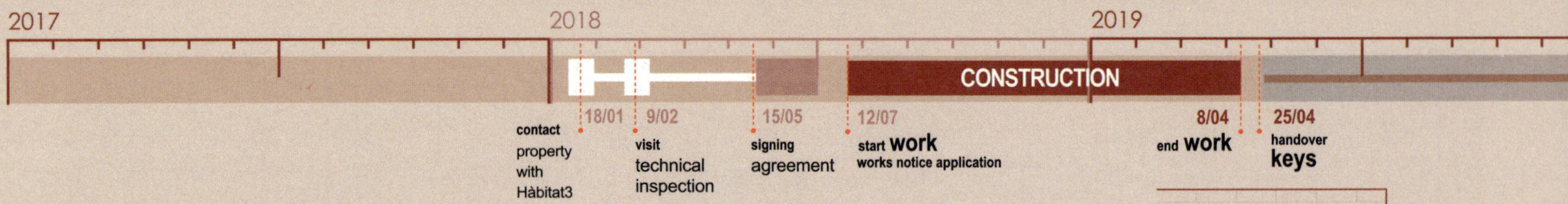

2 housing units / Poble-sec

Transfer programme / Fundació Hàbitat3

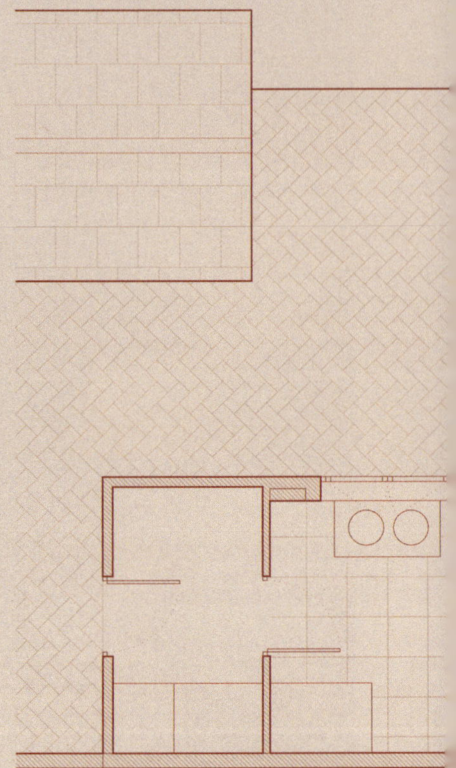

In the framework of a collaboration agreement, first with Barcelona City Council and then with the Barcelona Housing Consortium, Hàbitat3 acquires empty privately-owned homes and makes them available to people and families proposed by the Social Emergency Desk of Barcelona, thereby increasing the capacity of council stock to attend to situations of housing emergency.

The 373 homes currently in the programme were acquired by collaboration with private owners and, often, with the participation of estate agents and property managers. They are located in residential buildings throughout the city's neighbourhoods, which helps to integrate people in a context of social mix.

When adaptation or retrofitting of homes is necessary, work is carried out in collaboration with social organizations in the city that work with the social insertion of at-risk groups.

In all cases, with attention to possible vulnerabilities of individuals, social support is provided to monitor the proper use of the home, the fulfilment of contractual responsibilities and good neighbourhood relations.

Thanks to this programme, so far some 1,200 people have found decent housing with a rent that is appropriate to their income.

The programme's value lies in the fact that it brings an integrated approach to all the objectives: finding homes, negotiating to obtain market housing, financing and carrying out work, managing housing and providing personal support.

Hàbitat3 Foundation is a social housing management instrument made available to the local administration in a public-private collaboration relationship.

Interview – 2022

"As regards the flat, I like everything except the kitchen. It should go where the bathroom is, for example. And open directly onto the terrace."

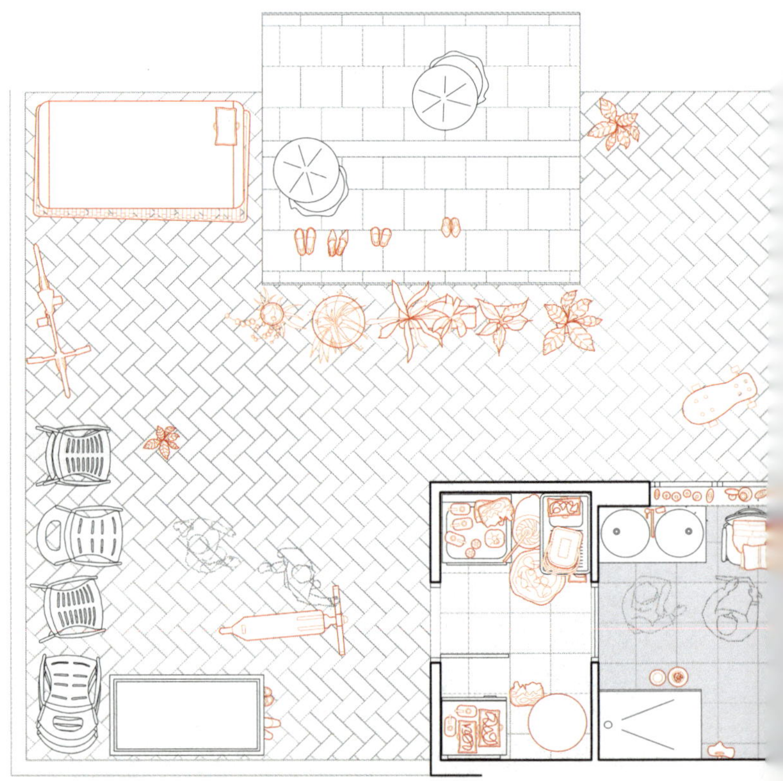

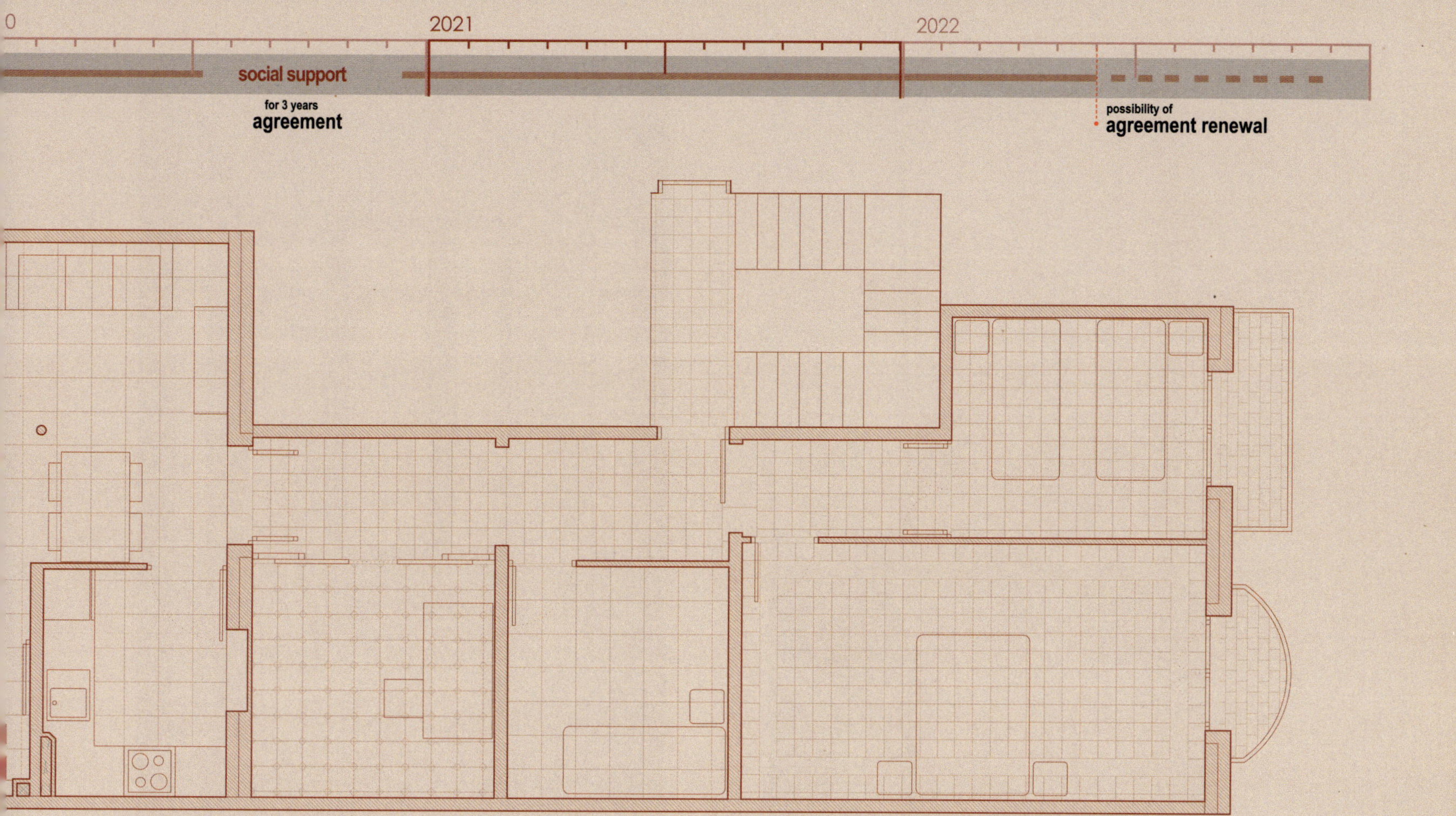

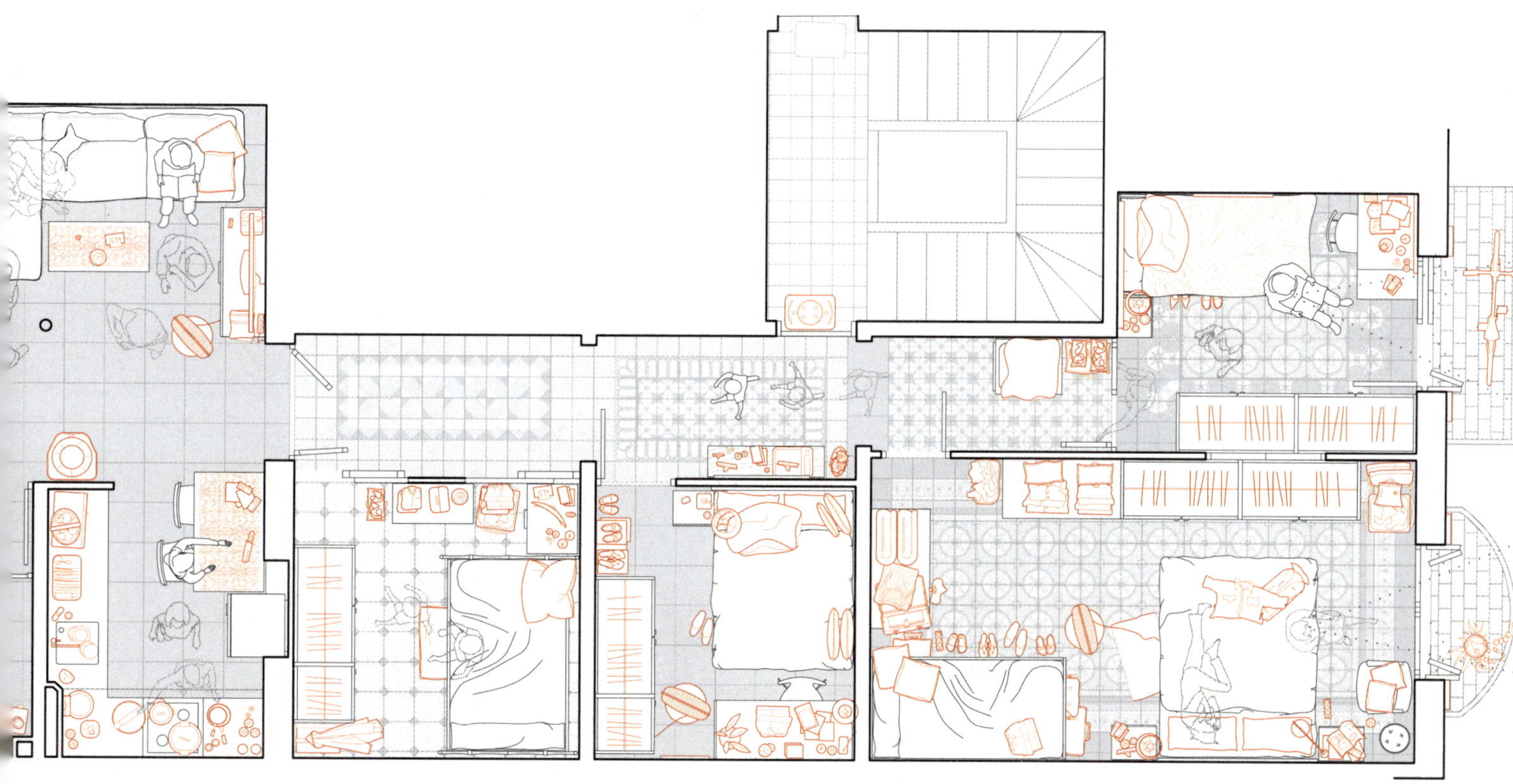

Lived-in floor plan 1:75

Photograph of previous state

Photograph at end of work

Photograph of previous state

Photograph at end of work

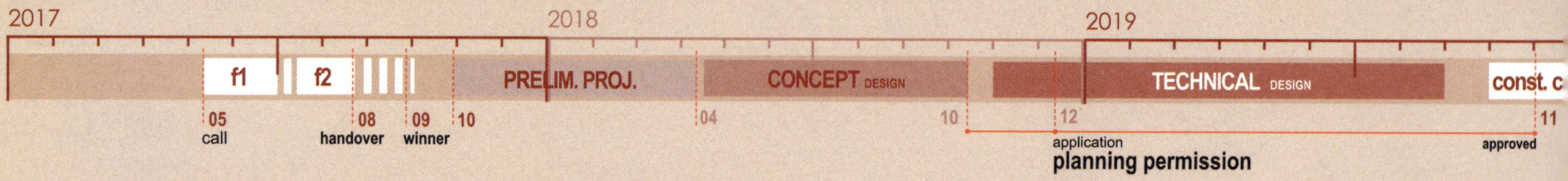

17 housing units / Casa Bloc Sheltered Housing

Estudi fàbric

Casa Bloc is an apartment building designed by the GATCPAC and constructed between 1934 and 1942 according to rationalist principles. In the course of those years, the Spanish Civil War brought work to a halt, preventing part of the original project from being carried out as planned: the first floors of block five underwent substantial modifications at the hands of the military, who demolished the layout of the duplex typology and built a residence in its place. In 2017, Fundació Hàbitat3 organized a competition to occupy these floors with a new project that respected the rules of the original architecture and proposed housing units in keeping with present-day needs.

The project is based on a simple premise: to use the original GATCPAC resources present in the building to create a new typology.

- The kitchens are opened up to connect with a dining area.

- The bathrooms are moved to the longitudinal axis of the building, coinciding with the pair of central pillars to take advantage of the pre-existing installation shaft.

- The central area is made bigger to maximize lines of sight and natural ventilation.

- Walkway access to the second floor is replicated, creating a new cross-ventilated typology.

- The materials, colours and various elements were reinterpreted in keeping with niches and detail studies: vitrified ceramics, rounded corners of partitions, painted plinths, original lamps and the colours in the woodwork.

A factorial decomposition of the elements of the original project is therefore proposed to recompose and adapt them to new ways of living.

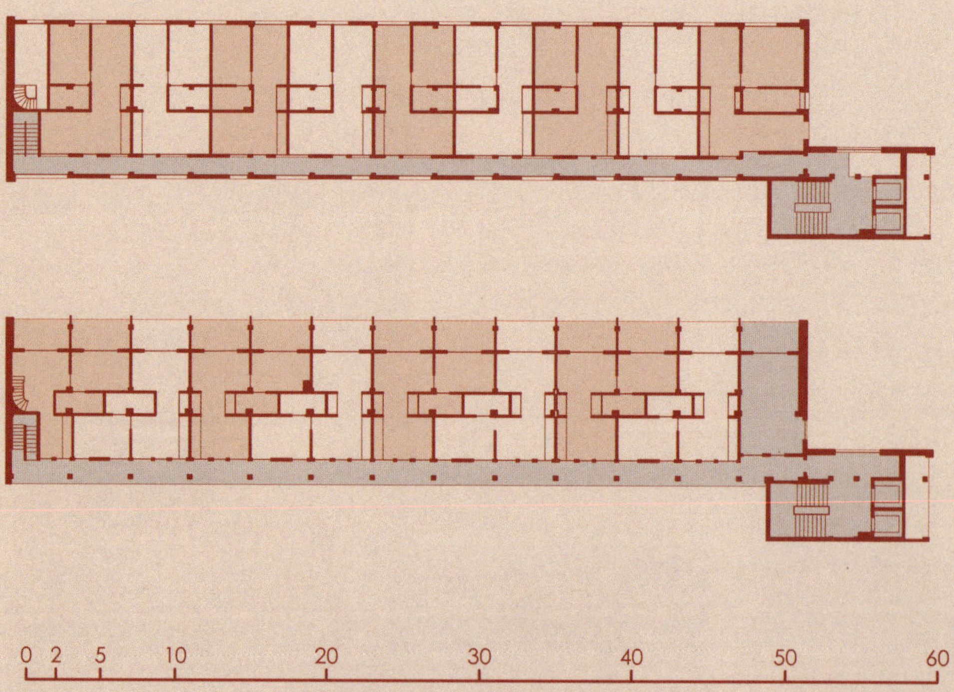

Location: c/Residència, 10. Barcelona. **Programme:** 17 homes. **Surface area:** 1,120 m². **Cost:** 614,083.18 € + VAT €. **Architects:** fàbric (Alain González, Pedro García, Javier Hernani, Pau Casanova). **Contractor:** Rècop. **Consultancy:** Rècop. (installations), Ariston (sustainability), Celinex (monitoring).

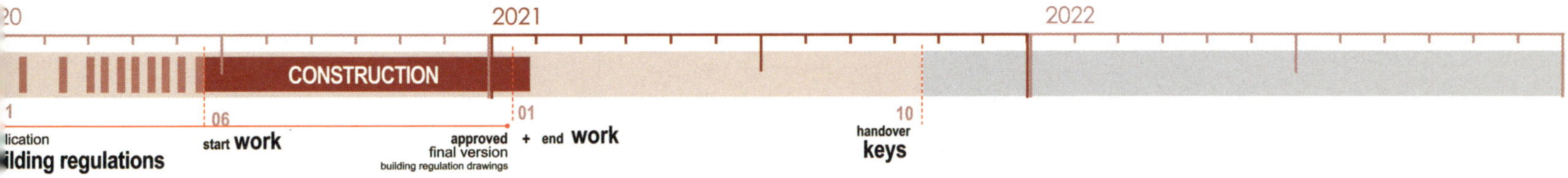

Photographs - Adrià Goula © - 2022

Floor plan of dwelling 1:75

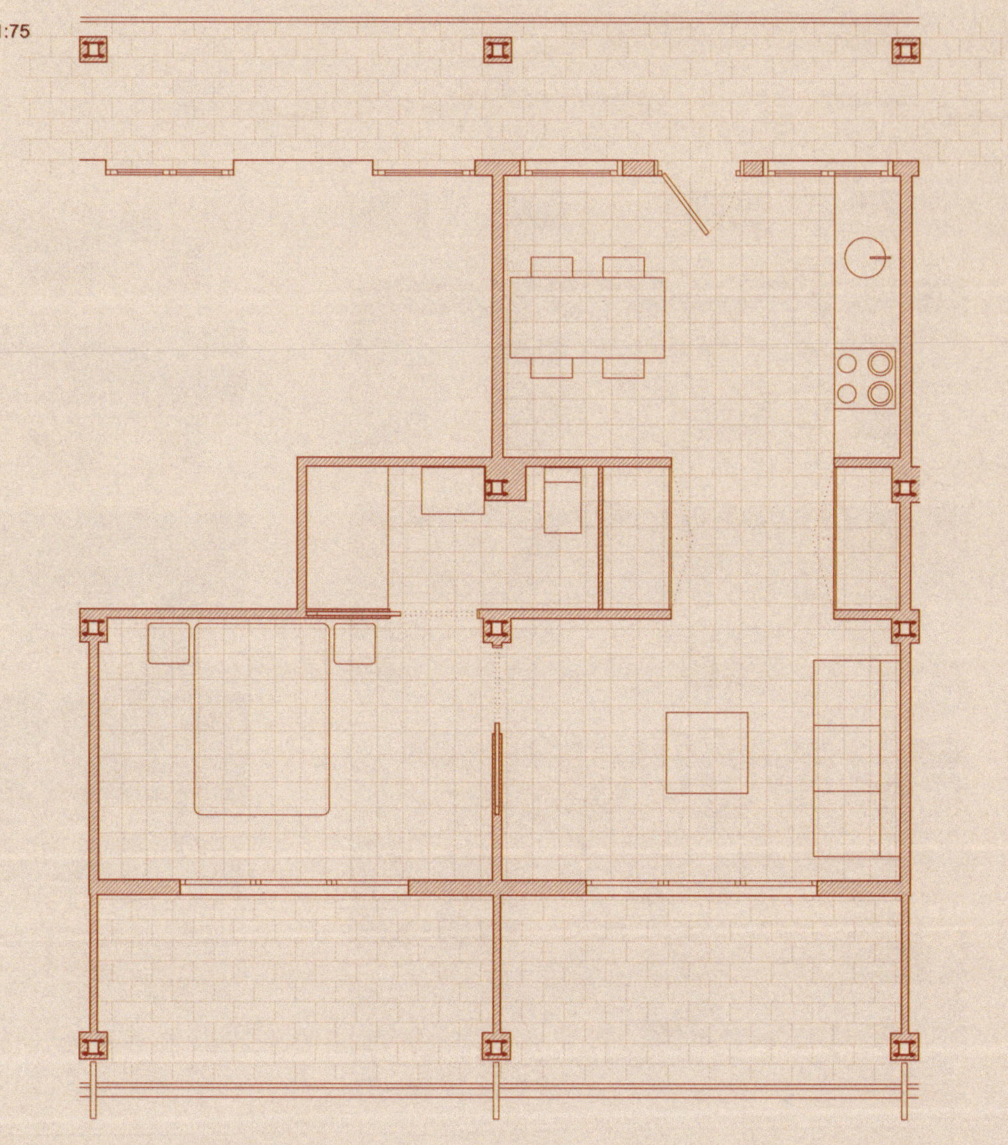

Typical floor plan – Competition phase

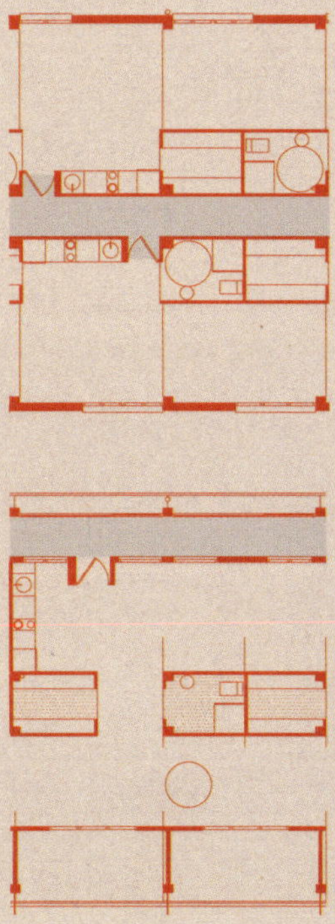

Typical floor plan – Concept design

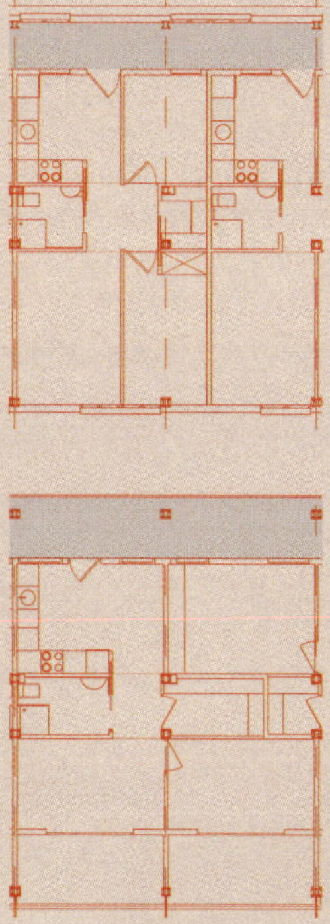

Typical floor plan – Technical design

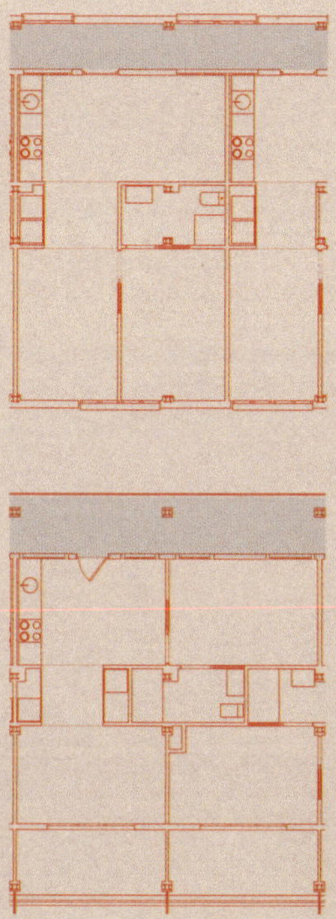

Lived-in floor plan 1:75

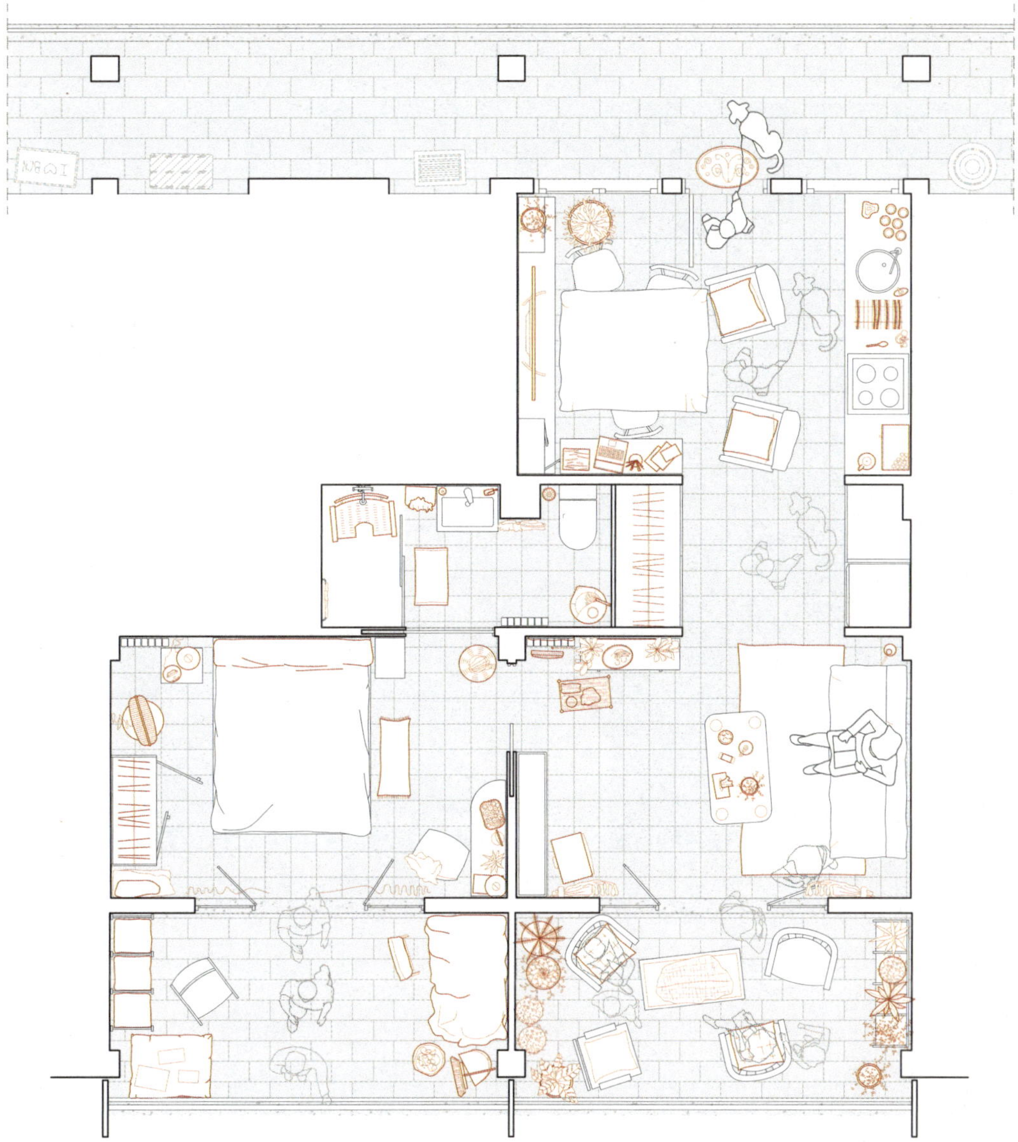

"We love it. There's one bedroom, but for the two of us, what more do we want? End of story. The basics. Dining room, bathroom and toilet..."

Interview – 2022

Photograph of work

Photographs of completed work - Adrià Goula © - 2021

Photographs of work

Photographs - Adrià Goula © - 2021

Photograph - Maite Caramés © - 2022

Mobilizing empty privately-owned homes in Barcelona

1 housing unit / Gran de Gràcia

Housing First / Fundación Hàbitat3

Since 2018, within the framework of an agreement with the Barcelona Housing Consortium, Fundació Hàbitat3 has negotiated the renewal of contracts with owners and acquired new homes for Barcelona City Council's Housing First programme.

This programme is based on the Housing First model, which sees access to housing as the necessary first step for a homeless person to improve their situation.

The homeless people taking part in the programme are characterized by a long history of life on the streets and a precarious state of health, and having functional autonomy for daily life, with an income or the possibility of having one.

Taking housing as the first step towards inclusion, the programme offers socio-educational support aimed at ensuring that participants can access the network of services and universal benefits, enjoy the economic and welfare subsidies to which they are entitled, and recover self-management skills, and family and social relationships whenever possible. Community integration is also promoted, and support is provided to monitor therapeutic treatments that may be necessary.

This support is provided by two organizations specializing in assisting homeless people, and Fundació Hàbitat3 deals with property management and housing administration.

At present, there are 49 individual participants in the programme.

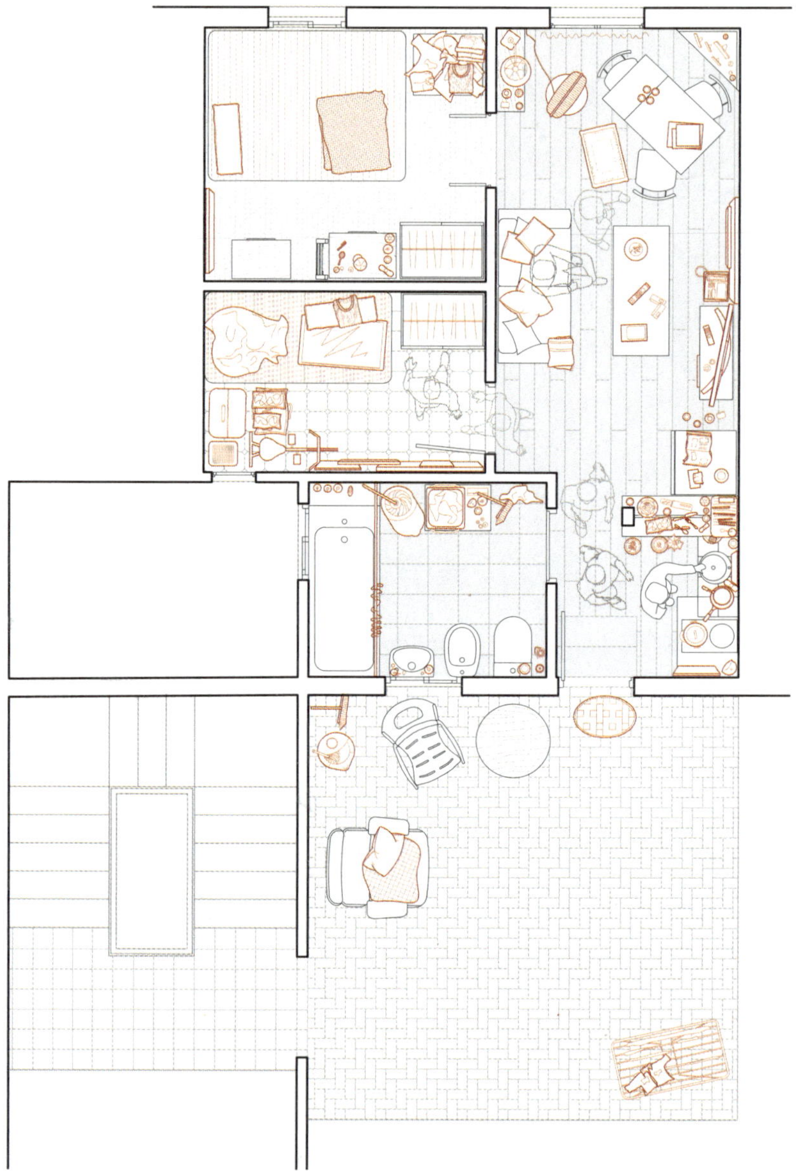

Lived-in floor plan 1:75

"It's great, I like the neighbourhood, the market is very affordable and there's a park... the squares are also very nice, and neighbourhood life is very quiet and very pleasant."

From temporary tourist accommodation to temporary housing

10 housing units / Independència

Temporary housing programme

One of the consequences of the Covid-19 pandemic was the decline in tourism in the city of Barcelona.

Barcelona Council took advantage of the situation to set up a programme to attract apartments with a tourist license for use as social rental housing. It contacted the operators of tourist accommodation interested in leasing their apartments to the Council, in order to increase the social housing available and accommodate people who were temporarily housed in pensions managed by the social services, awaiting the allocation of a social rental flat.

The temporary housing programme acquired 130 homes, situated in different districts of the city, to be available for between one and three years.

One of the first properties to enter the programme was Carrer de la Independència 287, which consists of ten two-bedroom homes, furnished and equipped with electrical appliances and household items. In this case, despite initially signing the contract for a year, the tourist operator has repeatedly extended it as the programme works well.

The cohabitation units taking part in the programme, as well as finding a home in keeping with their needs, had access to a social support team to assist them in managing the accommodation.

The temporary housing programme has accommodated some 400 people.

Interview – 2022

"I like the flat, it's very spacious, it's comfortable... The only thing is, really, that there's one bedroom for the kids, and I'd like Chantal to have her own room, but apart from that, everything about the flat is great."

Photographs - Adrià Goula © - 2022

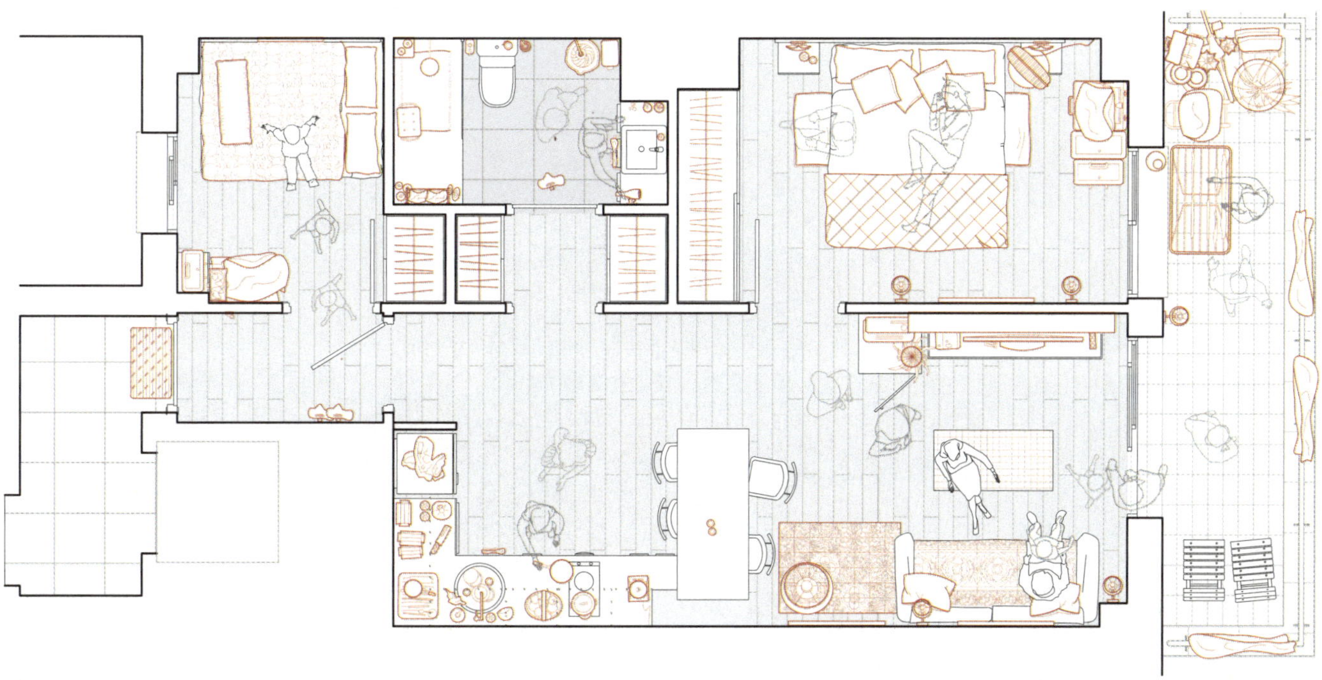

Lived-in floor plan 1:75

Professional participatory meetings at the COAC

As an action derived from this publication based on debate as a methodology, the curatorship team, with the support of the COAC, organized meetings about the gestation of social housing, at which the seven categories of housing strategy presented in the publication were represented by all the agents involved.

The purpose of bringing these agents together was to compare and contrast opinions and experiences to reflect on the work methodologies, programmes and projects of the municipal team, described in this publication, and to define to what extent they make them possible and qualify them. The meetings brought together 18 teams of architects with the directors of the Housing Department, Barcelona Housing Authority-IMHAB, the Municipal Urban Planning Institute, Foment de Ciutat, HMB, the industrial sector (Catalan Institute of Construction Technology - ITeC and the Constructors' Guild), foundations and the architects' association, COAC.

This is the ideal scenario for any of the teams of architects present when starting a project. The possibility of all the agents involved in the gestation processes sitting down together provides vital, hitherto unavailable information to understand the complexity of carrying out these procedures.

Two days of meetings were organized, grouping the seven strategies by the need for construction or retrofitting. The first session dealt with strategies involving work on an unbuilt plot, a brief defined by the IMHAB and unknown users: construction, industrialization, delegated public social production (Foundations and Zero Equity Cooperatives or FZEC) and delegated public-private production (Habitatge Metròpolis Barcelona, HMB). The strategies addressed in the second session changed these parameters to pre-existing construction (neighbourhood, building or apartment), with the presence of occupants as the main differentiating characteristic. They include the following categories: purchase and retrofitting, recovering vulnerable properties (Urban Regeneration Areas, URA; High complexity estates, HCE; Vulnerable interiors) and mobilization of empty housing (Exchange; Transfer; Housing First; Temporary tourist accommodation, TTA).

Another difference between the two sessions was the makeup of the meetings. At the first, most of the people involved were architects, mainly designers of the projects, though there were also technical municipal members of staff. At the second, the professional profiles were much more diverse, with a predominance of technical municipal personnel. This fact is directly related to strategic innovation: consolidated strategies are well known to many teams of architects, some of whom were responsible for developing them; the more innovative strategies implemented in recent years, meanwhile, still need the people responsible to be able to be seen.

The dynamic of the sessions involved presenting a series of topics to generate debate, in which each participant was able to have their say.

Administration: Project architects Delegated producers Industrial professionals COAC Curators

Department of Housing
IMHAB
MUPI
Foment de Ciutat

SESSION 1

30 JUNE 2022

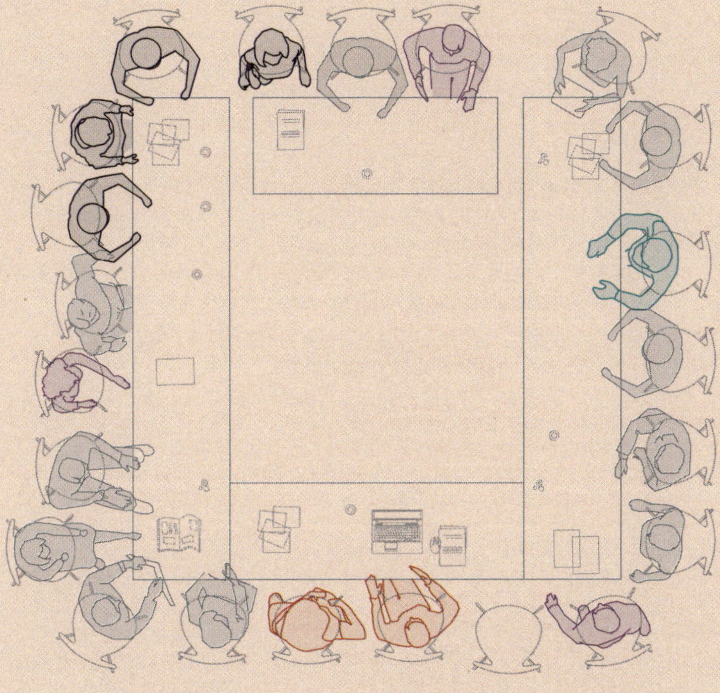

Enric Massip | Carme Ribas | Esteve Bonell
Eva Ortigosa | David Fernández | Javier Burón
Eduardo González de Molina | Joan Recasens
Olga Barrabés | Oriol Bosch | Donato Muñoz
Javier Ramos | Lluís Roig | Vicente Guallart
David Juárez | Jon Begiristain | Alfons Tornero
Manel Rodríguez | Mercè Berengué
Pere Joan Ravetllat | Guim Costa | Gemma Molas
Jordi Suñé | TIC Multimèdia COAC | Ibon Bilbao
Ignacio Urbistondo | Caterina Figuerola

SESSION 2

1 JULY 2022

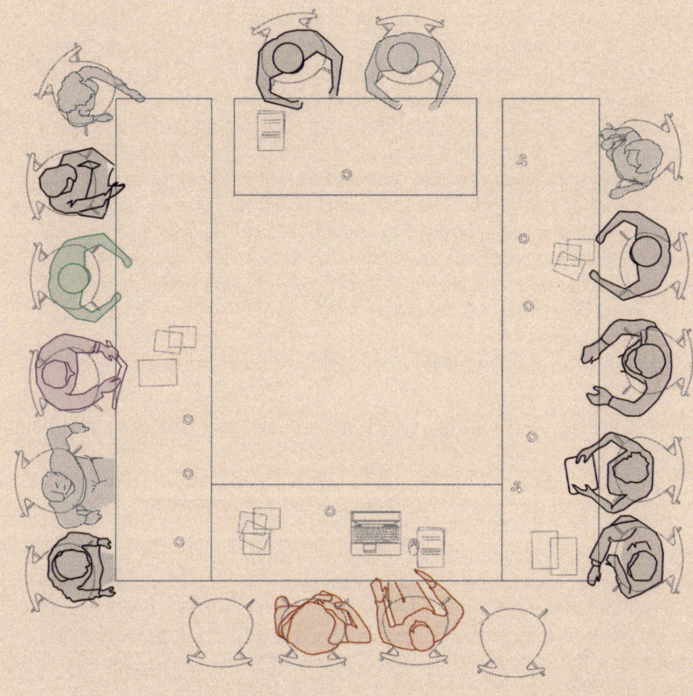

Eduardo González de Molina | Javier Burón
Javier Hernani | Josep Antoni Martínez | Oriol Gil
Xavier Mauri | Victoria Tous | Cristina Valios
Nuria Turró | Joan Recasens | Anna Rigalt
Oscar Frago | Enric Cremades | Gemma Molas
Caterina Figuerola | TIC Multimèdia COAC
Jordi Suñé | Ibon Bilbao | Ignacio Urbistondo

SESSION 1

As the main producer of new construction, the IMHAB opens the session with the history of the tenders.

Most of the projects featured in this publication were designed in a two-round competition model based on an initial curricular phase, where experience in multifamily housing was taken into account, and an initial graphic proposal evaluated by the Housing Board. This assessment was based on criteria such as creating the city, integration into the setting, environmental parameters, energy efficiency, ratios and construction systems. The same criteria were applied in the second round. In this first phase, the five or ten highest scoring teams were shortlisted to draft a graphic proposal in a second round evaluated by a jury made up of members of the municipal government, the COAC and, in some cases, neighbourhood associations. This model led to an open competition involving a wider range of participants, where experience was a given, without overlooking certain groups such as young people. The previous model tended to produce a repetitive list; this new model is more open, but everyone has to draw. We are currently considering two-round competitions: a first round with a very schematic proposal and a second, more detailed one. That's for the architecture competition, because then tenders for industrial production and construction are introduced, where the constructor and the architect go hand in hand. To maintain the architect's authorship, this model is deriving into a new formula with an initial tender to produce an architectural concept design and then a works tender, where the industrial company works directly with the architect at the technical phase.

From the moment the possibility of a site for a social housing competition comes up at the IMHAB, how long does it take to announce the call?

Quite a few variants come into play depending on the situation of the site. A plot of land with planning approval is not the same as one that has been transferred or is in the process of being transferred, if reparcelling is necessary, if it is affected by urban planning... The future purpose of the land and the planning to which it is subject are key to the architects being able to present a tender.

In all the competition strategies, it is important to maintain the quality of the competition that has to be reflected in architectural quality. When industrial professionals are involved in the competition, what is the guarantee that it will be maintained?

This is a complex process because it is based on an architecture project that has been scored, and, when the constructor starts work, to implement industrial methods and guarantee the quality of the system proposed in the competition, variations are introduced to speed up the process. The industrial specialist brings the system, and this means that the proposal has to be sufficiently open and flexible to allow for dialogue between the architect and the constructor.

As regards this process, why are there so many points in the planning? In terms of quality, knowing that we have to carry out technical projects in two and a half months, it is difficult to do the job well. This score, which favours the constructor because it allows them to finish earlier, is detrimental to the projects.

This is a result of the need to produce housing, but we have to define a period of time that works for both parties. If the conditions are clearly defined, can a technical project be carried out in three or four months?

In a traditional project, yes, but if you're introducing innovation and prefabrication, no.

The amount of time provided for the concept process is important, and increasingly so.

The competitions we removed did have tight deadlines, and short deadlines were scored. It's important to have a well-planned concept design so that producing it together with constructors can save us time. There's another handicap here, which is the building permit; no matter how fast we want to go, there are external conditioning factors.

In an industrial process, when you finish the technical project everything has to be defined; nothing can be changed during work, because the manufacturing process has already begun. The constructor's contracting process and the three or four months of the foundations could be optimized.

Formulas should be found for below- and above-grade licenses to be able to move forward with the foundations while the technical project is finalized. But most of all,

collaboration between the architecture team, the government agency and the constructor is vital in innovate processes.

You hear people saying "construction is getting harder and harder", and it's true. The main reason is the ever-increasing amount of bureaucracy and regulations it generates. This excess of bureaucracy and regulations makes architecture lose its cultural and humanistic values. Government agencies and architects' associations have to draw up regulations that are similar for everyone when formulating the conditions of entry of a competition. We are currently finding it difficult to make bids due to the lack of homogeneity in the process and the administrative documentation required. There are no clear rules; it is necessary to clarify, and this clarification has to come before the competition starts. It is the jury that has to establish the conditions of entry and answer questions. Someone in Switzerland asked me for a contribution: what was my experience with the Housing Authority in the Glòries building? The start of the competition and designing the project took four or five years, and that conditions the process. I don't feel like I suffered in that competition. Now I do; it's a mess, misinformation, excessive bureaucracy and always different entry conditions.

So what's the context, what's going on in the runup to the projects? First of all, size is important. For the public system, 100-200 homes is one thing; for this Housing Plan, the IMHAB is working on between 6,000 and 6,500 homes, with an investment of 1,000 million euros. That's a lot of stress on the system, which has to be able to digest it all. Then there's a housing emergency, with the Housing Department asking the IMS and the IMHAB to speed up, produce and innovate at the same time, which produces anxiety. Then, in legal terms, there are two parameters that work together and that also seem antithetical, though actually they aren't. One is a legal primitivism inherited from the 19th century, where steps go one after the other in time, without taking collateral actions into account –that is, a sequential administrative process that does not facilitate the management of complex processes. The other is a regulatory capacity of legislators that makes it impossible to keep up with affordable housing legislation. Planning also includes residential land in this process. Residential can take many forms: free-market housing, social housing for sale or rental, surface right, etc. The process of generating a raw material that is, at once, many raw materials is very complex. Then, all these types of land are patrimony, calling for procedures based on administrative law. The transfer of public patrimony to a private body sets off a chain of reflection; so the transfer of land from Urban Planning to the IMHAB is not straightforward either. And, in our case, many of the interventions we're involved in are financed by the public bank, especially the EIB, which also has certain technical requirements for a certain type of housing with a certain type of energy and environmental performance.

Right now, the Public Sector Contracts Act is designed for inaction, because it is based on price and mistrust.

Apart from tenders, there's another way of accessing projects, and that's through the FZEC or Foundations and Zero Equity Cooperatives Agreement and HMB.

The FZEC Agreement and HMB are interstellar gateways to another dimension. This agreement took five years, but now it's in place and has gone through all the filters, there are procedures for working with land and producing non-market housing that are not the usual ones, they're shorter. It's a long way round to get to a short way. Apart from this strategy, there are others: co-housing, surface rights, but the largest part is the tenancy for decades regime, this is the product that society is asking for. A simple kind of competition and legal structure is vital, because it is very difficult to combine speed, quality and simplicity.

This way of achieving quality in quantity is the objective we've been addressing with the COAC and the City Council.

This is Adamism –the idea of just starting one day, when the world already exists. To understand that the end of the story is that exceptional things are now being done, we need to ask ourselves how we got here

and put into context the things that helped us start to do exceptional things.

The first exceptional thing was an architecture act passed in 2013 that helped frame the fundamental idea of quality. The second was that innovation did not exist in the Board's competitions, nothing could be done. The argument was that a public company had to have a positive balance sheet, there was no public money, they had to be self-financed, which meant zero risk. What's the current balance? The relevant issue is whether today the Council invests money, what is the municipal budget for building homes or not, or buying buildings or not. Thirdly, the Council used to auction public land, not keep it, but at some point in history it was decided that no land would be sold.

This is the fundamental change: public land is not sold.

This is why the Council now has so much land, and it's now possible to have this volume of housing that's being talked about.To return to the second point: who pays for innovation, who invests? At each moment in history, the Council has invested where it thinks it needs to, in libraries, markets, car parks. But in 2014, realizing that building car parks no longer brought any added value, it decided to take out a concession and free up money for housing. This was quite exceptional, because it was a move from producing housing with zero risk because there is no budget and we have to produce buildings with a low risk because we have to guarantee that maintenance doesn't cost a lot, to, one day, you've got money to produce housing. And in the same way that I can create exceptional libraries and exceptional markets, I can produce housing that breaks with traditional brick and concrete solutions.

The fact of investing public money in housing production has changed the rules of the game.

In the case of tenders, the argument that we were making and discussed with the Housing Board had to do with the Council's climate emergency declaration. Yet buildings were still being made of concrete, a machine for making CO_2 financed by the budget instead of introducing other materials more in keeping with the bigger picture of the European Union and the climate emergency declaration. Then the Council announced some competitions in which a lower cost scored 10%, lower emissions, 25%, and shorter construction times, 25%, and this is exceptional. It was like that eight years ago. For governance, which writes the rules of the game, to change percentages is exceptional. Added to this was the experimental part we see in the TLA and in other buildings, which is also exceptional. Then there's another important part in the equation: the price per square metre, and being able to compare that with other government agencies. But this political vision, that doing it well is not good enough, we want to do it very well, on top of which we've made a climate emergency declaration and we're going to find the mechanisms, is both coherent and quite exceptional.

And finally, as for the joint architect and constructor competition, what the Council also did well was to fix the architect's fee so that it's not affected by the constructor's price cut. It was also a good to connect price bases. The experience of working jointly with a constructor from day one was very good, and this is important in the case of bold innovations. The formula of the competition up to the concept design should be tried with established building solutions like CLT, where the industrialization process is simple. We know that the traditional model is bad, because from minute one we're arguing with the contractor, making modifications and trying to get prices back up.So it's important to recognise how we got to this point, and the fact that the point where we are is exceptional. What we have to do now is speed it up.

What's the cost of innovation? Can we afford not to innovate in a context of emergency? You can't start a housing plan thinking you can only produce if you have 100% of the budget, that is absolutely basic. It's not a viable way to start a plan of work. The plan carried out in the last ten years has been produced with 50% Council capital, 40% partners and 10% other government agencies. When the IMHAB works with direct production, the land is free, the Council puts up 30% and the remaining 70% is financed.

In the gestating phase, the competition with a curricular phase is a barrier we've come up against several times; the joint curricular and ideas form, on the other hand, gives more teams access to public works. As for what social housing means, for us it's quality architecture, which is conditioned by the conditions of entry presented to the architects. Certain spaces are missing according to the type of housing, such as communal spaces, both in the case of cooperatives and social housing. It's also necessary to take into account the agents intervening in the tender phase, in the case of cooperative housing, that's groups of people, producers and engineering firms, and how they can be organized better. In the case of La Balma there was already an existing group of users; in the case of council housing, can the user be taken into account from the outset?

In the same way that the constructor has been included in the competition process, the user could be introduced,

as in the case of cooperatives, where it is very obvious. Well-drafted conditions of entry for a competition could produce greater richness in the project.

In this section on gestating, I introduce the figure of the producer as an intervening agent, a word that is difficult to mention in this house.

The property developer as the driving force,

as the prime intervening agent. Under this heading of developer or producer, I have five phases: a technical phase of drafting the project which then becomes the built work; a construction phase with the construction company; an economic phase: how much it costs; a financial phase: how it is paid, and a legal phase: what legal support is provided. The figure coordinating and directing these five phases is key, and it is the producer. The IMHAB is a housing producer; for the FZEC Agreement, an external producer was found, in this case foundations and cooperatives or a mixed company that carries out the whole process and is more agile than a public tender. It is important to emphasize this figure; it is chosen so that the process works in an integrated way, especially in the case of industrialization. As regards the next point, I've never understood how to draft a project without having a constructor lined up, because when I draw a line I need to know how much that line costs. I also need a financier by my side, because I need to know how I'm going to pay for that line, and legal support, because I simply cannot know all the existing rules. The phases are not sequential, they form a package, and even more so with industrialization. As for the financing, the model works because there are public resources. If you want to build quality social housing, two attributes that have been complete opposites for years, you need public money. In the case of foundations and cooperatives, this model is holding on thanks to subsidies –between 20 and 35% of the cost of the building. This has to be emphasized, and we have to continue to demand this of the Administration; if we want council housing, it is necessary to put up resources.

After the reflections about the overlap of quality architecture, quality housing, sustainability and the industrialization process on the course at the Sert School, and having taken part in several projects, we find it exciting to rethink competitions to involve industrialized architecture.

Competitions of this kind are an ecosystem of innovation per se,

it is a process that has nothing to do with other existing ones. Perhaps the implementation of this new way of doing things is expensive and creates anxiety due to the emergency, but once the system is created, production will be more efficient. There are lots of things to take into account in the competition phase: remuneration when passing a phase, the definition of project drafting periods... Remuneration must be sufficient to allow reflection. It could also include interaction with bodies like the Catalan Institute of Construction Technology in order to create a knowledge bank consultation space. The idea of the project that is first thought out and then built, a scheme anchored in the past, is also a concern. When working with industrial systems, there is no qualitative difference in the way of proceeding between a conventional project and an industrial one; today, everything is more or less industrial, it's a question of degree. A scheme where there is a concept design and then the constructor steps in can be valid, but it has to contemplate the industrial solution; the concept has to be flexible enough to absorb industrial solutions. For construction companies, there is also a learning process that allows new companies to emerge alongside those that are already recognized in the prefabrication sector.

All the points of the debate are inevitably interrelated. We are seeing that quality architecture, industrialization and project are inseparable parameters.

As regards the IMHAB, the HMB and the FZEC Agreement, and the idea that private bodies can potentially go faster, what is it that allows this? The IMHAB is a public body with stronger legal controls, but it is also a guarantee of more agents, more competition and more quality. In the case of private processes, can the same result be guaranteed in terms of final quality? Will all the architects who want to, be able to participate?

The empirical proof is that we delivered a production of 100 homes in 27 months as of the moment the site was tabled. Two months for a concept design, four months to process the license; while the license was being processed we drafted the technical design and the project was directly chosen based on a price for the iron, concrete and formwork for the structure, without knowing the kilos; 18 months of construction and three months for handover, which still seems madness to me. The architect was appointed by telephone, as were the engineers. With regard to quality, the overall process prioritized 100 families being able to live in a flat over putting the project out to tender to obtain a proposal that was surely better.

The agility is unquestionable; how to gauge quality is another matter.

The process of awarding a work at the IMHAB takes six months.

Today we're talking about industrialization, but retrofitting is the other big issue. When we get to the end of these municipal sites, we'll have to turn our attention completely to rehabilitation. I understand that the joint architect and constructor competition is much more agile, but I do think that it affects the quality. And, above all, you exclude lots of architects, because there is a natural tendency for a constructor that works well with a particular architect to keep coming back. An intermediate should be found, which could be the concept design. It might take a little longer, but it might be worth it to avoid excluding options.
The Architects' Association has already made an effort to link rubber-stamping and licenses, but there are still discrepancies. If they were unified, it would speed up the process.

Before, the architect was the client's point of reference; they chose the construction company and had the most responsibility. Now, these tasks are more diluted. Who's in charge?

The architect materializes what the producer thinks. It's the producer that provides housing for the users.

The architect is no longer in charge but they continue to have all the legal responsibilities.

The problem comes when the producer wants to be the architect and the builder wants to be the architect. The role of the architect has to be very clear.

HMB is a company that came into being as a result of a public tender, bringing together Greater Barcelona-AMB and Barcelona City Council, in which what was tendered was joint participation in a company with these two bodies. It was won by a company made up of Neinor Homes and Cevasa, NiCrent, which is a 50% partner; another 25% is AMB and the rest, the City Council. The aim of this company is to develop 4,500 homes for affordable rentals, a programme to be produced in the next six years, representing some 50 developments that are to begin in the next four years. This means you have to be able to produce where there is no room for exceptionality or singularity; otherwise, you have to turn this exceptionality and singularity into something systematic in order to guarantee quality and essential services, which is what we offer in our homes. As regards the tenders, an accreditation system is already in place to assess the curriculum and capacity of architecture professionals. For each production, three teams, already approved, will be asked to produce a preliminary project to evaluate who will be selected. This assessment will be based on architectural quality, surface performance and sustainability. We work on quantity, quality and also on price, not just on cost but on the price to be passed on to the tenant. Hereafter, it has to be made viable, built at the right price so it is financially sustainable. Even introducing industrialization so that it becomes routine.

If we want a more industrial form of construction that is more energy efficient and with a lower CO_2 footprint, we have to create an industry that is more powerful than at present, based on other materials, transformation and recycling.

If this more powerful industry is not created, it won't be possible to supply everything that needs to be done. It has to be created and promoted. For the moment, innovations will be singularities, since there is not yet a sufficient production chain in the sector to rely on these systems. When working with architects, we never tell them what to do so as not to interfere with their responsibility. We can make suggestions in the event of low performance, unsustainability, high energy consumption, excess emissions...

Everyone has to accept their responsibility. The architect has indefinite responsibility; we, as producers and owners, will always be responsible for the building from a qualitative, functional and economic viewpoint. In economic terms, rental housing is an activity with very tight margins and it has to be regulated; this is currently not the case. Subsidies are needed but so too are improvements in the tax regime. In fiscal terms, surface right contracts for rental housing, which is what many public administrations opt for, carry a huge penalty, much higher than for home buyers. We have to be able to correct and compensate this penalty by means of low management costs and efficiency; only in this way can we make it viable despite fiscal pressure.

You have to understand the complexity of producing housing in this country.

The problem of so many regulations and so little budget means that housing is not taken seriously.

The fact that housing is not part of the state's general budget is a basic problem. Countries around us are trying to address this with a renewable dynamic, continuously reproposing, whereas the process here has been stagnant for decades. On the part of producers, not architects, we should be talking about housing, not a product. To say "product" is to trivialize it. Housing is a very complex issue, the result of a process. A critical analysis of tender procedures has to be introduced –they used to be more agile– and it is important to remember that there are more possibilities of diversity than have been mentioned here; for example, tenders with mixed teams of architects that offer greater diversity. As for industrialization, we have to share experiences with other government agencies and procedures that have worked with it. It is not necessary to innovate in all projects; test projects can be designated.

Public production has to start this process of transformation and gain critical mass to make it viable.

Let's bring in typological innovation in competitions, with processes that start out with certain users, such as cooperatives, with industrialization. The impact of this typological innovation on the communal or collective spaces in the building that contribute surface area or complementary uses to housing.

The producer, in the case of cooperative partners, does not disappear, because we are the producers; we pay the cost of construction with our money and have a loan with an ethical bank that we pay back collectively over 30 years.

The architect acts as architect, but in the case of innovation there is a group of people who, together with the architect, decide how they want to live.

The partners are part of the process at the competition stage, defining the project, because we share a participatory process with engineers and architects. So there is also innovation in participatory processes and in the triangle between self-production and the cooperative, the team of architects and builders, and the public administration. Also related to innovation, as members of the solidarity economy, we try to promote the social market, and the teams and suppliers that form part of it. In the field of construction, it was difficult to find agents within this network, so we set up a cooperative construction company where the partners are on the governing board. We are therefore bringing innovation to the housing production process from the cooperative and solidarity economy sectors.

With typological innovation, we have to take into account two different types of projects: those that already have users, of the cooperative type, and others that do not. A known user will create the home of their dreams according to their possibilities.

For an unknown user, the administration should opt for trials, and offer citizens the possibility of discovering new ways of living.

When we see big developers advertising their products –and here it is a product– in the newspapers, they're absolutely antiquated and commonplace, when people have the capacity to live in other ways. We have to facilitate this possibility, and renting can be an important way to achieve this. What will it depend on? The duration of the contract. So how does HMB approach this contract?

Conceptually, HMB doesn't have a problem offering indefinite or long-term contracts because the price is regulated, but it prefers short-term rental contracts due to the uncertainty generated by legislation; what might happen in the future? For example, the rental sector disappeared in Spain in the 1980s due to regulatory changes. This insecurity is carried over to the tenant. It's just as important for the tenant as for the owner to have security; if the system is balanced, it will work. When we talk about the long term, we're not just talking about security; it's also the cost and the enormous fiscal burden of renting. Numerically, it is more profitable to buy than to rent, because of the fiscal burden; you end up paying more than 40% of the rental price.

Offering indefinite contracts would be a great thing, but the current legislative and fiscal situation is not favourable.

The duration of the contract is a very interesting instrument in social terms.

If the contract is short and the user lives there for a very limited time, they won't personalize their home; this is also an obstacle to reducing costs from the start, because certain things just don't get done. Longer-term rentals allow for personalization, which has to do with typological innovation: adapting the home according to changes in the family, creating a very basic kitchen so that it can be expanded or leaving a room unfinished opens up a range of possibilities for personalization.

As architects, when designing a building we have to think first about the parts. This is a very rigid procedure, and typological innovation involves rethinking the spaces in the house in terms of flexibility but also gender perspective. Some competitions still ask for an enclosed kitchen. All the spaces in a home's interior have to adapt to the way families grow and shrink, how they change over the course of 50-60 years. In the case of long-term contracts, taking possession of the home is key. This can be seen in cases like La Balma, where it is the users themselves who arrange the space thanks to an infrastructure of partitions. Typological innovation happens here, rethinking communal spaces.

In competitions there is not much demand for communal space, despite proof that it is a place for meeting and interrelation, and can even socially benefit the territory.

Creating communal space for a cooperative of 20 people who share the same philosophy is very different to community space in a building with 100 homes. The management of this space is very different, and it runs the risk of becoming a private reserve, with the deterrence and intimidation this can imply.

Managing rental also means managing the coexistence of people from different cultures and social levels without incidents, making communal spaces constructive spaces, and this can be more difficult than looking after the physical building.

If the future user is unknown, innovation involves finding a sufficiently flexible typological proposal, since administrative processes don't inform us about this. Spaces should be designed to be sufficiently flexible so that they can be adapted once you know who's going to be living there.

The problem of communal spaces is the management: if they're designed with a view to how they're going to be used, they'll work; otherwise, they won't.

A way to overcome the dichotomy between cooperatives and their buildings and the tenants of council stock is to

explore an intermediate situation: ask for volunteers among tenants who already live in a council building to take part in designing a future building and go and live there.

This has been explored in Bordeaux; there, the decisions made by the tenants in charge of the project were extreme in terms of aesthetics, quality, spatial layout, and so on, but it was the building they had chosen. They went on to form an association that is accountable to Bordeaux Council. Between the extreme position of prosumers (consumer-producers) and those who are on the register of claimants waiting for accommodation, there is this intermediate space. This strategy also means a rotation of council housing stock, as users move from one building to another.

For decades we've been working with an obvious idea; why are offices presented as empty infrastructures for the occupant to appropriate, whereas homes are offered fully finished?

A good design is better than something unfinished. The next user has limited options, and, besides, these homes are rotational. The private rental market asks for well-defined homes. We architects are supposed to know better. The focus should be on the quality of the project.

There is no council housing policy because we don't believe in it. A housing policy requires 12,000 million euros for 20 years in a row; the usual figure is between 300 and 500 million euros from the general state budget. This year, the Ministry is happy with 2,000 million, which is six times less than we need. Spain doesn't build housing because it doesn't want to; the exceptions are Catalonia, the Basque Country, Navarre and Valencia. Apart from the money, there is an issue of incompetence when it comes to managing rental housing over 175 years.

In the case of Cirerers, the tender was very helpful in producing a different kind of project,

a cooperative on a municipal plot of land in transfer of use, where the process helped to innovate in typology.

It opted for a community life project and energy efficiency, and for all the intervening agents to belong to the solidarity economy, thereby creating a zero speculation project. This provides guarantees, since the users look after their way of life and what they need. This whole process led to a series of decisions that wouldn't be possible in another procedure: changing the number of homes from 27 to 32, moving homes from one floor to another to design the communal spaces, construction solutions, communal facilities, prioritizing a wooden structure, solar protection design, assessing the building's life cycle –a whole series of choices and decisions that at no point diminished its energy efficiency.

In our experience of social housing in the public and private sector, where users have limited resources, we see that they appreciate homes that are as finished as possible. As architects, we have a fixed image of the desire for flexibility, when the user's expectation is different. In the case of Fabra, where the developer is IMHAB, we were surprised that the kitchen was the typological part that worked very well. Before, the kitchen was a functional segregated space, just for cooking; now it's the most social space in the house, and is positioned in the centre of the transitional space between the living and dining rooms. The fact that it is an open kitchen makes it a participatory space. Architects must design and define well; we get it right because we check more than users going to IKEA. We talk about non-hierarchical bedrooms; is it important that homes have two or three or one bedroom? Emergency housing, subsidized housing... what does our society really need? Then these homes are so small that communal space, which in our field we have little experience in managing, is important. In the case of cooperatives, what's the formula for the success of these spaces? Reclaiming the rooftops for common use, because this is the space in the building with the most value, and the homes are very small. People don't live with the minimum, emotionally we need more space, and in family homes of 40 or 50 m^2, the communal space is an essential complement if it is well managed. How do I see flexibility in a building? I see it in terms of structure. With housing, today we have a model, a size, but it can change, just like the use of the building can change. So we're not only working with buildings where the floors can be open-plan, we're even working with double-height spaces that combine mixed structures that are easy to disassemble or convert the building in the future. The long-term depreciation of the building has to be considered, especially if it is public. Finally, some good news within Spain: Catalan housing architecture has swept the board. Social housing prizes have been awarded in Catalonia, and most of them to developments produced by the public administration. The question is how to manage community spaces, because we don't have much experience in renting; in a cooperative it's easier. In the case of small homes, it's very important for the communal supplement to work. How is this space covered by rental contracts?

With the new habitability decree of December 2020, this communal space can be incorporated as a supplement within the useful surface area of the home.

But the question is, how will it be managed? It doesn't define that.

This would be typological innovation; moving part of the living programme outside the strictly private space frees it up a lot.

In 1972, doctoral theses were already looking to innovate. With the Frégoli building, 50 years ago we formed a cooperative of friends and relatives who bought a part. We found the site and built homes of 60 m^2 but you got to use 80. We managed this by building double heights; instead of ceiling heights of 2.70, we made them 4.20, gaining this extra percentage. A theatre was built on the ground floor on an initiative of the cooperative members. The good thing about these homes was that you knew the other owners before you went to live there. The structure meant that it was possible to make improvements and adapt the spaces to each user. It was a time of transition in regulations; by that, I mean that

typological innovation was linked to changes in regulations.

French legislation already stipulates sites for experimentation. The Administration assigns the city specific sites on which to experiment where regulations are not applied, they are tested.

The experimentation that we can allow ourselves is to build one or two bedrooms instead of two or three, and incorporate this space into the living room. Later, if the user wants to compartmentalize it, they can do so, because the layout of the home is prepared. But the reality is that almost no one has asked to create this extra room. Conclusion? More common space rather than more rooms. As outdoor spaces, we incorporate large terraces, but we haven't experimented much with the rooftop. As for the management of common spaces, we have a caretaker. Without a caretaker, common spaces in a rental development would be a major source of conflict. Maintenance: throughout the 50, 75 or 100 years of a home's life, we have to do maintenance, conservation, renovations, retrofitting, and we have to spend a lot of money.

On average, after 75 years, 140% of the initial cost of its construction has to be invested in a home.

Constant investment is needed, not just to maintain it but also to improve and update it, otherwise this asset is lost. This 140% is invested in retrofitting when there is rotation, in renewing installations, envelope and facings –that is, improving the building, not just conserving it.

In Spain, sheltered housing is not yet a permanent classification. In many regions, housing becomes free market after a few years. What has been achieved here –not selling public land or assets– is not yet the case in other places; land and homes are still being sold. Another reflection: expenditure is calculated by built square metres, whereas rental income is based on usable square metres.

The useful/buildable ratio is therefore basic; it has to be between 0.75 and 0.80 at least, and this penalizes community areas if they cannot be included as part of the home.

As regards management, the cost of managing housing is critical: the simpler the management, the better it adapts to existing models unless lines are established to subsidize a more social management of these homes, as in the case of Hàbitat3. These lines will have to be developed.

At TLA Glòries, our experience with prefabrication was quite positive. It was based on a concept design drafted by another team. We produced the technical design in collaboration with a constructor, which made construction very precise in terms of costs and deadlines, which surprised us compared to other developments. The technical design with the constructor took four or five months, and the constructor assembled all the containers in the factory and transported them to the site. Mounting and assembly of the containers took about eight months; they came with all fittings and finishes.

We're talking about 18 months to assembly 42 dwellings.

The deadlines could have been improved if factory work on the containers and site work had been overlapped. As for whether or not regulations help to innovate, in this case, the fact of not having to comply with habitability allowed us to work with the widths of the containers. The surface area of the dwelling is small, but the walkway leading to the courtyard at the centre of the street block offers a place to sit and socialize. This courtyard has good orientation and also provides this social function, since it incorporates an urban allotment, and the water cycle highlights the sustainable aspect. In terms of the building's life cycle, this system allows the homes to be moved to another location.

This corresponds to a new kind of typological innovation: if it is not covered by the habitability decree, a new figure of accommodation is created.

The subject of communal spaces calls for a publication of its own. I'm a teacher who has devoted many years to the subject of housing, and this academic year it just so happens that we ran a course called "how to share".

I prefer the word share to communal.

I think more attention should be paid to it in the programme, in terms of intention, from how a laundry or an entrance space is shared with a neighbour to how an undefined space is shared by 200 people. We need to work on scale and use, since not defining them is a source of problems. Sharing also means simplifying, reducing costs, improving socially. Sharing is a way of life.

In the case of Quatre Camins, shared spaces were already incorporated. As housing for the elderly, the user profile was known, and a company was awarded the management. Here, there's a management team of director, caretaker and social workers. Once the users are known and their needs detected, a use is assigned to the communal spaces. These same spaces, for other users of the same profile, could have another use, which is why it is important to know who the end user is.

In this respect, the success of our communal spaces in the cooperative depends on the self-management of some spaces that are already decided: shared washing machines, an eco-work room, a multipurpose room with kitchen. This cannot be extrapolated to the models being discussed. But if we have a maintenance firm for the centralized installations, a firm for lift maintenance,

why not incorporate a support team to help manage these communal spaces

not just for the elderly, but for all other housing productions? Why do we have these teams for technical aspects and not for more social and human issues?

Subsidized housing is a window of opportunity to introduce all these good practices that come from cooperatives,

from shared management to the option of participating in the design. This participation could perhaps involve not direct users but groups and associations of the collective for whom the development is intended. Even leave a percentage of the building out of the construction company's tender –principally these shared spaces– to allocate them to assisted construction workshops, actions similar to those carried out by Arquitectes de Capçalera or the example of Bordeaux. Barcelona Council has already carried out participatory processes, as in the case of Trinitat and Bon Pastor.

How long does this participation, which ultimately means a degree of personalization, last? To put it another way,

the architecture has to serve more people than those intended at the time of construction.

It has to be quite neutral so that it can be appropriated by more people. Extreme personalization is an added rigidity when we are talking about creating possibilities. More than personalizing, we need to talk about capacity for personalization.

And capacity for volume.

We need models that can be scaled and generate volume,

developments of 100 homes. The sectoral housing plan says that 300,000 homes have to be built in Catalonia in 20 years, two-thirds of them social or affordable.

Flexibility is the way to achieve personalization,

modular homes that allow various functions, like La Balma, where the structure allows for growth or decrease as needed. The three resulting sizes depend on whether or not an annexe is added. The new decree allows these community satellite spaces to be incorporated into housing.

Poem
In 50 years, how much tax will a home have paid, depending on its modality?
If you buy a home, you'll pay a total of 307 €/m^2.
If you rent a home from a private owner of the land, you'll pay €957/m^2, more than triple what you pay if you buy the home
If you rent a dwelling on a surface right contract, you'll pay 2,000 €/m^2 after 50 years, multiplying by three, six or eight times the fiscal cost of accessing housing
Yet our budget is not even 10% of what neighbouring countries invest in housing
As long as this is the case, we have a problem that is difficult to solve.

The COAC ensures good architecture and acts as a bridge to continue with the work we do.

SESSION 2

Differences compared to yesterday's session: strategies working with pre-existences, buildings, dwellings and users; support for people after adjudication; fieldwork identifies the need to support non-cohesive communities and rehousing.

Rehousing is a phase that is not involved in most cases of occupied housing rehabilitation policy, but in the case of the URA it is fundamental: we rehouse occupants to be able to rehabilitate, which adds another degree of complexity.

When talking about projects that address existing buildings, there are three main types, with different value chains and stakeholders. First, the IMHAB buys buildings and rehabilitates them for rent. IMHAB is in charge of the rehabilitation project, and the end user will be a council housing stock tenant, as well as subrogating existing rental contracts. Second, there are various programmes to find private housing for temporary public rental that often has to be rehabilitated, for which we work with internal and external teams. Rehabilitation is commissioned by the owner of the housing in the case of exchange or Hàbitat3 in the case of transfers. Third, a policy to promote urban rehabilitation and regeneration, where work is done exclusively on private stock with different programmes: non-profit investments intended for rehabilitation with some exceptions, where the community pays for building work and the suppliers are the industrial professionals. The form that affects most people in the city and the one with the most economic weight, 11,000-12,000 dwellings subsidized a year, it is the most private process: private owner and private contracting in receipt of a subsidy or not.

The constructors' guild carries out the three processes presented, some in the form of tenders and others in the form of an auction, which is what I have an issue with. When you apply for public tenders, you play by the rules of the game, but when you play in the private world, to choose a quote for rehabilitation for a community of owners, you're dealing with something very similar to an auction, given that all that really counts is the final price. Here, as a constructor, I'd like to point out the great error that appears when this happens. As constructors, we also face another difficulty, the user.

Eviction for relocation is not straightforward,

so we end up doing rehabilitation work with the user in occupation. Rehabilitation becomes complex when the user is living in the home, because we have to coordinate the circular nature of this work. In 2020 a royal decree was issued after the emergency shutdown decree. When we were once again given permission to work in communities, the word sectorization appeared. Lots of my colleagues wondered what sectorization meant in rehabilitation; it meant separating us from the occupants of a building. Rehabilitation has three protagonists: the building, the project and the user. Another thing about these programmes is the fact that there is a great demand in the case of subsidized users. In the case of public tenders for building renovation, banks should specify the correction coefficients associated with there being users in the buildings. This coefficient ensures that the price is correct and fair, and that the final quality is appropriate.

In the case of HCE, the Administration plays the role of producer and developer, but not in construction or the tender, which are carried out in the private realm.

The Administration is actively involved as a support and a driving force, as the private sector often doesn't take the initiative, and the relationship between private individuals, community and professionals can be complex in private contracting models. The Administration supports but does not execute.

In HCE it is technically the communities that contract, though functionally it is more like the relation between a residents' community with a URA than a residents' community that works with the guild and applies for a grant, since there is the legal advice agreement, the recognition of the residents' community, you're working in situ, and subsidies may be as much as 100%. As regards project quality, when 100% is subsidized you can control the result even if the contracting is done by the community, as support allows for this power relationship.

The main priority of rehabilitation in an owners' community is its needs: accessibility, structural pathology and leaks, rather than quality and energy efficiency as a separate area.

A grant announcement outlines a series of criteria, but it is not as robust a document as a public tender. It is the announcement that specifies the work to be done, and this is the same for any private individual, whether or not they are supported by the teams. Grants range from 35% to 100%. There are small properties where each user is in a particular situation, with the possibility of receiving 100% financing of work, via community subsidy and via private subsidy.

If budgets were bigger, would more properties be addressed as HCE? Communities would apply for these grants because they represent an economically relevant sum, and communities don't have many other options. In the case of communities that are not addressed as HCE, if the grant is applicable to the project for which they receive it, perfect; if the grant isn't applicable, it leads to discussion as to whether the grant can be made to fit or whether the community's own means should be used. This disjunction is almost never found in HCE, and in URA even less so. In communities that don't apply for grants, you don't see it; in HCE and URA, however, the quality of the rehabilitation work is apparent.

As a foundation, at Hàbitat3 we work on different projects: the empty flats programme, which consists of mobilizing empty private stock for temporary social housing, where people referred from the Emergency Desk can live; the tender for works direction for a housing interior design project; the direct rehabilitation of the Casa Bloc home, and the purchase of apartments with their respective retrofitting. The agent is important; when we find empty apartments, the position of the owner is relevant, because we have to reach an agreement, and it's a commercial agreement; we have to rehabilitate to achieve what we consider acceptable standards, and, ultimately, we have to start and end with certain sums of money, because we are pressured by the amount we have to invest. In the case of retrofitting, the sums are specified by the tender, but the agents, in this case, are the people living in the homes; they are the ones affected, they have a registry entry and, in the end, they have to return the money. The agent is important, whether they are a tenant or an owner; even if they are a tenant and therefore not affected by the economic aspect, they are demanding. This is the case of the Casa Bloc development: what we want to do is what we can do –it depends on economic viability, which, in rehabilitation, is less viable than in new construction. We are seeing this in a building transfer under the Foundations and Zero Equity Cooperatives Agreement, where the figures are very complicated.

In the case of acquisitions, investment in long-term maintenance has to be taken into account. Yesterday someone said that it could reach 140% of the initial investment, though this does seem a lot.

In the case of rehabilitation, unless it is complete, when we go into a building the cost is very high, because it is not the best housing in the city and it has gone for years without any kind of rehabilitation. Plus we work in buildings where we intervene in just one dwelling, and lots of these buildings have no maintenance whatsoever. It's like paying a toll;

if rehabilitation is piecemeal, maintenance is much more expensive.

We calculate 500-600 €/year per dwelling; you just can't compare complete and isolated rehabilitation.

Would it be possible to combine the vulnerable programme with URA or HCE programmes, and address interiors like vulnerable homes, and communal areas like HCE and URA?

In URA and HCE, work is done on communal elements, but URA also goes inside homes for good practice; work is being done in practically all the bathrooms due to the presence of cement pathologies and damaged installations.

HCE funding is exclusively for communal elements and it doesn't address home interiors, but we do have an overview of certain dwellings with pathologies because we create a census of the homes we have entered to repair the structure. Having detected them, we can direct users to grants for vulnerable areas or to the social rental exchange in the case of empty flats, where they can access subsidized repair work and adaptation. Now, with the Next Generation fund, we are seeing a line of subsidies that integrates communal elements and energy efficiency of interiors. This is a step forward.

As architects, we shouldn't lose sight of the social component. Unless we work with the inhabitants, we're going nowhere. We're dealing with inhabited buildings, very run-down buildings with no maintenance, with a group of people who are not easy, starting with the complexity that exists within the communities. Apart from that, we have to encourage the communities to actually do rehabilitation work.

As architects, we focus a lot on the physical rather than the social side, and in the URA and HCE programmes it is vital to get the community excited and involved, to bring it together.

Ultimately, in HCE the producer is the community. In URA, it is the Administration that carries out the work. In the case of home interiors, we find that it's necessary to give a value to the space in which they live. Until now, they occupied a space without giving it any more value than the fact that they weren't sleeping outdoors. When you carry out a major renovation of the building, you're valuing the space in which they are living. Although we only work on the communal elements, the intervention is so intensive that the occupants get excited and want the interiors of the homes to have a value, they want to rehabilitate their home. If there is a rehabilitation policy, we explain how they have to go about it. The fact that these vulnerable people make an extra effort to update their homes –change the kitchen, rewire the place– is a complete change of attitude and means added value. This is a variable that we cannot lose sight of. In the gestating phase, proactivity in the rehabilitation of occupied housing is very important. In the neighbourhoods where we're working, the work that needs doing has to be very serious for the residents to tackle it themselves. They sometimes have structural problems and live with a prop in the middle of their home; it's not just that they can't do anything about it, they don't even question it. The fact that the Administration tries to get them involved, and even takes the step to do it, is a big thing.

Of all the strategies you're carrying out, which one allows you to control the final quality? And what do we mean by quality in these cases? How do we define quality in these types of interventions? Because including the user, treating them well in the process and ensuring that they have suitable support, is quality in itself, over and above whether the plastering is sound. In these strategies, the decision to include the user is a defining parameter of quality.

We're architects who offer solutions in the field of housing, above all in the Raval district. We work with communities who are trying to access the HCE programme, but we're also developing another programme called Punt Raval, which we've been working on since 2017. On the subject of home interiors, there are two basic aspects covered in this book that we find when working with families with a high degree of vulnerability: one is including the time factor of the intervention and the other is the action of living. Two fundamental issues that bring quality to the process yet are not normally taken into account in the architecture processes. We find that many of the inhabited buildings are occupied by tenants who live there while work is being carried out. They are people who normally have no idea what's going on or how long it's going to take, and they live in totally unsanitary conditions. The fact that the outside of the property is rehabilitated is of course a step forward, but with this programme, we offer solutions not for the building but for the person. Architecture is a tool to provide quality and offer quick solutions for these people, to give them some hope. In the end, apathy and disenchantment set in, and they end up hating the walls that surround them. We offer low-cost, quick-to-implement levers, alongside what the Administration does, as a fast response to problems of healthy living conditions, while realising that we cannot solve all the problems they have in their homes. Architecture is also a tool to negotiate with owners, since they have the responsibility of maintaining private housing stock. Along with the HCE and URA programmes, the pedagogy of maintenance and rehabilitation as a responsibility should be promoted. We often talk to owners who say "let the City Council come and do it for me". With this project, with the help of the Architects' Association in the form of grants for cooperation, we work with these people. As for

quality, our work consists in making people feel good about the place they're living

and feel that they've got support.

Keeping a control of quality is very complex, and now, with the Next Generation European funds, it will be even more so. And then the owners often forget that they are the ones responsible.

Is there a difference between owner occupiers and owner landlords?

Absolutely; sometimes it's even insulting, especially in the Raval; you go into someone's home and you think: this person shouldn't be living here.

Is there a difference in maintenance between a landlord who lets a home and a landlord who lets business or office premises?

Users who rent premises are more demanding because their business depends on it. In the case of a person who rents their home, the power relationship is very different; it's not that easy to move to another one. At the same time, the tenant is afraid to ask the owner to do maintenance work in case the rent goes up; they're at risk of exclusion. Sometimes their safety is even endangered. This is abuse, and there's no one to protect them. The only solution is to go to court, and they won't do that, apart from any other reason because it costs money. Instruments like building inspections and the certificate of habitability should control this situation.

In the case of grants for common elements, an initial report is drafted by building specialists and a final report by the municipal technician, stating whether it has been carried out correctly and the grant can be given. If the work is not carried out according to the initial report, there will be a reduction in the subsidy. This can be controlled by our infrastructure. In the case of Next Generation, apart from having a major goal and having to reach many more homes, we only have the same human resources, and we won't be able to write these reports. The role of external technicians will be very important: building engineers, architects and property managers. The quality we're talking about begins at minute one, when a citizen decides to apply for these grants. It depends on the applicant being well informed and aware of both the project and the tenants' application. These applications normally respond to accessibility and structural pathology, which in principle is not included in Next Generation, but now is the time to act by unifying interventions.

HCE are properties that were detected by means of a study carried out by the UPC. This study provides indicators that these estates probably have the kind of profile we're looking for. We almost certainly find that the obligation to maintain the property has not been met, for multiple reasons: economic, cultural, etc. The idea is to introduce a culture of maintenance so that in 15 years the Council won't have to go back to it. After rehabilitation, what we do is organize a more pedagogical part for the owner community, addressing aspects of administration, management, dealing with conflict, and even building maintenance. Another thing is that before, in the world of rehabilitation, there were actors who were at the centre, while the people really involved, the users, were not considered.

It is important to put people at the centre.

Another two ideas: someone commented that the call for subsidies for common elements and HCE were guided by the same logic, but the degree of control is not exactly the same. HCE is an intervention that has to be carried out in the framework of a tender that outlines certain technical aspects, specified by the license and the Architects' Association, but the control is not the same as if it were a public tender, like URAs. There is a control at the start, then a monthly control, as the advance payment system accompanies the progress of work, with each certification checked according to the work carried out, and then the final control with the corresponding final work report. The last thing is the issue of tenants; as a public administration one of the tools we have in the framework of the call are clauses that we introduced to ensure that owners who wish to receive the community part of the subsidy adapt the rental price and the duration of the contract. This has helped to regularize and formalize a number of informal and illegal rentals, and increase the duration of the contract to three and even five years.

With regard to quality control, in the case of URAs we have ways of controlling whether or not certain quality levels are met. As producer, we do set high levels; the physical project and the social part have to be differentiated. If the social side is not promoted, you're going nowhere. As for the architectural side, as promoters of the projects, who commission the projects and monitor them, we ensure a basic quality that is, ultimately, very acceptable. There's another point to add to the debate: the question of cost. We come across buildings that, due to a lack of maintenance, for many and varied reasons, are in a very, very bad state of repair; to bring them up to date –not just carry out a decent rehabilitation but to really comply with present-day regulations– we'd be talking about a rate of investment per home of 60,000 euros. If we think about the buildings we have and the population that cannot meet this expense, 60,000 euros per home is huge, but this really is what they need to be brought up to date. We have façades in a dreadful state, structural problems, damp, and on top of that there're the issues of accessibility and the energy vector, which is not cheap. Complying with today's regulations, principally the

Building Code, calls for work on the envelope that eats up 20-30% of the budget. These are investments that have to be brought up. Unless the Administration makes a huge effort, which it is already doing, the private sector and vulnerable areas simply can't meet this level of expenditure. In keeping with quality, quality is expensive. We are now in the phase of optimizing those 60,000 euros, reducing investment without losing quality, but in the end we're talking about very significant amounts. We've tried to combine one-off subsidies with financing, part of these subsidies has to be paid back over a period of time. The Council tries to achieve this kind of loan, because we think that if something is given away, people don't appreciate its worth. When you go along and do up a building where there has been a flagrant lack of maintenance, if you pay for 100% of rehabilitation work, the occupants just aren't aware of the economic sum you're paying, whether it's 10 or 1,000, it's all the same. This is why, from the outset, we say that citizens should always pay something, in the form of registration or payment on the home, or directly in the form of a loan to be paid back in instalments, because otherwise they're not aware of the work that's being done.

This ties in with what we were saying about people's demands, because there's no awareness of the costs involved.

At the construction phase, we're trying to ensure that there's no interaction between occupants and constructor; the Mupi is the delegated owner, and the works management dialogues with us. We told them: we'll set up a site monitoring committee, but please, let the constructors work, otherwise the residents will pile on the pressure. We're just starting work on the first project and in a year we'll be able to evaluate it, but initially our intention is this: to provide a firewall. Although the occupants are in their homes, and we'll relocate them when we have to work on the structure and return them when work is not yet complete, it will be us and the works management that ensure that work is carried out correctly.

When you say 60,000 euros per home, do you mean complete rehabilitation of the building?

Yes, but excluding all the previous tasks such as drafting the project, licenses, if any, the suitability report since in this case we don't pay taxes, relocation and furniture removal, surveillance, fitting out the relocation apartments... all this is separate and is paid by the Administration. As for actual construction work, our intervention includes structural reinforcement to address the buildings' cement pathologies, replacement of all the downspouts, the communal part of the water and electricity network, the entire thermal envelope including façades and roofs, replacement of all the windows, waterproofing and installation of a lift. All this produces that figure of 60,000 per home.

In the case of the Casa Bloc home, the scope of our work begins with the competition. Our profile is much more technical, and we're not familiar with all these procedures. But as regards the procedure that does affect us and the mechanisms to guarantee the quality of the project, the competition had two categories: spatial quality and contextualization. Both have a more or less objective part based on regulations, though it is interpretive. In this case Catalonia is quite exemplary, because it has developed mechanisms to assess these categories that are quite common in the profession and are reflected in the bidding process. This is a really key point in the overall process:

depending on how the project is tendered, one kind of production or another will be generated for both the design and the construction processes, and then for maintenance of the building.

As regards the tendering process, whether it is carried out jointly with a construction company or otherwise, for me the kind of work you achieve is crucial. In my case, the experience was bad.

Yesterday we were talking about processes that start out jointly with a construction company, specifically the industrialization tenders, but architects said it might be more appropriate to have a good concept design and then have the construction company come in at the technical phase, rather than at the end –for the concept design to be the architect's proposal, and the constructor not to be as involved at this point.

If project and construction are tendered and scored by quantity, there's a part that corresponds to the construction company, in terms of execution and money. The economic part is important, but it's impossible to judge if the cheapest project is the best, because the construction company makes an offer based on a preliminary project, without surveying; it gives an approximate rate. And then the task of redoing the project 20 times over at the technical design stage to make it fit eats up the architect's fees that were established right at the start.

Really, the problem is not so much construction company versus architect as how the work is tendered, whether it's public or private. A private tender can be at least as demanding as a public one.

Working as you said, first on the concept design and then jointly with a constructor, solves almost all future problems.

In the end, it's a joint task; the problem is how the price is decided. It's the result of the idea of what the architect wants to do and the idea that the contractor has, economically, of the architect's idea; it's almost witchcraft. In a project, we have to imagine what the designer imagined; then we have to imagine it in place, how much it costs, and pay for it. The contractor is not really to blame; the contractor is the paid victim of the situation, because if the project has to be improved by the contractor's work, we've got it wrong, and if the contractor has to improve their own economy at the expense of the project, we've also got it wrong. As regards the cost and maintenance we've been talking about, work shouldn't be given away nor people subsidized so much: let's not penalize those who do well, let's not penalize those who maintain their buildings, let's not reward those who don't maintain their buildings. From the outside, subsidies can seem like prizes for people who abandon their building. I constantly do maintenance on my building, and have never received a subsidy. It's impossible, because I comply with everything that's required of me. As regards maintenance and its cost, how it's paid for, I explain it to communities like this: you don't have to ask for financing to pay for something today, you should have paid for it yesterday and you didn't; you didn't get any money and you didn't pay any. As for maintenance of Hce, I'd recommend going to organizations that already do it. Barcelona Council and the Generalitat Catalan Government have spaces in the city where intensive rehabilitation has been carried out; let's see if the maintenance was done. Someone said that the ideal is not to go back to a building to do rehabilitation work, but we will, because people are used to it: if they do rehabilitation work, they'll be back to do it again.

The two interventions, Hce and Ura, are valid for the public administration, and both have their pros and cons. In the case of Hce, they're doing rehabilitation work; this is a differential fact and we don't know whether, in 15 years, it'll have had the desired effect.

The final building file is very important in these cases of rehabilitation. After rehabilitation work, this file outlines maintenance that needs to be carried out, so that people know how often the railings have to be painted, claddings checked, and drains and installations inspected. As for quality, in the case of HCE, rental exchange and vulnerable homes, when there is public investment it's monitored, but in the private sector, quality, which should be the responsibility of specialists, which the client doesn't pay for because they take it for granted, is watered down.

We do a lot of pedagogy with regard to the building file, not as a boring document that ends up in the property manager's drawer, but something that is really accessible to the community. It should be like a mobile app that all the residents are familiar with. In terms of pedagogy, the thing is that

with the rotating population that we have today, teaching about maintenance at community level is not as effective as doing it at social level.

In terms of subsidies, it's great that the Council is taking advantage of grants to communities to make improvements to the city, not just maintenance and conservation, but also energy improvements, issues that might not interest owners as much, but that are very important at city level. In the case of vulnerable owners who live in their own homes, if they have other flats, the rent of one flat could be used to rehabilitate another.

The scale factor linked to the economic issue; retrofitting a single flat, doing microsurgery, has a different impact to the comprehensive retrofitting of a building or even a neighbourhood. Is this scale factor important in economic and structural terms?

The tender and the economics are dependent on this level; retrofitting a 10-dwelling building is not the same as a 300-home community; neither the implementation nor the means are the same. Everything changes, and this is what I was complaining about, the tariffs and these coefficients.

Could Hàbitat3 make a bid for a batch of 20?

Firstly, flats turn up as and when they turn up; if 50 came in every month –and that's a lot– it would be an option. Secondly, when they do turn up, you're not ready. For example, we've made purchases from other municipalities, bought 10-15 at once, and then we weren't ready for the bid; it's the scale. In our case, since acquisition is small-scale, retrofitting is small-scale. It involves a very high cost and is very inefficient. Yes, there is a standard retrofit, but in the end you have to adapt to each case. The other option would be for a few of us who do retrofitting to get together and make a joint bid. In the public-private sphere it would be very complicated, but in the third sector we could consider it. Retrofitting a building, like when we rehabilitated Casa Bloc, is different; it's a different scale and the company is also different. The company we work with is an insertion company that works at this small scale; if four homes turn up it's overwhelmed.

It's also good to have different types of construction companies: small, medium and large.

With the segregation into different types of company, the Council has experienced this situation with us. When we need to apply to the rental exchange, we look for a certain type of company; with HCE, we go for another type, and some firms are in them all and for some tenders we all apply. We have our labels because everyone knows where they're most comfortable. If a company doesn't work in a given area, it moves away.

It's natural selection; each firm knows what it can handle. At this scale, companies localize, they work on the same neighbourhoods and the same districts.

Here we should point out that the city of Barcelona has a stigma: anyone can work there, but Barcelona natives can't work anywhere. A contractor from the city of Barcelona goes to Terrassa and they get thrown out; a contractor from Terrassa comes to Barcelona and is camouflaged, submerged in this cosmopolitan city.

The issue of the scale of work is really important. The price corrector of the Construction Data Base has a minimum scale of 0.4 million. This is larger than the productions we're talking about. Should there be a very small scale?

We're talking to the Catalan Institute of Construction Technology to get these prices, and we're all working with them to make the prices closer to the reality of the scales. As of 400,000, perhaps there aren't so many projects.

In our case, all the works except Casa Bloc are under 400,000 euros, most are 30,000 and less. Not having this price regulation is a shortcoming.

When you come down to a certain level, the tender no longer has a given price; you end up setting the prices yourself.

We all propose the lower prices and yields ourselves, based on yield studies, not from a book.

In projects like URAS, where the interventions are ultimately a catalogue of proposals for the envelope and structure, wouldn't it make sense to have regulated prices?

Barcelona Provincial Council and Barcelona Council created price lists to be able to do very low-cost work on flats, such as changing toilets, some kitchens, very specific things. The budgets were very tight, but they were more flexible, so there was always a price of implementation or site visits that compensated. But it wasn't very successful.

With these prices, which we applied to vulnerable interiors, apart from the price, which is pared right down, other factors come into play in the tender: volume and timing. The way vulnerable interiors began, it's impossible to break even, but it's a different situation now if you tender a batch of 50 homes to be carried out in a year with set terms of payment.

In our case at Hàbitat3, we've got a price list that is updated, though unexpected expenses always crop up. The function of this price list is to try to ensure that there's no competition between the insertion companies, that it's a fair price, but there's always the question as to whether these prices are fair or not. Having a price list works well for us, because when acquiring flats, negotiating their purchase, we have to have an idea of the costs, because it's a lot of money. Then if you have a relationship with companies where there isn't this competition, the companies are also more flexible and you can create greater continuity. In a public tender, where everything is much more regulated, there's not much room to negotiate this payoff between present and future work.

There is no payoff in public tenders.

An important issue to consider is typological and technological innovation, or energy efficiency in the case of Next Generation. We might carry out an inspection and see that addressing just health and liveability problems eats up the budget; how can we address energy efficiency when the most basic needs are not covered?

Next Generation "covers" two fronts: interiors and communal elements. For interiors, it's 3,000 euros, but the other part can go up to 18,000 or 21,000 with a margin of 80%. Then there's the technical and technological requirement of reducing emissions; it seems quite complex to comply with these requirements. I don't think it'll have too much impact on the most vulnerable groups. We participate with other foundations in what we call express rehabilitation, with limited funds. We do some improvement work but there's no major impact on energy.

In the case of the most vulnerable people, these energy improvements have two aspects: technical comfort and energy costs.

Non-fossil energy is also a requirement.

It seems that habitability and health will get left behind. There are grants for rehabilitation that used to be directed at maintenance, but now, unless a project incorporates energy improvement issues, it's overlooked. What are we to do? If you start out from a baseline of moderately decent conditions, it makes sense to incorporate energy improvement measures, but if you start out from a situation of poor housing, what sense does it make? There's already a law on the right to housing. The question is, why isn't it applied more, and why is substandard housing not corrected by existing legislation?

Improvement projects on buildings with few homes in vulnerable neighbourhoods, like the one we did in Foradada, basically involve energy improvement. In these types of homes, innovation in energy improvement of the envelope, with the money available, ends up being either an ETICS or filling air cavities in the case of an exposed construction with two facings. There's little else you can do, because you have to change the roof, then the beams have concrete pathologies... You can make the roof more energy efficient, but then you don't go inside the homes to change the heating and cooling system. So what sort of technological innovation can you introduce? If you do all this, you're doing a lot in these buildings. You come across cases of what were initially healthy cross-ventilated homes that are no longer healthy because the owners have invaded the exterior spaces and turned them into interiors. What are we to do? How do we incorporate these interior spaces that are no longer aired? We go inside the homes, repair the structure and, in this case, end up doing what we talked about before, retrofitting the bathrooms, which tend to create the microclimate that produces concrete pathologies in the beams. In one tender, we went in to carry out building inspections in a part of the Besòs district. The buildings are fine, they're cross-ventilated, but the users didn't air them, despite the fact that it was very straightforward, because the windows are big. The homes are healthy in themselves, but they cease to be healthy because the people who live there are not used to airing them.

All this has to do with maintenance. In the case of Hàbitat3, the homes are remodelled, the users come in and, three years later, when it's time to rotate, we find flats full of mould caused by condensation. The homes have not been adequately aired, despite being cross-ventilating. In this case, because there is social monitoring, users are advised to ventilate for so many minutes, so many times a day.

I'm surprised by this debate that's arisen about innovation, technology and efficiency when we're talking about social housing, and what we're assessing is liveability. In new builds, yes, you may be able to assess the new technologies implemented, but in all the programmes we're working on, existing housing stock is poorly maintained and owners who do rehabilitation work do the bare minimum. In the rental exchange we have a grant of 20,000 euros per home, but in many cases that's not enough, and the owner doesn't want to spend anything. In the case of transferred flats we can put rehabilitation expenses down against the fee we pay the owner. But in the end, the owner pays for it, and the lower the fee, the better.

There's no culture of investment in housing or maintenance,

at least in the social housing we get to work on in these programmes. So talking about technological innovation is a bit like science fiction.

So, we're saying that the new build has a shelf life because one day there'll be no more land; retrofitting, meanwhile, goes much further, the entire city has to be retrofitted. If we can't come to retrofitting with these funds and this new premise of energy efficiency, we have a problem.

Conceptually, Next Generation is a good idea; we want to achieve energy efficiency in existing homes and we have a subsidy policy, but we need to come at it in a different way: we're dealing with vulnerable neighbourhoods. Policies to exclusively insulate the building envelope according to specified limits are perfectly in line with homes in perfect condition that require a leap in quality. In that case, the limits are reasonable, and the target efficiency levels are reasonable. To achieve an 80% reduction and get an 80% subsidy, you have to be working with A- or B-rated buildings. We're starting with F- or G-rated, and it's impossible. The energy savings associated with being able to achieve this subsidy percentage involve such a high level of investment, not just in envelopes but also in energy-production systems, that it's unfeasible in the buildings we're dealing with here, in vulnerable neighbourhoods and environments. As for subsidies, they're very acceptable; we're talking about a 60% subsidy. But, in the end, you have the ceiling of 14,500 euros per home with an expenditure of 60,000 euros. It just doesn't add up. With this horizon, thinking about innovation is science fiction. These are buildings with a very low baseline: energy consumption is minimum because they don't have washing machines, lots don't have hot water or they heat water using butane, they don't have heating, they don't have dishwashers or powerful ovens or air conditioning; in this sense, their energy consumption is zero.

Optimizing energy consumption in these buildings is very complicated because the initial consumption is very low.

When we started the urban regeneration programme, one of our ideas was to set up a construction laboratory with the school of surveyors, working together to achieve improved construction solutions in terms of energy efficiency and costs, but it hasn't been implemented yet.

We're drafting a project in the Besòs neighbourhood and we're going into flats with majorly unsanitary conditions, in run-down districts with zero maintenance culture, with some flats that are privately owned but the owners still think that the Council should fix them. You're presented with a very complicated situation, and when you try to achieve what Next Generation is asking for, it's so complex that you can't innovate, you just have to take action on the front that's open to you. We are seeing that PV could be a good option, because at least you're not going into homes; you can work on the building as a whole. But it turns out that the certification programmes only take into account energy savings in the building's lighting and heating consumption. It's very difficult for us to access Next Generation. There are solutions like ETICS, simple solutions that offer a thermal guarantee and that you know will work, but in terms of costs they're just not possible. I think we're in a privileged position because we're working with projects for the Administration, with a greater capacity and a bigger economic commitment. For a community of owners in a similar situation, that wants to do this without the support of a public administration, it's science fiction. Who, today, is in a position to invest 600,000 euros in their building to access Next Generation and see if they can get a 40-50% grant with limits that is light years away from the investment they'll have to make? Homeowner communities will struggle to get started. Next Generation looks great, but it's complex.

The aim of the fund shouldn't be just to get everything free; it should

insist on people being responsible for doing work in their buildings.

The aim of funding should be for housing to be compatible with our present-day ideas about sustainability and comfort, not just to get the money. We have to be jointly responsible. The other thing is that we now have a vehicle and an opportunity to achieve it –the funds– which exist today and may not exist tomorrow. Property administrators are happy because they are now being rewarded for doing work that in the past they weren't, but they must also remember that their administration didn't encourage or promote all the maintenance they were obliged to do as secretaries of homeowner communities.

Sometimes there's no need to innovate so much; innovating can also mean finding the most suitable solution and starting to systematize. Also, it seems that every time a community commissions a project, it has to start again from scratch when a lot of previous work is lying in a drawer.

One of the things that Next Generation funds have done is make us realize that building inspections don't exist because they've become necessary; they've always been necessary. Building inspections should be formalized rather than waiting for them to be a legal requirement.

They often got left in a drawer out of fear of presenting them to the Housing Agency. Then they have to be done again, and then, as technicians, we have to carry out the inspection again, because it was done before but not presented. In this area there's a lot of fear in homeowner communities.

This would be a way of forcing maintenance and retrofitting; if you start but don't see it through, that's when people let it slide and give up.

The Catalan Agency has released a circular stating that there is a penalty of between 9,000 and 90,000 euros for not carrying out a building inspection. People say, will I be fined 90,000 euros? I tell them that they should already have paid that amount.

I think it's interesting to consider that

now is a golden opportunity for us to share knowledge,

because we're entering a territory where every small contribution goes a long way towards meeting these requirements for making a community work better. We have to share experiences because our colleagues can learn a lot from them, from how we were able to survive in a project like this. We shouldn't always be starting from scratch.

Before, we said "let's redefine the term quality in the context we're working in and introduce the user as a concept of quality", but perhaps the concept of innovation here is sharing this knowledge. The innovation is not so much the object as the procedure.

Innovation is also working together with residents,

for the Administration at least, because we're used to calls for proposals with projects that respond directly to physical reality, and residents are left a bit on the sidelines. I would also add the way of working the project.

You said before that during the construction phase you aimed to create a firewall between the constructor and the residents.

During the construction phase, yes, but there's a preliminary phase of months and months of reaching a community, encouraging it and gaining its trust. After all, it's the Administration that's going into their homes, forcing them to do things they don't want to. They want the council to fix that beam that's propped up and remove the prop, but they don't want you to get into issues like tampering with the electricity meter, regularizations... You have to get them to see what's really needed. Then you draft the project, explain it to them, they respond, you go into all their homes. You're working with the residents for a year or a year and a half. When we've agreed on the project and explained in every possible way what needs to be done, we start the technical design phase, when the occupants have to let us work; this is no longer the time to comment on technical solutions, because now they have all the information. It's during the construction phase that the firewall has to exist.

I take my hat off to you! The problem we have is interacting with that occupant who interferes, questioning or criticizing what an expert with their four or six years of studies has done.

Some of our public programmes involve the most complicated urban fabrics with the most difficult communities to work with, and will continue to do so, because the market won't have workable solutions for the parts of cities where social fabric has received least attention. It's like social rental housing: it's the administration that does that. In terms of financing, it seems that there's starting to be instruments that can be used, like soft loans, and what we don't have and will lose the opportunity to generate are public-private companies that are permanently dedicated to retrofitting and regeneration with mixed capital. Right now, that's not on anyone's agenda, and in a context where subsidies come and go, with an Administration that if it has money, looks after certain areas of the city, and, if it doesn't, does nothing, it's impossible to generate a system. We have a structural problem; how much money is needed to rehabilitate the pre-1950s housing stock?

The tradition in rehabilitation, in Barcelona at least, except in extreme social cases, has been the responsibility of homeowner communities. Perhaps innovation means creating specialized companies that are more efficient and, therefore, more profitable.

There are two points at which private capital comes to a halt. The first is when talking about affordable rental housing: the answer is, in theory yes, but we'll talk about maintenance tomorrow. The other is to invest with the Administration in areas such as photovoltaic energy: it stops here, but in the middle, in existing homes and rehabilitation, there is no context.

If the commitment to energy rehabilitation is real, as it seems to be, the international context doesn't stop here; 10 times more is needed. So if we are looking not at the present but at the future, now is the time to learn, and the processes being begun by the city of Barcelona are instruments for this learning process.

The question is whether society will really learn from this need for retrofitting.

As regards ownership,

the problem in this country is that rental property ownership is unprofessional;

the owner who has five, 10 or 20 flats doesn't have a professional vision. Companies that are devoted to housing management will have a very correct vision of maintenance; the rentier owner, meanwhile, is not interested. For someone who has a vision of reinvestment, of improvement, of tenants paying for this improvement, this more business-minded approach makes sense, but there are very few of them.

There is a major problem that's difficult to solve: small property owners who manage a real-estate asset by putting it on the market, but not with much economic rationality: they don't do annual accounts, they have an income, they pay some tax if they actually declare it, they don't set funds aside to rehabilitate the property over a period of time. There's a large percentage of small owners who are completely ignorant of what this involves. I don't know to what extent an information or training campaign could be organized. This would involve talking to the small property owners association, which says it represents the sector, get them involved and offer training to their members to talk about the responsibility of conservation.

The word we need to explain, and that until we haven't really thought about, even in the context of the activity, is pedagogy: a pedagogy of social care, a pedagogy of how to use housing, of how to use and manage the building. The good news is that it is a very intense step towards something that aims to create a habit, a situation that we didn't know how to manage before. This is why what we're doing now is working on emergency, which is the first thing we have to attend to. But if we continue with the dynamics of understanding what's happening in this meeting, which is very different to yesterday's, professionals and the Administration alike must decide to commit to these three strategies to achieve social housing. A message for the Architects' Association: this meeting is proof that, here, we have diversified as professionals. The way we work now as architects is very different to 10 and even more, to 20 years ago. This is good news because it means more possibilities. We've taken on board the building file, but not the home file; no one gives you a manual about how a home functions and is managed, and the fact that, when it's used incorrectly, user errors occur. In academia, in the Administration and in the professional world, we're seeing that this is the case.

The problem is, people think that we build pyramids, and that they'll last a thousand years. The sector is also heading in this direction; guarantees of materials are getting longer and longer, as if they were eternal. We have to get across the idea that

we build machines, very complex machines that need a maintenance manual.

This is the social problem we have. The concept of the home file is very necessary.

Seeing the home as a machine with its own functioning is quite right; day/night, winter/summer, it has a way of working that's not on anyone's inventory. The user thinks that their home functions the same 24 hours a day, 365 days a year, and this is not the case.

As well as focusing on maintenance by owners, we mustn't forget maintenance by tenants who, because it's not their home, don't make good use of the property, and this is evident when the flat is recovered. This pedagogy has to be applied to everyone.

Yesterday, someone asked about the indefinite leases of Cevasa, the company that manages the most rental housing in Spain. The answer was yes, an indefinite lease would be preferable to avoid changing users, but the current fiscal burden and the uncertainty of "what will happen to me as an administrator" don't allow this, which is why short contracts are offered. If a user has an indefinite contract, they'll take good care of the home, whereas someone who lives there for three or five years won't invest. So legality doesn't make it easy.

There's a difference: at yesterday's meeting there was a private producer, at today's there isn't. This is one of the structural problems we have. The Administration is taking action when there's no alternative, favouring a particular preventive medicine for the city as a whole. Professionals in the sector and industrial professionals are represented, but

there are no rehabilitation agents.

Contractors are not producers, and companies that evict people are not producers, because the point of their business is not to retrofit and manage, but to push out the current actors, increase the property's value and produce new assets.

The problem is that we don't have private companies that carry out rehabilitation work as a business. Volume is important; it's difficult to make rehabilitation pay at the small scale, but it is possible if there's a certain volume and the means. For example, we tend to give little importance to the fact that Spain has a huge mortgage market, because historically we've built a lot of housing and, in general, it's been sold and paid for with mortgages. We've got that, but not a circuit of producers, providers of services or financing of rehabilitation on a massive scale. However, we are on the way to creating a critical mass.

What would the system have to be like for them to earn money?

Very long-term financing, say 30, 40 or 50 years.

The clients would be the owners of the homes, who would pay a fee to cover expenses.

There's also the deal where you do so much retrofitting and they let you build so much. You say to the owners: I'll do retrofitting in exchange for a small fee, but I get to keep the new uses. There are companies in the professional association that are trying to make this leap of scale and professionalize rehabilitation, but a bigger scale is needed.

These retrofitting companies could be seen in the same way as lift maintenance firms, where you pay a fee to guarantee that maintenance is carried out regularly.

Today's payment is what you haven't spent and investment in tomorrow.

If it's not coercive, it doesn't work; lift maintenance happens because it's required by law. As long as construction and production are associated with big profits and fast bucks, it's very difficult to imagine companies that are financed in the long term and seek sustained profit from rehabilitation. That's why I said it was a social phenomenon: if society doesn't start to really see housing stock in a different way, we're going nowhere. A case in point is the cooperative: a small part of conscientious society that wants to do it properly and work well.

Coercion is important, but promotion is more efficient. It's a question of culture.

There's no social awareness that we're doing this to make the world better, not in the case of vulnerable situations or in situations of high income levels. Residents' communities don't think about making the most of a façade renovation to improve energy efficiency; as long as the façade is attractive, that's enough.

Bringing it closer to home, here, and in this profession, seeing that there are now architecture practices that live from their dedication to a different kind of architecture, working on crosscutting projects with users, perhaps things are progressing and changing.

What are the profiles of these architects?

Young people, studios that introduce the social factor into their way of doing things, working alongside users. They're not people trying to do what previous generations did but with less money; they're trying to do it in a different way, and this is what is important if the methodology is to change. Climate crisis is here to stay, and mechanisms have to be designed by the Administration, by the profession and by industry, to address it as fast as possible. Today's meeting is more innovative than yesterday's, with the exception of the cooperatives, because 10 years ago it wouldn't even have been considered, much less at the headquarters of the COAC. In this book we talk not about certainties but about the new issues facing us, which are of such complexity that we need this coming together and this crosscutting approach. New issues that, until now, no one was talking about in the Administration, or the profession, or society.

The following index is the script of topics that was used during the sessions:

INDEX
Experience and conclusions of the process

Gestation phase:

- Start of the process: drafting the different bidding procedures: two-phase competition, industrial construction competition... Quality of the competition
- Project: outlining the proposal: designer-producer-constructor dialogue
- Works tender: construction companies and contract execution budget
- Construction work: professionalism of constructors to implement the starting parameters

Effect of the parameters defining architectural quality on each of the phases of gestation:

- Working with pre-existences: object and subject
- Typological innovation / replacing, parasitizing, reusing
- Industrialization / Scale factor
- Energy efficiency, sustainability, decarbonization, environmental parameters and life cycle
- Maintenance

Relevant aspects at each stage of gestation:

- Background and unforeseen incidents
- Designing for an unknown occupant, where the occupant enters at the living phase, vs designing with an occupant, where the occupant enters at the gestating phase
- Project competition and subsequent construction work tender vs project and construction competition (designing with an industrial professional)

Living phase:

- To what extent are the project proposals ratified?

Maintenance

- Crosscutting parameter in gestating and living
- Effect on project definition
- Effect on the building's life cycle

Published by:

Barcelona City Council

Barcelona Housing Authority

Architects' Association of Catalonia-COAC

Edition and Publishing Board of Barcelona City Council:

Jordi Martí Grau | Marc Andreu Acebal
Águeda Bañón Pérez | Xavier Boneta Lorente
Marta Clari Padrós | Núria Costa Galobart
Sonia Frias Rollón | Pau Gonzàlez Val
Laura Pérez Castaño | Jordi Rabassa Massons
Joan Ramon Riera Alemany | Pilar Roca Viola
Edgar Rovira Sebastià | Anna Giralt Brunet

Director of Communication:

Águeda Bañón

Director of Publishing Services:

Núria Costa Galobart

Resources, Distribution and Marketing:

Núria Mahamud de la Peña

Editing:

Oriol Guiu

Production:

Òscar Carreño

Department of Editorial Services
Passeig de la Zona Franca, 66
08038 Barcelona
Tel. 934 023 131
barcelona.cat/barcelonallibres

Collection:
"Barcelona, Architecture and Urban Planning",
curated by Carme Ribas

Housing and Rehabilitation Management of Barcelona City Council:
Javier Burón

Manager of Barcelona Housing Authority:
Gerard Capó

President of the Architects' Association of Catalonia-COAC:
Guim Costa

Director of Institutional Relations and Communication:
Clara Llensa

Director of the Open Architecture Centre:
Josep Ferrando

Coordination of edition:

llindarquitectura -
ibon bilbao caterina figuerola arquitectes
Collaborations:
Carmen Chacón
Júlia Duran Vilalta
Roser Roca Panicot
Ignacio Urbistondo

Coordination and technical revision:

Joan Recasens
Eduard Cabré
Núria Colomé
Eduardo González de Molina

Translation:

Elaine Fradley

Linguaserve Internacionalización de Servicios, SA

Graphic design:

Ignacio Urbistondo | llindarquitectura

Retouching and graphic production:

Xavi Parejo

Impression:

Ce.Ge

Distribution:
Actar D, Inc. New York, Barcelona

New York
440 Park Avenue South, 17th Floor
New York, NY 10016, USA
+1 212 966 2207
salesnewyork@actar-d.com

Barcelona
Roca i Batlle, 2-4
08023 Barcelona, España
+34 933 282 183
eurosales@actar-d.com

Barcelona, 2023

ISBN: 978-84-9156-498-0
DL: B 10066-2023

Also available:
Spanish-language edition: *Gestar / Habitar: Estrategias para la vivienda social en Barcelona*
ISBN: 978-84-9156-497-3

Catalan-language edition: *Gestar / Habitar: Estratègies per a l'habitatge social a Barcelona*
ISBN: 978-84-9156-487-4

Acknowledgements

In a collective publication like this, there are many acknowledgements to be made. If we were to name one by one the people who have been involved, it would be a very long list. The contribution of each person is what has helped to shape a book like this, where the richness of the diversity and content of the documents is the result of this multi-collaboration.

Thank you to the Management team of Barcelona City Council and to the COAC for the initiative of producing a publication like this; to the municipal technicians for carrying out the various strategic programmes; to the teams of architects for providing project documentation; to the article writers for their reflections; to Maite Caramés and Adrià Goula for capturing with their cameras such thought-provoking scenarios as the ones they have shown us; to the occupants for opening the doors of their homes to us; to the professionals attending the participatory meetings for their debate, and very special thanks to Ignacio, Roser, Júlia and Carmen for their involvement and their daily support.

This diagram compares the timing of each of the projects presented in this book, ordered according to the seven strategies described. Efforts have been made to collect the same data for all the projects, although, as they respond to different methodologies, the procedures are also different. The diagram reflects the complex gestation processes involved in each of the strategies and makes it possible to highlight the work of all the agents involved.

To understand this complexity it is important to realize that the construction of housing by public tender, according to the traditional model, involves a great many phases. In the case of most of the projects presented in this book, they were developed one after the other: project competition, competition ruling, awarding of the draft project and construction to the architect, project design, rubberstamping, building permit, bidding for works, awarding of building work to the construction company, building work, completion of building work, reception of the work by the developer and, finally, handover of the dwelling to the user. This succession of phases is drawn out in time and may therefore be affected by multiple singularities that prolong the process and excessively extend deadlines. This diagram features two historical moments that completely conditioned the initial planning of the projects: the economic crisis of 2008 and the Covid-19 health crisis. It was important to highlight these critical moments, since, in some projects, they were decisive in calculating the time factor. Further, this long, complex timeline encountered new challenges arising from a whole series of climate and, very directly, housing emergencies. It is the response to these challenges that characterized the design of the new strategies, one of their main objectives being to shorten the process of gestating social housing.

1
- 68 housing units / Sancho de Ávila II — BAAS - Jordi Badia
- 105 housing units / Glòries — Bonell i Gil / Peris + Toral
- 44 housing units / Can Fabra — Roldán + Berengué
- 81 housing units / Josep Pla — Estudi Massip-Bosch
- 61 housing units / Bon Pastor — Pascual-Ausió
- 44 housing units / Quatre Camins — Ravetllat-Ribas
- 47 housing units + 20 accommodations / Tànger — Coll-Leclerc

2
- 17 housing units / Raval — MIAS Architects
- 114 housing units / Encuny — MSA+A

3
- 12 accommodations / Ciutat Vella — Straddle3 / Eulia Arkitektura / Yaiza Terré
- 42 accommodations / Glòries — Bestraten-Hormias / Javier Ramos + Lluís Roig
- 40 housing units / Arriassa — Guallart Architects

4
- 20 housing units / La Balma Cooperativa — Lacol / LaBoqueria Taller
- 32 housing units / Cirerers Cooperativa — Celobert
- 44 housing units / Fundació Salas + Fundació Nou Lloc — 011h

5
- 63 housing units / Ulldecona — Musquera Arquitectura

6
- 24 housing units / El Besòs and Maresme — Estudi d'Arquitectura CODI
- 5 housing units / Gòtic — Heres Arquitectura

7
- 18 housing units / Floridablanca — Borsa de Lloguer + Compra
- 2 housing units / Poble-sec — Fundació Hàbitat3
- 17 housing units / Casa Bloc Sheltered Housing — Javier Hernani - Estudi fàbric